Trail Riding & Pack Trips

In Washington

Where To Ride. . .
And How To Get There

Dick and LaDonna Woodfin

Woodfin, Dick.
    Trail riding and pack trips in Washington : where to ride
and how to get there / Dick and LaDonna Woodfin.
    p. cm.
    Includes bibliographical references.
    Preassigned LCCN: 97-60935
    ISBN: 0-939116-44-8

    1. Trail riding--Washington (State) 2. Washington
(State)--Description and travel.   I. Woodfin, LaDonna.
II. Title.

    SF309.28.W66 1998   798.23'09797
                                         QBI97-41605

Published by:
    Frontier Publishing
    Portland, OR

Fulfillment by:
    Runnin' W
    14355 S.W. Bell Road
    Sherwood, OR 97140

Printed in the Unites States of America

ACKNOWLEDGMENTS

We sincerely acknowledge the support of U.S. Forest Service Trail Coordinators and Staff Specialists. Their recommendations clarified the text and added content that is important to trail riders.

The encouragement to produce *Trail Riding and Pack Trips in Washington* came from Ruth Vanderhoof and Lyle Wilson, authors of *Trail Riding Oregon*. A special thank you to Pat Yoes Badnin for her enjoyable, technical and artistic help. To a couple of pairs of special friends Dean and Pat Fitzwater, and John and Beverly Horn, our trail riding partners, thanks for your support.

Along with good friends, we remember those four-legged partners, who packed us for over 3,000 miles during the past 20 years. Our saddle horses Barb and Miley carried us across trails that ranged from simple and easy to those so difficult they barely clung to the mountain side. Down shale, over snow fields and through blowdowns, up and down too many trails to count, they could be depended on for whatever was asked of them. Good horses are like good people, there aren't enough of them! And we definitely had two of the best trail horses that anyone could have wished to have ridden.

What has helped keep it all together has been the support of a couple of excellent farriers, Patrick Henry and Bill Evans who trimmed, nailed and repaired broken hooves in order to keep us on the trail.

Many thanks to all of them and to our family members who take care of the place while we trail ride!

Cover photo by John Horn

Overview of Trail Map Locations

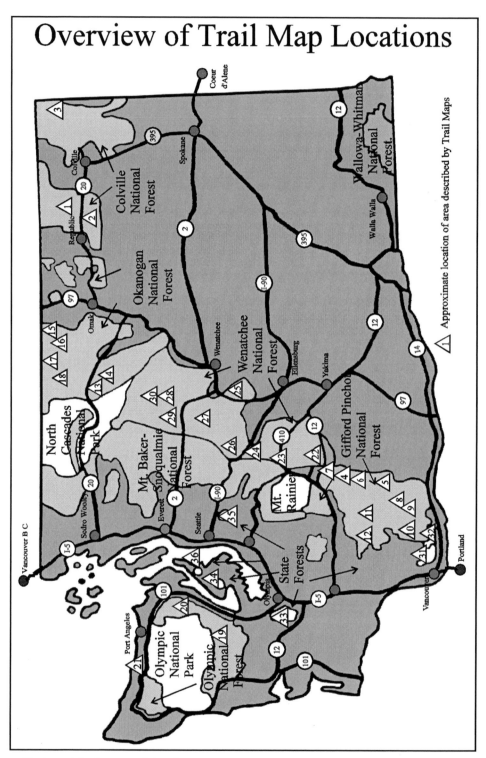

Legend of Key Features on Trail Maps

Trail	$\cdots\cdot\cdot^{1209}\cdot\cdots$
Road or Highway	62 or Hwy. 12
Pacific Crest National Scenic Trail	PCT 2000
Trailhead is Described	U
Site or Facility	•
Horse Camp	
Mounting Assist Facility Available	
Mountain	
Lake	
Pass	| or ~
Trail Map Area in Washington	
Map Scale	1 Mile
Map Orientation and Compass Declination	N 20° TRUE MAGNETIC
Stock Not Permitted on Trail	••
Campground	

ABOUT THIS BOOK

When you want to trail ride and visit new areas, for us, the important questions become: Is there a wide selection of trails to ride? Can we make loop rides? How do we drive to the trailhead, and can we park a four-horse trailer there? Is there a place to camp with horses? What are the specific regulations for the area and what maps should we carry? We have tried to make *Trail Riding and Pack Trips in Washington* a book that helps answer these questions.

Our goal has been to give trail riders a different look at what is available across the state. The selection of areas and trails across the state range from the Gifford Pinchot National Forest in the south to the unique scenery of the Olympic National Forest in the west, to the Colville National Forest on the Idaho border and Okanogan National Forest and the Pasayten Wilderness on the Canadian border. The Wenatchee National Forest in the center of the state offers many trail riding opportunities with access to the east side of the Mount Baker-Snoqualmie National Forest.

The 36 Trail Maps include 30 from National Forests and 6 from Washington State forests that have horse camps or horse-use trailheads. Combined, these trail maps show more than 150 specific trails, with a total length exceeding 1500 miles. Each of these trails is described by a Trail Guide following the map which gives you information on parking, regulations, maps and so on. In addition we describe 100 or so other trailheads and more than 30 designated horse camps. You will find numerous other trails, without Trail Guides to describe them, on the 36 Trail Maps. These are left for you to explore. Some are close to a major highway or forest road; others may require hours of travel to reach. The trails range in challenge level from Easiest to Most Difficult based on the U.S. Forest Service new rating categories (Appendix

4). For our friends who need a Mounting Assist Facility, we have identified horse camps and trailheads that provide that service. State Forests, are an outstanding example of "lands of many users" that meet the needs of trail riders.

This book is unique in that it may possibly be the first on horse trail riding to include a full chapter on how to use a compass. It provides basic knowledge about maps and how to use a compass with a map. Several map and compass examples are presented that may apply to your own trail rides.

The National Forest sites have been reviewed by forest personnel as to the sites' designation as horse trails and camps. *Trail Riding and Pack Trips in Washington* uses documented resources about the trails on public lands. Information on where trails are located, routes to the trailheads and the distances to travel came from personal rides and pack trips, U.S. Forest Service and Washington State trail guides and recreation and wilderness maps.

However, a word of caution: Roads, trail conditions, trailheads, camps and parking areas change due to weather, use, limited maintenance, reconstruction and closure. In fact, there is a road closure program underway on some National Forest lands. This may mean some access roads will not be available to drive but they could open up for riding. Check with the local Forest Service office for road conditions. When visiting state forests, check with the State Department of Natural Resources (DNR) as to the trail status and current use requirements.

Care was used to review and compile this information to ensure accuracy. However, because of changes that are outside our control, we cannot accept responsibility for errors and omissions that result from change in trail status or condition. An essential part of being a good trail rider is to take responsibility for the safety of yourself and your party. Know your ability and that of your horse so you do not over extend beyond either's physical limits. Check out the appropriate federal or state land management agency permit requirements for the area you camp and ride. Use caution. Ask about road and trail conditions and stock use requirements at local Forest Service offices.

We especially do not want a trail rider or reader to feel halter led over every creek and around every turn in the trail. Therefore, the Trail Maps and Trail Guides intentionally leave room to experience the unknown and unexpected. We hope you will agree with us that there should be room for a few pleasant surprises during wilderness and back-country trail riding.

When you try the routes, trails and camps in this book you take responsibility for your safety. All the changes in weather, roads, trails, stream levels and structure conditions have the potential to impact your trip. Trail difficulty categories are broad and cannot cover every condition that can develop on a trail. Be careful and be prepared! Whichever trail route you try, have a safe ride.

Camping at Basin Lake

Photo by Dave Welch

TRAIL RIDER INFORMATION

Recreation Fee Demonstration Program: Changing resource conditions are evident to most serious trail riders. It is visible in trail and camp conditions or closures. It is also evident in a pilot or demonstration program mandated by Congress and scheduled to run through 1999.

For the first time in the history of the Northwest, trail riders and others will pay a fee to park vehicles at trailheads and ride trails in some areas. Winter sport users have paid a "Sno Park" fee for a number of years, intended to cover costs to remove snow from parking areas. The new recreation fee revenues similarly are targeted for operation and maintenance of trails and trailheads.

The "Trail Park" pass fee of $3 per visit or $25 per year which began in eight forests in Washington and Oregon in summer 1997, is meant to fill the gap in recreation budgets for National Forests. The Forest Service Pacific Northwest Region (Washington and Oregon) "Trail Park Pass" is one of 50 projects across the nation that were included under the initial Demonstration Program. There are over 500 trails and trailheads covered by the pass in Washington alone. The Colville and Gifford Pinchot National Forests were not included in the first year's effort, but you can expect these Washington forests to be included in future years. Some variation in fee structure may also exist between the individual National Forests.

Land managers say the legislation allows the U.S. Forest Service to retain 80 percent of the fees at the local forest for trail and trailhead related work. The Forest Service hopes this fact will promote public acceptance of the program and provide much needed funding for the extensive system of trails in the Pacific Northwest. For trail riders a plus of the program may result from having someone check on compliance at the trailheads. This could mean extra security for trailer rigs left unattended for several days.

Mounting Assist Facility: Accessibility to outdoor recreation for disabled Americans is expanding, in a limited way, to horse camps and trailhead with stock facilities. The guidelines for Universal Access to outdoor recreation have resulted in equestrian facilities being constructed to include accessible paths, transfer platforms (mounting assist ramps), access to horse-care facilities, and camps and toilet facilities.

The U.S. Forest Service, Northwest Accessibility Specialist provides the leadership to develop these campgrounds and trailheads. For example, on the Lake Wenatchee Ranger District of the Wenatchee National Forest there are two accessibility campsites at the new Chiwawa Horse Camp. They may be reserved by calling the District Office.

In this book, we list four National Forests and four State Forest horse camps or trailheads that currently have mounting assist facilities. Each trailhead with horse facilities or a horse camp reported to have some form of mounting assist is identified on the Trail Maps. However, National Forest and State Recreation maps identify many more trailheads with accessible picnic, camping or restroom facilities.

Mounting Assist Ramp at Chiwawa Horse Camp,
Wenatchee National Forest

—Photo by Authors

Trail Riders' Responsibility: When you leave a camp, would it pass your inspection if that were your job? Would you want to be the next visitor to use it?

Every year Leave-No-Trace (LNT) gets and deserves more attention from trail riders who ride the back-country. Enjoyment of back-country forest and wilderness trails carries a number of responsibilities that can be easy to ignore. Today every use of natural resources is under a magnifying lens and it is essential that we as trail riders take LNT seriously. The two broad topics related to LNT most often demonstrated at clinics, cussed and discussed or written about are methods to reduce the impact on each area visited and the need to do some easy maintenance like cut or move a log from the trail or pick up a piece of trash left by others.

Just like volunteer trail work and horse camp construction, LNT efforts take time and work. They may mean getting off the horse, but these efforts are the right thing to do and may result in benefits that are hard to measure. Many trail riders and outfitters have already taken on similar responsibilities, like clearing trails in the spring, and are leaders in the Leave-No-Trace effort. When put into practice, LNT guidelines for stock should help ensure that horse use and horse camps continue to exist and even improve on the National Forests.

Here are some accepted recommendations for trail rides:

(1) Use existing fire rings whenever possible. Burn only fallen dead wood, or even better, carry a portable stove for cooking.

(2) Pack out—do not leave or bury—garbage. Remember, many food containers and wrappers will not burn.

(3) Dig and use the "cat hole" toilet technique to bury human waste at least eight inches deep and over 100 feet from water.

(4) Check with the local Forest Service office to determine maximum group size permitted in an area (referred to as maximum number of "heartbeats", meaning riders and stock). Regulations change each year and vary between forest and wilderness in Washington so check for the latest information.

(5) Camp and keep horses and pack stock at least 200 feet from lakes and streams except for watering purposes. Some wilderness areas in Washington now require camps be no closer than 0.5 mile of lakes.

(6) Hobble, high-line or picket horses instead of tying them

to a tree. Some horse camps and stock trailheads now have high-lines in place that must be used for holding stock.

(7) Spread the horse "apples" (manure) before you high-tail it from a camp or leave a lunch stop. This simple act will go a long way to helping trail riders get along better with the land managers as well as hikers and bikers.

Be a Team Player —
Join a Trail Riding Organization

There is another effort that is important to all trail riding volunteer groups which could also be called a responsibility. It is described in trail riders' newsletters. That is to become active as a 'trail riding citizen' and maintain a membership in organizations such as the BackCountry Horsemen of Washington (BCHW) or similar trail horse riding groups in Washington and other states like Oregon Equestrian Trails (OET). Then, as a member, support the goals of that organization and, as an individual, let state and federal legislators know of your concerns and use of trails. Express your concern to legislators for funding support to the appropriate land management agencies. It just makes good sense to keep everyone who enjoys the back-country working together, not against each other's type of recreation. This is the type of message emphasized in literature prepared by the BackCountry Horsemen of Washington, an active trail riding organization of over 30 chapters throughout Washington. They keep tabs on legislation which may affect horse use and are dedicated to: "Preserving the rights of American people to use horses for recreation on public lands; Protection of our priceless back country environment; Expanding and improving trail riding and other back-country recreational opportunities; Development and keeping trail riding opportunities in urban areas." Contact Jim Murphy, Executive Director (BCHW), 360-876-7739, for further information.

TABLE OF CONTENTS

Chapter 1

TRAIL RIDING HORSE SENSE

Nearly every recreation book on trail horse riding, hiking, biking, climbing or white water rafting deals with the issues of clean campsites, disposal of human waste, campfires and packing out trash. One asks whether this material is used just to fill space or to meet a social need of the book, and, if it is even read. Does it really get the message across and educate the novice and influence the messy among us? How much do you think about these areas as you plan a trip or day ride? A lot more than given credit for we expect!

Trail riding in Norse Peak Wilderness, Wenatchee National Forest
— *Photo by Authors*

Mules Included

To those who favor trail riding on a mule, please accept our use of "horse and stock" as terms that include the way you enjoy a trail ride. We just have very little experience riding and packing mules.

This section offers some good old-fashioned trail ride practices that are still acceptable and do not get in the way of the experience we want. They represent common sense; some are required by regulations.

Hopefully, safe and approved practices are part of any trail ride and campout. That means you choose routes that are suitable for horses, and that the back-country areas you visit can accommodate stock. Provisions you carry into the back-country should be packed in containers that can be flattened (no glass) and packed back out with non-burnable trash. A shovel for toilet use is a standard item on any trail ride even if it is only one that folds up and fits into a saddlebag. Pick up trash—even that left by someone else—so the campsite will look even better when you leave than when you arrive. (Maybe your actions will set an example for the next camper.) Campfires are always drowned with water and stirred to make sure they are dead out.

Since trail riders probably don't have to work as hard as the hikers and backpackers, there is no reason for us to cut a switchback just to save a little distance. Ride the trail and enjoy the changing views the switchback presents.

When you start up the trail from a horse camp or trailhead make sure you take time to register even if a wilderness permit is not required. You know the hikers all register so their numbers tally a high count. Be counted as a horse rider. Let the agencies know we trail riders are using the trails and camps.

Spread the "Apples": When your party breaks camp and cleans up, someone needs to take a stick, walk the grazing and high-line picket areas and spread the horse apples (manure). Just like dragging the arena or pasture at home, this allows nature to break them down faster. Besides, they are not as obvious to the next visitor. Also, remember the trailhead or horse camp is not the place to clean out our horse trailers. Pack it back home or use the manure bins if they are provided at trailheads.

Meeting Hikers: Any trail rider knows the feeling of riding a horse along a narrow trail and having the horse get spooked at some scary log or rock. This same thing happens to some horses when they meet a hiker or backpacker. It pays to make a practice of speaking to the backpackers you meet. A question to them gets an answer and lets the lead horse know that lumpy thing is a person.

The guidelines in horse books and Forest Service literature commonly recommend that the backpacker or hiker step below the trail. Hiking books don't always offer the same advice, but since a horse will more likely shy and move up slope, the safest place to be is below the trail. However, for many hikers who do not ride, being on foot below that big animal is worse than above so they feel safer stepping uphill onto loose or steep footing.

This is the time for us on horseback to take it easy, keep talking and give the person on foot enough time to get good footing and be in a safe position before riding past. Leave a word of greeting as you pass, a friendly "Hello," or a "Please pardon the dust."

This is also a good time to ask if there are more in their hiking party further on the trail. Or tell them another rider or two in your group will be right along. A friendly visit never hurts. After all each one is enjoying the great outdoors. It's just the method of transportation that is different. Trail horse riders know who has the best method!

Other Riders on the Trail: Old trail customs and the way of doing things that existed for pack strings make sense today. Non-pack string groups would pull off the trail at a safe place to let the string pass. The same guidelines work for a line of trail riders meeting other riders. Old guidelines say an uphill group of riders or pack string gets the right-of-way over a downhill pack string.

In areas with heavy use, like horse camps, incoming traffic to the trailhead gets the right-of-way until noon and outgoing traffic in the afternoon. But in reality trail riders know there is no such thing in trail riding as right-of-way—common sense and courtesy are what work best. The one who can get off the trail the safest and easiest is who should do it.

When Nature Calls: Some overused back-country campsites are so popular it makes one wonder if there are enough rocks and trees or places for anyone to dig a private "cat hole" toilet spot behind. Whatever toilet route you take, take a shovel that allows you to dig a hole at least eight inches deep. This depth should be the minimum in camping. Cover it fully after use to allow soil micro-organisms to do their job. Stay over 100 feet from lakes and streams.

Campfires: Much has been written about the presence of fire rings at popular camping areas. Following Leave-No-Trace guidelines means using existing fire rings, spreading the ashes and fire ring rocks when you leave. Recommendations by the Forest Service and back-country groups suggest using the existing fire rings rather than building another one nearby. When your campsite has never been used before, it is time to practice your best LNT skills. Build a fire on bare soil, then later spread the cold ashes and put some dirt over the burned spot. Before building a fire in a grassy spot, remove a very thick piece of sod so the roots will survive when it is replaced. When ready to leave, spread soil over the burned spot and replace the sod piece.

Another approach is to use a ground cover of fireproof material, cover it with a few shovel scoops of soil to hold the fire. They do not burn, they protect the soil and make it easier to spread ashes around. Several of these products are on the market including one that uses discarded forest fire fighter shelters that have been cut into 3'x3' sections.

Firewood is in short supply in many heavily used camp areas. This, along with fire closures in late summer has prompted many riders to invest in a good one or two burner propane cook stove. Some areas now even require that propane-type stoves be used. Test your stove at home using the appropriate fuel container in order to learn how long you can cook, make coffee and heat water on one container. Trail riders without hot coffee can be downright dangerous!

Step off the Horse: There is an old story about folks who kept walking around a rock rather than removing it from the road. Wealth was hidden under the rock for whomever moved it. Getting off your horse to move a limb, cut a downed log or move a rock off the trail may not bring a prize but it makes good sense. Someone has to do it. Let the trail crews use their limited time to repair trail damage. Trail riders can help keep trails free of obstructions and prevent trail damage by others who might ride around the obstacle.

A tool that can help is one of the excellent 26-inch pruning saws carried in a scabbard that fits under your stirrup leather. You'll never know it's there but having it available could mean getting through a blowdown without having to leave the trail or even save miles of riding back because of a blocked trail.

Have A Horse To Ride in the Morning: Hobble, high-line or electric fence? Horses may get to graze loose or on hobbles at the end of the day but we want them tied up at night. Usually it is to a high-line. It is not a difficult process to get a horse used to grazing in hobbles. Horse trainers and many trail riders can handle that training job. A set of leather or nylon Figure-8 hobbles are light, easy to carry, put on and remove. Grazing hobbles

Grazing Hobbles
— *USDA Forest Service, Pacific Northwest Region, illustration*

with their chain connector between the leather straps allow a horse easier movement but they are heavier and awkward to carry on a saddle.

It is a good practice to keep at least one horse tied up while the rest graze unless you are very certain there is one that can always be caught. Sooner or later we all learn that a horse on hobbles can outrun a person! A bell on the boss animal lets you know where it is even if it grazes out of sight.

The picket line method of putting a horse on a front foot hobble with a soft cotton rope tied to a swivel pin is not for everyone. It takes more equipment and a longer training time, but is a popular way to keep one horse nearby. The boss or dominant animal is usually the

Front Foot Picket Line
—*Photo by Authors*

one to picket, while the others graze loose or with hobbles. Some outfitters never hobble their stock. They prefer to keep one or two on a picket and put a bell on a dominant animal that is allowed to graze loose. The outfitters then wrangle them up in the morning.

New horse camps being built with the help of volunteer groups have high-lines in place. These are either poles or trees with rings attached. A rope is strung between the rings or a cable is already in place, and lead ropes are tied to that. Either way, a horse on a picket line should only be able to

High-line and tree-saver straps
— *USDA Forest Service, Pacific Northwest Region, Illustration*

get its nose down to the ground to feed. A lead rope tied too long is an invitation to serious trouble when a horse lies down. If your saddle horse did not get a chance to roll when you unsaddled, it may roll when tied to a picket or high-line. Keep that sharp knife handy for a rope-cutting emergency.

More riders are using portable electric fences to hold horses in the back-country. The flexible nylon-wire fence material and light posts are easy to carry, roll up and reuse. The high visibility of the two to three inch wide white fencing material reduces the chance of deer or elk running through the fence. Batteries and the charger unit are getting smaller and last longer. You do, however, have to pay attention to how long horses are left fenced in on a piece of ground to avoid over-grazing. But it allows you to keep track of stock and allows them to move around and find tree shelter to help keep warm on a cold night. A fenced area can be made to include grassy areas and some timber. Here again, it is essential that trail riders know the regulations about holding stock for the specific area they are enjoying.

Use hoof pick to help remove an
Easyboot™
—*Photo by Authors*

Lost Horse Shoe: The decision to carry spare horse shoes and equipment depends on your skill to replace a shoe. Also extra horseshoes and shoeing tools are heavy.

Another choice is to use the Easyboot™ to replace a shoe. We have used them numerous times and now make sure we carry one to fit each horse. One packhorse traveled over 100 miles with an Easyboot™ and did not even come close to wearing it out. The trails were rough granite, very rocky, steep and sometimes boggy. The boot came off only twice, both times in bogs. Now we paint the boots fluorescent yellow to make them easier to see on or off the horse. Also, we drill four small holes in the bottom to let water and grit drain out of the boot. Try the boot on both a front and hind hoof to make sure it fits the horse before it is needed.

Trail Horse Hints: What makes a good trail horse? Everyone has an opinion and trail riders put a great amount of trust in the horses or mules they ride. A good part of enjoying a ride is not having a battle with the saddle or pack stock. Good trail stock is not an instant product. Wet saddle blankets and miles are often what counts. Because over the miles the horse gets a chance to deal with many trail conditions and circumstances. To our way of thinking, the following are some of the things a trail horse should do that mean safety to horse and rider:

•Load, haul and unload easily
•Not walk off while you are getting aboard
•Approach water easily, cross it willingly and cross bridges
•Meet hikers, motor bikers, mountain bikers and back-packers
•Be led over obstacles and let you lead another horse
•Be hobbled or tied to a high-line
•Let you ride off alone
•Not spin around when startled by something like a grouse flying up

•Let you get on and off either side and be maneuverable on a narrow trail.

There are, of course, other things a good trail horse should do, but these are some that make a difference in rider safety.

A horse should let you dismount or mount from either side. This can be necessary on a steep, narrow trail. When it is necessary to turn a horse around, whether you are on the ground or in the saddle, the safest way to turn is usually considered to be when the horse faces the drop off, not the uphill side. This lets the horse see where the trail edge is so it doesn't step off the edge with its back feet.

It is getting more common to meet a group of llamas being led as pack animals on the trails. When horses are not used to this critter the results can be a lot of action in the wrong place, like a narrow trail. Give your stock a chance to meet and be around llamas sometime to lessen that problem on the trail.

Make Stock Care Easy: Trail rides and pack trips are taken to enjoy the ride, take in the great Washington scenery and have a break from everyday pressures. One of the best ways to make

Horses with "Scrim" nose and hay bags

—*Photo by Authors*

sure that happens is to be prepared for easy care of your horses at a trailhead or camp and have access to good horse feed.

A day ride may mean a horse will only be tied up a short time during a lunch stop. But still pick a tree at least eight inches in diameter to tie to so there is no damage to the bark. Carry a lead rope long enough to fit around bigger trees.

We like to remove the bridles and put our horses on hobbles whenever we stop for a short lunch break in an area that is suitable for grazing. Carry the hobbles around the horse's neck or tied to the saddle so they are readily available. Again, spread those horse "apples" before you skedaddle from a lunch stop.

On overnight trips, you need to know about the availability of adequate grazing and whether or not you need to carry pelletized feed. In many areas, it has become necessary to supplement over-night grazing with a good measure of pelletized feed. (Grazing regulations vary and are specific for some back-country wilder-ness areas. Check at the local Forest Service office.)

Experience has shown that giving horses a small amount of pelletized feed just before dark helps them settle down when tied up for the night. A light-weight nosebag made of "Scrim," the fabric used to cover greenhouses, will save feed and help keep it clean.

Remember to give your horses a chance to drink before put-ting them on a high-line for the night. When you take thirsty horses to water be prepared for an unexpected jump or pushing

Horses made comfortable with blankets
— *Photo by authors*

for position. More than one good trail rider has gotten injured while on foot at the watering spot.

Not every camp has a good night-time tree shelter for horses. If you are making day rides from the horse camp or trailhead you can use a good horse blanket on a cold night. But most blankets are too bulky and heavy to take on a pack trip. What is worth its weight in mountain riding is a light, Thinsulate-lined horse blanket. Use them on cold windy nights.

Each blanket only weighs about four pounds, rolls up easily, and takes up little space in a pack. Make them fairly rain resistant with any good tent waterproofing spray. Using these blankets means the horses are quieter, and since they rest better, we sleep better. Sure, it's not traditional to think about blanketing in the back-country, but our personal sleeping gear has gotten a lot more comfortable over the years, why shouldn't the horses'?

How Much To Pack: For trail rides that require pack stock, you should have at least one pack animal for every two riders. It makes good sense to take along as few head as possible to reduce the amount of feed you have to carry and to reduce the impact on land. This becomes particularly important when the number of riders in a group increases and the number of "heartbeats" is limited.

Impact on the land can also be reduced if pack stock carry a full load. Some professional outfitters recommend that a pack animal carry about 20 percent of its weight. That means a 1,000-pound horse in good condition could carry 200 pounds, including pack saddle and blankets. However, everything left over should not be hung on the saddle horse. There are many good commercial trail riding accessories on the market such as canteens, coolbags, saddle bags, cantle bags or horn bags; they allow a rider to manage what they carry on the saddle. The problem starts with putting too much stuff, which means weight, into large saddle bags or hanging it off the saddle horn.

Added weight behind the saddle on a long ride will be very uncomfortable for your horse, and carrying an unbalanced load adds to the horse's job of getting the rider back home safely. Large, heavily loaded saddle bags pound on a horse's kidneys. And, when there is a need to dismount in a hurry, all that stuff gets in your way. When thinking of what to take on a trail ride, think light and compact. Give as much attention to what you carry as you do to making sure the horse blanket is clean and the riding saddles and pack saddles fits the stock properly. If you have never checked out your saddle's fit, get someone to show you how to make this very important check.

Try a Pack Trip: Somewhere along the way after a few years of trail riding most of us want to try a pack trip with our own horses. There is no better way to see the back-country for several days. You can find plenty of help on what to do and how to do it if that is your goal.

Start with a couple of good books like the one by Smoke Elser in our reference list. Learn a simple lash tie like the Walker hitch. (It is easier to tie than the diamond hitch). Get yourself to one of the packing clinics that trail riders sponsor each year, usually in the spring. Start with the basics and decide if you like to use pack boxes or wrap up your gear in mantee loads.

This is the time to borrow a sawbuck or decker pack saddle and try your hand at packing. Some folks put a pack saddle on a horse or mule and never bother to learn how to tell if it fits. There are good articles in the western magazines and monthly newspapers that describe how to fit and shape a pack saddle to an animal. We put some white marks on our pack horses before we learned to fit a saddle, not just add more pads.

You can turn most trail rides into pack trips with some careful planning. We started with everything on our saddle horses for one night trips. Because we wanted to go further and stay longer we added a pack horse. Now it is two pack horses with trips that last 7 to 10 days and go over 100 miles in length.

Stock Feed and Conditioning: In some popular areas, grazing for stock can be difficult to find late in the trail season; in some camping areas it is even non-existent. This is usually not a problem for day-long trail rides, but you must plan for it on overnight trips. Using pelletized feed, while bulky to carry, greatly expands the areas trail riders can camp with reduced impact. Introduce horses to one of the pack pellets or complete horse rations prior to a lengthy trip, if pellets will be their primary feed source. (In the first-aid chapter, note the vet's comments on changes in feed.) Making day rides from camp or the trailhead will allow you to use more bulky hay as feed, but that should always be certified weed free to prevent spreading noxious weed seed along the trails. Note that in many areas only pelletized feed can be taken into the national forest.

Like most riders in the springtime, horses are soft and out of shape. A horse's conditioning is important to your safety and the horse's, as well as being fair to the animal. Riding or packing a soft or inexperienced horse invites a slip on a difficult trail or in a scramble over rocks. An out-of-condition horse is also more likely to get a cinch sore. Know what you are asking the animals to do and carry. Help them to muscle up with some use before taking an extended trail ride or pack trip.

—Illustration Courtesy of USDA Forest Service,
Pacific Northwest Region

Chapter 2

STOCK FIRST-AID

By Dr. Greg D. Fischer DVM
Newberg Veterinary Hospital, Newberg, OR

Since a vet or a doctor is not readily available on a back-country trail ride, it is important for someone in the group to have basic first-aid training and to understand basic care items for stock. The following first-aid section by Dr. Fischer covers several of these.

Common Trail Injuries and Emergencies: Even if you are an experienced horseman, horse injuries and emergencies happen. These situations cannot only ruin a ride, but can become life threatening if not attended to. When you have to deal with a medical situation, always think of your safety, while tending to your horse's needs. Contact your nearest veterinarian for consultation as soon as possible.

In preparation for a trailer or trail ride injury or emergency, have some basic first-aid supplies on hand. General treatment and restraint techniques should be reviewed prior to leaving for a long ride. Your local veterinarian is an excellent source to answer any questions you may have on procedures or treatments.

A functional first-aid kit should include the following:

1) Veterinarian's name and phone number
2) Several rolls of 4-inch vet wrap
3) Several telfa gauze pads
4) 4" x 4" gauze pads
5) Cotton-tipped applicators
6) 1' x 1' foam rubber piece for padding chafe injuries
7) 2" or 3" Elasticon tape (2-3 rolls)

8) A roll of duct tape
9) Tweezers, the sturdy type
10) Thermometer, non-glass type or glass in a container
11) Syringes (4 of each size) to flush wounds
12) 1 pint Betadine or chlorhexiderm scrub
13) Saline solution to clean eyes
14) Antibiotic ointment (Nolvasan, nitro furacin, Betadine)
15) Non-steroidal ophthalmic (eye) ointment (BNP)
16) Electrolyte replacer (Entrolyte)
17) Non-steroidal Anti-inflammatory (Phenylbutazone, "bute," paste and Banamine paste)
18) Fly spray or wipe
19) Hoof pick if you don't carry one on the saddle
20) Instant ice for leg injuries

Pack a condensed version of these supplies when traveling and the rest can stay with the trailer. Remember to use plastic containers not glass when ever possible. Check to see what others are carrying to avoid leaving something at the trailer.

While enjoying your ride, stay in tune with your animal to recognize the early onset of problems. Timely treatment can be the difference between success and failure in medical situations. The following are some common equine injuries and emergencies with general guidelines for treatment.

Subsolar Abscess and Penetrating Wounds of the Foot: Both of these injuries are a non-weight-bearing lameness. Subsolar abscess can be a result of stone bruise, poorly placed nails during shoeing, dry cracking hooves, "seedy toe" or separation of the hoof laminae from previous laminitis. In most cases, this condition results in fluid accumulation or active infection within the hoof. Treatment usually involves a veterinarian opening the infected area and applying an antiseptic solution and antibiotic dressing.

When necessary in the back-country, you can reduce the animal's pain by thoroughly cleaning the sole and applying gauze pads held in place with duct tape. In addition, one to two grams of Phenylbutazone paste (bute) per 1,000 pounds of animal weight, can be given orally for pain, until the horse can be evaluated by a veterinarian. It is important to thoroughly flush any draining areas with a strong antiseptic such as Betadine or chlorhexiderm solution. Have your veterinarian examine the injury as soon as possible.

Laminitis (Founder): This condition can result in permanent damage. Most commonly it is caused by a dramatic change to lush feed, such as mountain meadows or excessive grain, but can also be caused by excessive water consumption, colic, and hoof trauma from hard surfaces. The result is decreased oxygen supply to the tissues of the hoof which can cause death and separation at the cellular level.

Signs of founder include shifting leg lameness, usually more pronounced in the front feet. Horses will attempt to put more weight on their hind feet by placing them more central and underneath. Additionally, you may notice increased warmth in the hoof wall as well as bounding pulses in the extremities. To treat the condition on the trail, remove all the bearing weight (pack and rider), pad the soles as described above and orally give the horse one to two grams of Phenylbutazone per 1,000 pounds of animal weight. Always keep in mind that animals with laminitis can be in extreme pain and may be hazardous to handle and bandage. Because of the seriousness of this injury, veterinarian assistance should be sought as soon as possible.

Cuts, Scrapes and Chafing: These are the most common injuries on the trail. Most can be successfully treated by thorough antiseptic cleansing, medicating with antibiotic ointment and proper bandaging. The same procedures can be followed for a more serious injury that involves joints and ligament. Excessive bleeding must first be controlled with firmly placed pressure. Clean the wound thoroughly once the bleeding is controlled.

In the case of a break or tendon laceration, the limb must be stabilized by a splint. As a rule splints should extend across the joint, above and below the injury, whenever possible. You cannot go wrong using plenty of padding and bandage material. Annual vaccinations, including tetanus are a must and should be kept current as a prevention for other problems.

Colic: This term has been used to describe generalized gastrointestinal (G.I.) pain of the equine. The majority of conditions that cause G.I. pain are medically manageable and in some cases subside with time. However, this condition can be fatal and should be treated with the utmost concern. Rapid changes in the type and amount of feed, dehydration, intestinal parasites, water consumption, exhaustion and environmental stress, such as heat stroke can all cause colic.

Horses with colic generally appear nervous, lick and bite at their side, and frequently attempt to go down and roll. The simplest prevention for rolling is continual walking. The horse should be watched closely to prevent injury if it attempts to roll.

Banamine (flunixin meglumine) paste is a successful treatment for gastrointestinal pain. This drug binds some toxins that may be absorbed into the blood during an attack of colic. If the horse has no relief from pain within 45 minutes of giving it Banamine, seek veterinarian attention immediately. If the horse appears to return to normal, slowly return the animal to normal feed after 12-24 hours. By monitoring the consumption of feed, maintaining good hydration, and following a regular rotational worming program, colic can usually be avoided.

Exertional Rhabdomyolses (Tying-Up), Exhaustion and Heat Stroke: This muscle-cramping condition can be caused by either a change in feed, a change in exercise, and possibly by some genetic predisposition of the animal. Metabolic conditions, such as excessive fluid and electrolyte losses, along with a build-up of waste products, such as lactic acid, cause this ailment.

Horses experiencing this condition exhibit a range of signs depending on the severity. Most commonly there is general muscle stiffness and a reluctance to move, indicated by a stiff painful gait. In addition the muscles of the rump may feel firm to the touch. There is usually an increase in temperature, pulse and respiration. Sometimes there is red urine associated with the breakdown of muscle tissue. This condition often goes hand in hand with exhaustion and heat stroke. Treatment for both is essentially the same.

Affected animals should be rested and cooled out slowly until vital signs return to normal (heart rate 30 to 50, respiration 8 to 22, and temperature 99.5 to 102 degrees). Rehydration with up to eight to ten liters of electrolyte solution will return lost minerals and help restore muscle function. In addition, give the animal Phenylbutazone at two to four grams per 1,000 pounds of animal's weight to reduce pain and restore movement. Find a shady area and apply cool water to help in the recovery.

Proper conditioning and regular use of your horse will help

prevent this and many other conditions. If your horse shows signs of depression, appetite loss, or a reluctance to drink persists, contact your veterinarian as soon as possible.

COPD (Allergic Bronchitis): This condition is similar to human "hay fever". It is brought on by atmospheric irritants, such as pollens, molds and trail dust, that can trigger persistent attacks of coughing and labored breathing. Douglas-fir pollen appears to be one major culprit in the Northwest.

Treatment usually involves removing the animal from the source of the irritant and having your vet administer antihistamine, steroids or allergy shots. This is often a life-long affliction and it is important to know if your horse suffers from this before asking it to do hard trail work.

Thumps Synchrondous Diaphragmatic Flutter: This condition may develop in addition to fatigue and loss of electrolytes. It gets its name from the thumping sound generated as the horse's diaphragm contracts consistently with each heartbeat. The horse should be given plenty of rest and eight to ten liters of electrolyte solution (Entrolyte or Lifeguard). The best preventive measure is to provide plenty of opportunities for your horse to drink throughout the ride.

Snake Bites: Snake bites are a serious medical emergency, requiring immediate assessment and treatment. Often bites occur on the neck, head and nose, resulting in swelling which hinders respiration. Until a veterinarian is available, apply cold compresses to decrease swelling. Only under experienced hands should tourniquets be applied in 15-20 minute intervals to prevent the spread of venom from extremities.

Ocular Injuries: Eye injuries are common on the trail and include foreign bodies in the eye, corneal abrasions, and bruising of the eyelids. To treat foreign bodies and corneal abrasions or punctures:

1) Thoroughly flush the injured eye with a sterile saline solution.
2) Apply a non-steroidal antibiotic ointment (BNP).
3) In severe cases, cover the eye with a protective gauze eye patch. Treat eyelid bruises by applying cold compresses for 15 to 20 minutes at a time. Do not attempt to wipe or rub the eye, always wash. Do not apply an ointment con-

taining steroids (for example, Hydrocortisone) unless directed by your veterinarian. Eye infection and trauma can result in permanent vision damage. Seek professional help as soon as possible.

Washington State Health Certificate Requirements

Horses entering Washington must have an official health certificate issued by your veterinarian. The certificate requires a blood test to show the animal is free from infectious and communicable diseases. You should also have proof that a negative test for equine infectious anemia has been made within six months. Horses moving from Oregon to Washington are excluded from test requirements according to WAC 16-54-071, but it is still a good idea to have the health check done for your own information. WAC 16-54-071 also states that horses with equine health certificates acceptable to Washington State and the state of origin from certain other states, including Idaho, may enter Washington for rides or other events. Check with a local veterinarian about specific state health requirements. These requirements can change suddenly if there is an outbreak of a disease.

You should also carry a brand inspection certificate for your horse even if it is not branded. The goal of brand inspection is to deter theft and deny easy markets for strayed or stolen stock. This inexpensive proof of ownership can be obtained from local brand inspectors on an annual basis or as a lifetime certificate.

Chapter 3

SOME BASIC STUFF

Our Rules for a Trail Ride: You could call these our 'don't make the same mistake twice' rules. A hot summer day in Wenatchee can be matched by a cold rain or even snow in the Pasayten Wilderness less than 75 miles away. A warm sunny morning can quickly turn into a day with a cold rain, or snowstorm in the mountains. Situations like this are expected by many who ride in the northwest and take pack trips. Because of some learning experiences with weather and equipment over the years we put together what has become "Our Basic Rules" for a trail ride. How does it fit with your list?

- Have a map for the area.
- Never, never leave camp without a jacket and/or rain slicker.
- Be prepared with the 10 essentials to stay out overnight on any trail. (See the essentials list in the map and compass chapter.)
- Carry water and purification pills.
- Turn and look back where you've ridden.
- Note the landmarks you pass, odd trees, rock outcrops and streams.
- Pack a cantle bag or saddle bags with the extras like an Easyboot™, hobbles and a tool to cut a wire or pull a nail.
- Wait for your partners to water their horses. Don't ride away.
- Share the dust, take turns being the leader.
- Pack it out and more.
- Tell someone where you're going. Leave a note face down in the truck.

Hypothermia: We have said very little about personal injuries, but one danger we want to note is hypothermia. Sitting on a wet saddle, soaked to the skin from a cold rain, is a sure way to be exposed to this injury. It does not take frostbite temperatures to cause hypothermia.

Hypothermia is not restricted to winter or to mountain climbers and snowmobilers. Any time of the year anyone can be affected by the rapid loss of body heat that results in the lowering of body temperature. Just a few degrees loss in body temperature is all it takes to cause exhaustion, and affect your judgement. You need to recognize the early signs and symptoms of hypothermia in riding companions and know what care to give them.

Since the weather will not ask if we are prepared before sending a cold rain or summer snowstorm, always go prepared to protect yourself. Warm clothes, hat and rain gear can make a cold day both tolerable and safe. It is most important to stay dry and protected from the wind to avoid hypothermia, according to cold weather injury specialists. Most hypothermia cases are reported to develop in air temperatures between 30 and 50 degrees. Riding along shivering in rain-soaked jeans, boots and a denim jacket makes you a candidate for hypothermia before you realize what has happened.

Tips for Riding and Camping in Bear Country: Problem encounters with bear are rare and that is the way we want it to remain. But it is a fact, Washington can be considered bear country so learn these easily followed guidelines to reduce further the chance of having a bear visit camp. The black bear is more common than the grizzly bear. That piece of information alone makes most of us a lot more comfortable in camp. However, the Salmo-Priest Wilderness in northeastern Washington is home to not only the mountain caribou and gray wolf, but also the grizzly bear and black bear.

Advice from wildlife specialists include these practices when camping in bear country. They also may be regulations in some grizzly bear habitat areas:

Keep a clean camp.

Store food, garbage and cooking gear at all times.

Prepare food away from the camp sleeping area to keep clothing, tent and gear free of cooking odors.

Sleep in different clothing than that worn around the food area or during cooking. Never cook in the sleeping tent.

Especially, do not burn or bury garbage, pack it out. Bears find buried food and associate it with humans.

Consider leaving the trail dog home on trips into bear country. Dogs may provoke aggression or disturb a bear and lead it back to you or your camp.

Lay out camp to keep personal gear and the sleeping area at least 100 feet uphill from the cooking area.

Store your food and horse pellets either in bear proof containers or suspend items at least 10 feet, 15 is better, above the ground.

The following U.S. Forest Service diagram can be used to identify bear tracks.

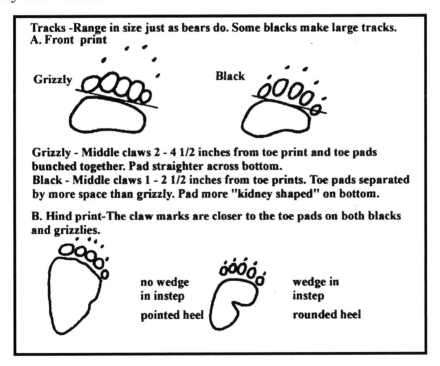

Tracks -Range in size just as bears do. Some blacks make large tracks.
A. Front print

Grizzly   Black

Grizzly - Middle claws 2 - 4 1/2 inches from toe print and toe pads bunched together. Pad straighter across bottom.
Black - Middle claws 1 - 2 1/2 inches from toe prints. Toe pads separated by more space than grizzly. Pad more "kidney shaped" on bottom.

B. Hind print-The claw marks are closer to the toe pads on both blacks and grizzlies.

no wedge   wedge in
in instep   instep

pointed heel   rounded heel

Watch for obvious bear sign along the trail, like tracks, fresh digging, or scat. Try to avoid possible encounters with a feeding bear by being alert as you ride through huckleberry patches, since, like us, the bears may be having a snack. Watch for a feeding or sleeping bear in such spots.

It's a personal preference but in grizzly bear country we carry one of the large pressurized pepper spray containers designed for serious bear encounters. But beware, the wind can also blow the pepper back to you and your stock.

Another piece of wildlife that gets our attention is the cougar. Trail Map 21 and the Trail Guide for Mount Muller Trail 882 notes some recommendations to follow if a cougar is sighted. Ask about wildlife at the local Forest Service office.

Chapter 4

HORSE CAMPS IN WASHINGTON

This section of *Trail Riding and Pack Trips in Washington* presents campgrounds and horse camps designated for trail riders and their stock. They are organized by National Forest and State Forest, include directions to the camp and a section, township and range map location. Certainly there are many more additional horse camps and dispersed camping sites across Washington but these represent many of the best horse camps and trails at these locations. Do your part to help keep them clean and in good repair.

Some horse camps in the most popular areas are overused to the point of being in the need of repair, or have no space available on a weekend. The increase in trail riding at all these popular locations also means more evidence of impact. You have the opportunity to try new areas and spread the use around the more than 30 horse camps referenced in this book. Horse camps are noted on the Trail Guides when they are close enough to a trail to be considered as a place to stay. Horse camp locations are identified on Trail Maps by a horse figure.

COLVILLE NATIONAL FOREST

Walpaloosie Forest Camp is designed for horse use but is not restricted to stock users. It has a very large parking area with a circle drive that is convenient for trailer rigs. There is a heavy log-built combination feeding and tie stall area that handles up to 6 animals. Facilities include tables, 3 fire pits, toilets, loading ramp, stock water and a high-line that at last use required a bucket to stand on to reach the tie cable.

Tie area and feed bunk at Walpaloosie Horse Camp, Colville National Forest

—*Photo by authors*

From Kettle Falls, take Highway 395 west about 2 miles to Highway 20. Follow Highway 20 west for about 20 miles. Make a right turn north onto Road 2030 (Albian Road) and travel about 3.8 miles to the trailhead in Section 31, T.37N., R.35E. **See Trail Map 1.**

Jungle Hill Forest Camp is also designed for horse use but is not restricted to stock users. Facilities include 5 pull-through camps, metal hitch rails, toilet, a feed-tie stall location, poles for high-line tethering, loading ramp, loop drive with adequate parking for 6-10 rigs, stock water at the creek but no potable water.

From Kettle Falls, take Highway 395 west about 2 miles to Highway 20. Turn left and follow Highway 20 west for approximately 20 miles to the junction with the Albian Hill Road 2030, this is about 2 miles before you reach the top of Sherman Pass. Turn north on 2030 (right, if coming from Kettle Falls) and go about 0.5 mile to the trail sign at the edge of the gravelpit site. The trailhead is 0.2 mile west across the meadow. It is located in Section 8, T.36N., R.35E. From Republic, take Highway 20 east about 11 miles. Turn north (left) on Road 2030 the Albian Hill Road. **See Trail Map 1 and 2.**

Gypsy Meadow is not a horse camp but a forest camping site (or dispersed camp) used by trail riders going into the Salmo-Priest Wilderness. The only facilities at this trailhead are toilets and adequate parking for 6-8 rigs. Use the trail junction with Road 2220 at Gypsy Meadows. There is a stream for stock water but no grazing (in spite of the name Gypsy Meadow) or potable water. Area also used by many non-trail riders.

Travel 5 miles from Metaline Falls and follow Road 22 (Nordman-Metaline Falls Road) for about 6 miles until it turns south at the junction with Road 2220. Follow 2220 another 7

Looking into Idaho from Salmo-Priest Wilderness

— Photo by authors

miles (13 miles from Sullivan Lake) to reach the 511 Trailhead on the right. These are good roads with one lane turn-outs to let traffic pass. Be prepared to use turnouts on forest roads. **See Trail Map 3.**

Old Stage Road Camp and Lambert Creek Forest Camps are designed for horse use but are not restricted to stock users. Each trailhead has adequate parking for 4-6 large trailer rigs and both have a loop drive and some pull-through sites.

Old Stage Road Trailhead, Colville National Forest

—Photo by authors

This covers two camps and trailheads at opposite ends of the Old Stage Road Trail. The Old Stage Road Camp at Trail 75 has stock water in a stream, hitch rails, tables and fire rings. From Kettle Falls follow Highway 395 to Highway 20, about 2 miles. Take Highway 20 west for approximately 22 miles to the junction with Road 2030 (Albian Hill). Travel 2030 approximately 7 miles north to the trailhead in Section 13, T.37N., R.34E.

The Lambert Creek Campground at Trail 1 Lambert Creek Road 2165 has hitch rails, loading ramp, tables, fire rings and toilet. However, check with the Republic District Ranger Station for camp status. This trailhead was involved in a recent forest fire and was considerably damaged though not closed, in 1996. For Trail 1; From Republic take Highway 21 north to County Road 546 which becomes Road 2156. It is about 5 miles on Road 2156 to the trailhead located in Section 4, T.37N., R.34E. **See Trail Map 1.**

Thirteen Mile Campground is located on Highway 21 about 12 miles south of Republic near the boundary of the National Forest and the Colville Indian Reservation. This camp has a large parking area and a loop drive. There are toilets, fire rings, 4 table areas, loading ramp and hitch rails. This camp is also open to all users, not just those with stock. Trail 23 from the camp is access to Kettle Crest Trail 13 to the east. **See Trail Map 2.**

GIFFORD PINCHOT NATIONAL FOREST

Falls Creek Horse Camp is west of Indian Heaven Wilderness on Road 65 in Section 31, T.6N., R.8E. From Carson go north on the Wind River Road for 5.5 miles to the junction with Road 65. Go north on 65 about 15 miles. Parking is adequate, there are toilets and stock water but no drinking water or corrals. This camp is heavily used and is often taken up by non-riders. The back part of the camp is boggy. **See Trail Map 8.**

Lone Butte Sno-Park is near the Indian Heaven Wilderness on Road 65 north of Falls Creek Horse Camp. This is a winter recreation parking area so please remove manure from the asphalt parking area. Although this is not a horse camp it is available for overnight stock use. It has toilets, stock water, warming shed, tables and stove but no potable water or loading ramp. The location is ideal for group use such as a barbecue and there are numerous areas available to ride. The Lone Butte Elk Habitat nearby has dispersed riding and Trails 20 and 21 are at the north end of the habitat area. It is located in Section 6, T.6N., R.8E. **See Trail Map 8.**

Crest Horse Camp is located in Section 21, T.5N., R.8E. south of the Indian Heaven Wilderness on Road 60. From Trout Lake follow Highway 141 west for 5 miles to where it becomes Road 24. Continue on for about 2.5 miles and at the junction of Roads 24 and 60, turn left onto Road 60. The camp will be on your left after about 9.5 miles. This 3 unit camp has a hitch rail and pit toilets but no other facilities. There is parking for several rigs. Take water for yourself and horses because there is none close. The Pacific Crest Trail goes through camp. **See Trail Map 8.**

Little Goose Horse Camp is located in Section 5, T.6N., R.9E. northeast of Indian Heaven Wilderness on Road 24. From Trout Lake, take Highway 141 which turns into Road 24 at the Forest boundary. Follow Road 24 for 10 miles to the campground. The horse camp is on the south side of the road and Little Goose Campground is on the north side. The only facilities at the horse camp are a turnaround and a large area to park. Toilets and stock water are nearby. Potable water is available at the campground across the road. Used as an overflow camp by non-horse riders. **See Trail Map 8.**

Kalama Horse Camp with a mounting assist facility, is located southeast of Mount St. Helens in Section 28, T.8N., R.4E. Access is from Highway 503 west of Cougar. Take I-5 Exit 21 at Woodland to 503 East. This goes to the north side of Lake Merwin. Follow Highway 503 to Cougar, turn left (north) onto paved Road 8100 (81) about 1 mile before Cougar. The horse camp is about 9 miles on Road 8100 and up a short spur road. This excellent horse camp is a tribute to the working relationship between Washington BackCountry Horsemen and the U.S. Forest Service staff in this area.

Camp facilities include 13 trailer parking spaces, 6 single vehicle spaces, large staging area at the trailhead, loading ramp, a mounting assist ramp with tie area and a picnic site with horse-shoe pits. Other features are a stock trough with running water, horse lungeing area and campsites that include 6 double trailer rig sites with four 10'x10' corrals, 2 single trailer rig sites with corrals, 2 group sites that will hold 3 or more rigs and four 10'x10' corrals. Campsites have a table, fire ring and nearby toilet access. This is a donation campground. A donation can be made to help maintain the facility. Place manure in bins and clean up any excess feed. A camp host may be available to assist with cleanup equipment if needed. **See Trail Map 12.**

Keenes Horse Camp is on the Randle District. Take Road 23 north from Trout Lake or Road 90 east from Swift Reservoir. Road 90 ends at Road 23. From either route, you turn east off Road 23 onto Road 2329. The camp is about 6 miles down Road 2329 in Section 34, T.10N., R.10E.

It can also be reached from the Randle area off Highway 12. Take Road 23 south from Randle to the junction with Road 21. Follow 21 to the junction with Road 5601 and turn right, this road has sharp switchbacks. It connects with Road 2329 in about 4 miles. Follow 2329 6 miles to the horse camp. Facilities there include loading ramp, corrals, new high-lines, 14 campsites, water trough, vault toilets, and tie stalls at some campsites. Be prepared to get there early or find another camp as this one gets and shows heavy use. This camp, renovated in 1997, is now a " haul your manure away" camp. **See Trail Map 6.**

Lewis River Horse Camp, with a mounting assist area, is within the Mount St. Helens National Volcanic Monument and is located in Section 18, T.8N., R.8E. Trails are open to horses, hikers and mountain bikes. The available rides range from those only a few hours long, to overnight and week-long camping with route combinations and loop opportunities. The Dark Divide, Lewis River, Wright Meadows and Spencer Meadows trail systems are all accessible.

To get there, take I-5 Exit 21 at Woodland onto Highway 503. Travel east on 503 through Cougar (about 30 miles), Highway 503 ends and becomes Road 90. Continue on Road 90 past the Pine Creek Information Station at the east end of Swift Reservoir. At the junction of Roads 25 and 90 turn right (east) to stay on 90. Two miles past Lower Falls Campground at the junction of Roads 90 and 93, turn left (north) onto Road 93. Travel 0.1 mile and the horse camp entrance will be on the right. It is approximately 27 miles from Cougar.

This camp is designed for horse use with parking and camp units for at least 15 trailer rigs. The picnic area has fire pits, tables, horseshoe pits, and toilet facilities. There are four 10'x10' corrals, loading ramp, mounting assist area, and a horse warm-up area. Campsites are available for 3 double units and 5 single trailer units. In the camping area there is another group of 10'x10' corrals. Each campsite is equipped with fire ring, table and a high-line. Potable water is available at Lower Falls Campground. **See Trail Map 11.**

Morrison Creek Horse Camp is on the south end of the Mount Adams Wilderness in Section 2, T.7N., R.10E. From Trout Lake take Road 17 north for 2 miles then continue on Road 80 for 3 miles to the Road 8040 junction. Take Road 8040 6 miles to the camp; the road becomes increasingly rutted and narrow. The horse camping area will be on the left with parking for 4-5 rigs. An old corral is across the creek behind the camping area as are the toilets. Check for current stock tethering requirements in the area. Facilities at this camp are in poor shape but it continues to get steady use and maintenance by trail riders. **See Trail Map 5.**

Walupt Horse Camp is located in Section 19, T.11N., R.11E. off Highway 12. Take Highway 12 for about 11 miles east of Randle to Road 21. Turn right (south) and proceed on Road 21 about 14 miles to the junction with Road 2160. Follow 2160 for approximately 4 miles to the horse camp one mile west of Walupt Lake. Facilities are a loading ramp, hitch rails and campsites for 11 units with pull-through or pull-in parking. High picket tie-line units are available. This is a fee camp with recent rates of about $10.00 per single unit. There have been charges for extra vehicles and the camp fee doubled for the multiple unit campsites. **See Trail Map 4.**

OKANOGAN NATIONAL FOREST

Twisp River Horse Camp facilities include loading ramp, hitch rails, toilets, stock water at the creek and 12 developed sites with permanent high-lines. It is located in Section 19, T.34N., R.19E. on the right side of Road 4435 before the end of the road. The sign there reads, "Horse Camp 3/10 mile". This camp is well planned and worth a visit but it fills early on holiday weekends.

Connecting trails are 428 and 1243, a National Recreation Area (NRA) Trail. To reach the camp from Twisp, take Road 44 about 22.6 miles to the South Creek Campground. Road 44 becomes 4430 on the way. Note that when you cross over to the other road along the west side of the Twisp River, the road is 4430 then 4435 after Reynolds Creek. **See Trail Map 13.**

Andrews Creek Horse Camp is located in Section 20, T.38N., R.22E. A day-use area is on the right side of the road and the horse camp is on the left. The day-use has loading ramp, hitch rails, parking and turn around space. The area is not large and with 5-6 rigs it could be hard to turn around. The horse camp side has 2 corrals, 5 hitch rails, pens, toilet, fire rings, a large area to park several rigs, and water at the creek. A sign reads "Coleman Ridge 9 Miles, Andrews Pass 12 Miles, Boundary Trail 15 Miles".

The camp is located north of Winthrop. Take the West Chewuch River Road 1213 to the end of the pavement. It is about 23 miles to the trailhead. After you enter the National Forest the Road is 51. **See Trail Maps 15 and 16.**

OLYMPIC NATIONAL FOREST

LeBar Horse Camp, under construction by the BackCountry Horsemen of Washington (BCHW) and the Forest Service, was dedicated in 1997. It will replace Brown Horse Camp and is expected to be ready in 1998. Facilities at the camp will include potable water, high-lines, toilets and campsites for 18-20 rigs. It is located in Section 4, T.22N., R.5W. To reach the trailhead, take Highway 101 for about 6 miles north of Shelton to the Skokomish Valley Road. This is also about 7 miles south of Hoodsport. Turn west onto the Valley Road and go about 5 miles to Road 23. Take 23 for 9 miles to the junction with Road 2353, then travel about one mile on Spur Road 100 to the camp. **See Trail Map 19.**

Mount Muller Camp is a converted gravel site and the only facilities there are toilet, ample parking and an information board. There are no horse facilities available. It is located in Section 28, T.30N., R.10W. The camp is 31 miles west of Port Angeles on Highway 101. Turn right (north) at highway mile post 216 onto Road 3071 to the trailhead. **See Trail Map 21.**

Ken Wilcox Horse Camp at Haney Meadow is located in Section 13, T.21N., R.18E. of the Cle Elum Ranger District at the 5400' elevation level. This camp is another example of cooperation between volunteer users and the Forest Service. It carries the name in memory of a long time volunteer trail worker and the founder of BackCountry Horsemen of Washington. Ken's unique efforts were to bring the horsemen, Forest Service and other land management agencies together for a common goal of developing horse camps and trails. The authors had the pleasure of working with Ken on a national trail organization for several years.

Access to the horse camp is by Highway 97 north from Ellensburg about 30 miles to Blewett Pass (shown as Swauk Pass on Forest Service and state highway maps prior to 1996). The camp is located about 10 miles south of Highway 97. Follow Road 9716 about 4.5 miles to the junction with Road 9712. Take 9712 approximately 5 miles to the horse camp at Haney Meadow. There is extensive parking.

Cabin at Ken Wilcox Horse Camp,
Wenatchee National Forest
—*Photo by authors*

Do not use Road 9712 beyond the horse camp as a route from the camp back to Ellensburg.

There are a number of trails that cross this area, known as Table Mountain, including 1205, 1209, 1372, 1373, 1381 and 1601. Camp facilities include 19 campsites, loading ramp, hitch rails, single and multiple camp units, and a large gathering area. There is no potable water. Stock water is available from a stream but forage is not available at the camp so be prepared with feed. The drive to the area offers spectacular views and the area gives you vistas into the Tronsen Drainage. An old cabin near the camp-

Ken Wilcox Horse Camp

View from ridge above Ken Wilcox Horse Camp

ing area adds to the enjoyment of this area. **See Trail Map 25.**

Chiwawa Horse Camp, with a mounting assist ramp, is nearly new and an excellent place to stop. It is located on Road 62, the Chiwawa River Road. You reach this area by taking Highway 2 north from Leavenworth to the junction with Highway 207. Follow 207 for about 4 miles to the Road 62 junction. Continue about 14 miles on Road 62 to the horse camp located in Section 36, T.29N., R.16E. It is about 2 miles past the Finner Campground.

High-line poles ready for use
— Photo by authors

The camp has pull-through parking sites, barrier-free ramp, hitching areas, high-line poles, loading ramp, toilet and trail map. The Rock Creek Tie Trail and the Estes Butte Trail were relocated in 1996 to make them more suitable for stock.

A trail guide sign there lists the following horse trails: 1508, 1509, 1511, 1515, 1519, 1527, 1528, 1530, 1538, 1539 and 1561. There were also these signs posted: "Estes Butte Tr. 1527, Rock Creek Tr. 1509", and "Finner Tie Tr., Bridal Tr." **See Trail Map 30.**

Trinity Horse Camp located in Section 21, T.30N., R.16E. is a new (1996), small horse camp with four campsites, high-lines and hitch rails. Stock water is at the creek. Take Highway 2 north from Leavenworth to the junction with Highway 207. Follow 207 for about 4 miles to the Road 62 junction. Take Road 62 to Road 6200 and the Phelps Creek Campground, about 18 miles. At Phelps Creek Campground take Road 6211 to the trailhead. **See Trail Map 30.**

Alder Creek Horse Camp is located in Section 12, T.29N., R.17E. It is off the Chiwawa River Road 62 about 2 miles northeast of Fish Lake in the Lake Wenatchee Ranger District. The horse camp is now showing wear and only light horse use. The campground is open to horses but is no longer managed or maintained for stock use. It has 3 horse corrals each with 8 stalls, but is large enough for 24 horses. There is a loading ramp, group campsite with table, fire ring and toilet. Parking will handle 4-6 rigs. The 11.3 mile Trail 1548 leaves from camp and goes north along the east side of the Chiwawa River. Motorbikes use the trail as it ties into off-road vehicle (ORV) Trails 1524 and 1534. **See Trail Map 30.**

White Pass Horse Camp is located in Section 2, T.13N., R.11E. at Leech Lake off Highway 12 at White Pass past the ski area and about 18 miles east of Packwood. Facilities include spring water, 6 dispersed campsites, toilets, loading ramp, hitch rails, a capacity for 24 horses and adequate parking for trailer rigs. This site gives access to the Pacific Crest National Scenic Trail 2000 which connects to 79 to the south in the Gifford Pinchot National Forest, and to Trails 1106 and 1107 to the north in the Wenatchee National Forest. In the same location, **White Pass Trailhead South**, has a loading ramp and space for 4 rigs. The water source here is at the White Pass Trailhead. This is also the access to Trail 2000 to the South. **See Trail Maps 22 and 7.**

Lion Rock Springs, on the Cle Elum Ranger District of the Wenatchee National Forest, is one of several campsites that have limited horse facilities but no overnight horse-holding facilities. Lion Rock Springs is an older camp located in Section 4, T.20N., R.18E. This is 23 miles north of Ellensburg off Road 3500 on Spur Road 124. There are 3 camping units with table and fire ring, toilet, tie and loading facilities, a stock watering trough but no potable water. There is ample parking for horse rigs.

This facility is in a good area for riding but it is rather primitive and a bit worn. At last visit there were no signs or camp names apparent. It can be reached over Road 3500 off the 9712 Road into the Ken Wilcox Horse Camp at Haney Meadow, however, that 5 mile segment of the Road 3500 from the 9712 junction is rough in stretches.

Paved Road 35 north from Ellensburg also leads to the south end of Road 3500 and Spur Road 124 over to Lion Rock Springs. This is about 21 miles and a more direct route than from the south.

This is open and generally flat country while on top of Table Mountain and the terrain of the area prevents some access but the views from the rims are good. It is not advisable to drive past the camp as the turn around space is limited even for a single vehicle. This is the site of the old lookout and it is worth a ride to look over the area. **See Trail Map 25.**

Cayuse Horse Camp gives access to the two horse trailheads located in Section 16, T.22N., R.14E. at the Salmon La Sac Campground. In addition to both the Cayuse Horse Camp and Salmon La Sac Trailhead, which have facilities available for horse riders, there is a large campground for non-horse use.

Cayuse is a fee horse camp, and fees have ranged up to $12 with an extra vehicle charge of about $5. This horse camp is an extensive camping opportunity in connection with the Salmon La Sac Campground. It is located on the north end of the Cle Elum Lake at the end of the Cle Elum Valley Road 903, 18 miles north of Cle Elum. Facilities include potable water, flush toilets, community kitchen, stoves, tables, camp host station, a 15 unit horse camp with group and single corrals and loading ramp. There is a 3 horse limit per campsite. The horse camp entrance also has a large turn-around site that makes for an extra safe entry from the road. Forage at this camp location is limited.

Trails accessed from the campground include: 1307, 1309, 1310, 1311, 1315, 1324, 1393. A sign at the horse camp reads, "Salmon La Sac campground 1/4 mile, Salmon La Sac Trailhead 1/2 mile, Tucquala Lake 10 miles".

The Salmon La Sac Trailhead has more than 10 parking spaces suitable for long rigs. There are fire pits, toilets and a loading ramp with hitch rails but no camping or tables. This is a large trailhead. **See Trail Map 26.**

Deep Creek Horse Camp and Trailhead is also known as the Blankenship Trailhead and is located south of Bumping Lake in Section 29, T.15N., R.12E. To reach the trailhead, take Highway 410 north from Naches or east from Pomeroy over Chinook Pass. About 4 miles west of the junction with Road 19 (1900) take the Bumping River Road 1050. Follow 1050 to Road 18 that goes south past Bumping Lake. It is about 17 miles from Highway 410 on a gravel road to the trailhead just down off the road to the left. Washouts from 1996 have been under repair on this road and some rough sections may remain.

Bumping Lake, Wenatchee National Forest

—Photo by authors

There are at least 8 dispersed horse campsites in a good setting with 6 hitch rails, loading ramp and large turning area. Toilet facilities are only available at a campground 0.8 mile further up the road. Parking at the horse camp will handle 3 or 4, 4-horse rigs. Water is available at the horse camp in Deep Creek and at Indian Creek on Highway 12 to the south. Horses are not permitted in either the Deep Creek or Indian Creek Campgrounds. Trails skirt these areas.

The north end of Trail 1105 starts at Deep Creek and serves as a connecting trail for access to several loop rides south into the William O. Douglas Wilderness. It also reaches Highway 12 to the south near Indian Crossing Campground and the White Pass Horse Camp. A popular loop ride from Deep Creek is south to Blankenship, Pear and Apple Lakes but be prepared for mosquitoes. **See Trail Maps 23 and 22.**

Caution: There is a critical feature of this nice secluded camp that riders should be aware of when handling horses in camp or allowing children to ride alone around the camp. The military uses this canyon as part of a training flight path for very low (tree top) flights. Jet planes appear suddenly over the tree tops and roar across camp, an element of great surprise and terrific noise! We experienced this problem while there and confirmed the situation with the Forest Service.

Buck Meadows is the site of the old Buck Meadows Horse Camp on Road 3100 along South Fork Manastash Creek, 24 miles west of Ellensburg in Section 22, T.18N., R.15E. The facilities there include tables, fire rings, pit toilets and 4 campsites but no horse facilities. There is stock water but no potable water. The parking area is large enough to turn a 4-horse rig although the old parking area tends to be muddy in the spring. The Shoe String Lake Trail 1385 and trailhead are about 1.8 miles from camp.

A new multi-use camp is planned for construction by 1999 in the same vicinity. The purpose is to protect the wet areas that are in the vicinity. A camp host will be in residence during seasonal use. This project will restore the adjacent meadow and wet areas and create improved camping. **See Trail Map 24.**

Black Pine Horse Camp is located in Section 2, T.24N., R.15E. on the Leavenworth District near the end of the Icicle Road 7600. This is about 17 miles out of Leavenworth. Road 7600 goes south out of Leavenworth past the National Fish Hatchery. The horse camp is close to the end of Road 7600 where the trailhead is located. There is no parking for trailer units at the end of the road, but near the turn into the horse camp there is a large stock unloading area with additional hitch rails and a loading ramp. The horse camp has 8 campsites, potable water, hitch rails, fire rings and toilets. A maximum of 6 horses are allowed per campsite and a camping fee may be required.

Trail 1551, the primary trail from this area, connects with other trails and offers several loop ride opportunities into the Alpine Lakes Wilderness where permits are required. **See Trail Map 27.**

WASHINGTON YACOLT BURN STATE FOREST

Rock Creek Horse Camp is 9 miles southeast of Yacolt in southeast Washington off I-205. Take the I-205 Battle Ground Exit for Highway 503. Follow 503 north for 14 miles and turn right onto Road 12 past the Moulton Falls, then turn right onto Dole Valley Road. Rock Creek Horse Camp will be on the left after about 5 miles. The location is Section 9, T.3N., R.4E. Facilities include 19 tie stalls, 6 picnic tables, group shelter, toilet and drinking water.

The Rock Creek area offers 25 miles of trails. Trails lead to views of Rock Creek Canyon and the Camas City watershed, and travel through forests and high brush on the way to upper sections of loop trails. The loop trail connects with many logging roads, so carry a map and know how to use your compass.

The low bridges that cross the wet areas and creeks do not have high side rails so horses should be well practiced at crossing a wooden bridge. It is an easy place for a nervous horse to slip or step off the bridge into the bogs. Some sections of the trail are steep and lead to rocky ledges and shale.

This is a high-use area, endurance riders train here in the summer so the camp fills up fast. It is possible to call the Department of Natural Resources (DNR) for information about availability of space which is distributed on a first-come basis. **See Trail Map 31.**

WASHINGTON CAPITOL STATE FOREST

Margaret McKenny Horse Camp with a mounting assist ramp, is located in Section 28, T.17N., R.3W. Take I-5 Exit 95 (south of Olympia) and head west on Highway 121 for 3 miles to the town of Littlerock. Keep going straight west 0.8 mile to a "T" junction. Turn right and travel less than 1.8 miles to the Margaret McKenny campground. You enter the horse-use portion of this camp off Waddell Creek Road and the entryway takes you through the non-horse section of the camp. All roads are paved.

The road into the horse campsite invites many non-horse visitors to stroll into the area so this can be a good time to spread some goodwill between horse campers and others. A sign at the horse camp entry notes "For Horse Use Only". We hope this regulation is respected by others.

Facilities at this horse camp include potable water from an old-fashioned pump, toilets, 6 first-come campsites, stock water, 12' x 12' corrals with concrete pads, back-in parking and a loop drive. There is a manure bin at the site to use when cleaning up the corral before leaving. Be sure and cooperate in this effort.

Waddell Creek is reached by a short 0.5 mile ride out to Trail 6a. It is a safe place to water horses, or you can carry water from the pump in camp. Expect to see spare rigs parked to save a camp spot for a late arriving friend. **See Trail Map 33.**

Porter Creek Horse Camp is located in Section 12, T.17N., R.4W. It is reached from the north off I-5 by taking Exit 88 onto Highway 12 west through Rochester and Oakville to Porter. About 20 miles from I-5 go right on Porter Creek Road for 4 miles to the Porter Creek Campground. Facilities include two large corrals, parking area and campsites away from the corrals. The trail system for horses goes east and south from camp. Long loop rides are apparent by studying the map of the Capitol State Forest. **See Trail Map 33.**

Fall Creek Trailhead Day-use Camp, with a mounting assist ramp, is located in Section 24, T.17N., R.4W. **Fall Creek Horse Camp** is in the same vicinity. Both are reached by taking I-5 Exit 95 (south of Olympia). Head west on Highway 121 for 3 miles to the town of Littlerock. From Littlerock go west to the Mima Falls Road and turn left (south) to the Bordeaux Road as if you were going to the Mima Falls Trailhead. Continue west on Bordeaux Road past Marksman Road to the Bordeaux entrance and the end of the County Road, now called D-Line. Continue on D-Line to Road D-3000. From Marksman Road to D-3000 on your right (north) it is about 5 miles. Turn onto D-3000 and go 3.8 miles to the Falls Creek camps.

Facilities at the horse camp include 8 campsites with 12' x 12' stalls, 7 picnic units, potable water, forest stream and toilets. Get there early as these camps fill quickly. **See Trail Map 33.**

Camp Wedekind (for group gatherings) is located in Section 21, T.17N., R.4W. It is accessed from the north off I-5 by taking Exit 88 onto Highway 12 west through Rochester and Oakville. Go 2.8 miles past Oakville to where D-Line Road starts on Highway 12. This is the same road that goes to Fall Creek. Signs read "Cedar Creek Entrance". It is less than 2 miles on D-Line Road to D-1000 NE that you take for about 6 miles to Camp Wedekind. The camp sets in the junction of D-1000 and C-Line roads on Monroe Creek.

Facilities at the horse camp are hitch rails, parking area for 2-3 rigs and campsites. It is a camp for group gatherings and really not a place for overnight camping. This camp is about in the middle of the State Forest and horse trail system. **See Trail Map 33.**

Mima Falls Horse Camp is located in Section 4, T.16N., R.3W.

It is reached by taking Exit 95 off I-5 south of Olympia. Follow Highway 121 for 3 miles to Littlerock. Go straight through town heading west for about 0.8 mile to the Mima Road junction. At this "T" junction take the road left for about 1.3 miles to Bordeaux Road. Turn right onto Bordeaux Road and follow it 0.8 mile to Marksman Road. Turn right (north). Mima Mounds geological area will be on your right and the horse campground is a little over 0.5 mile further on Marksman Road. Camp facilities include 5 campsites, drive-through parking, 12' x 12' pole stalls, toilets, 2 picnic sites and trailhead access. **See Trail Map 33.**

WASHINGTON TAHUYA STATE FOREST

Tahuya River Camp in Section 21, T.23N., R.2W. is the only designated horse camp in the Tahuya State Forest. It has 11 campsites that fill quickly during the summer and for horse events. There are 20 horse corrals provided. The camp is primarily used by horse riders although ORV and ATVs are permitted. Drinking water is available. From Bremerton take Highway 3 south to the junction of 3 and Road 300. Follow 300 (North Shore Road) approximately 6 miles to the junction with Tahuya Road.

The Mission Creek Trailhead in Section 35, T.23N., R.2W. provides a day-use-only staging area with adequate parking. There are no restrooms at Mission Creek Trailhead. **See Trail Map 34.**

WASHINGTON GREEN MOUNTAIN STATE FOREST

Green Mountain Campground must be accessed by trail for both trail riders and hikers. Since there is no overnight camping at the trailhead, all users have access to the trails and the camp located in Section 3, T.24N., R.1W. Washington DNR has provided for horse riders with 12 corrals, potable water, 13 campsites and 4 toilets available to campers at Green Mountain Vista. **See Trail Map 36.**

Chapter 5

TRAIL MAPS AND TRAIL GUIDES

Volunteer Work: BackCountry Horsemen of Washington member clears large blowdown from PCT in Gifford Pinchot National Forest
—*Photo by authors*

Map 1

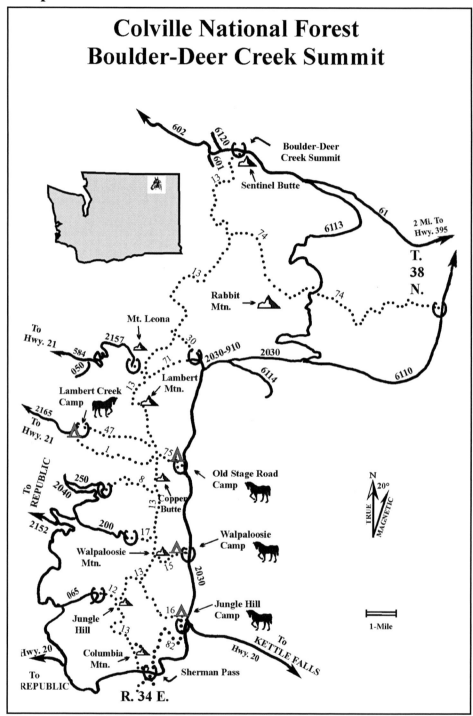

Colville National Forest
Boulder-Deer Creek Summit

602

6120

601

13

Boulder-Deer
Creek Summit

Sentinel Butte

74

6113

61

2 Mi. To
Hwy. 395

T.
38
N.

Rabbit
Mtn.

74

Mt. Leona

To
Hwy. 21

2157

584

050

30

71

2030-910

2030

Lambert
Mtn.

13

6114

6110

Lambert Creek
Camp

2165

To
Hwy. 21

47

1

75

Old Stage Road
Camp

To
REPUBLIC

250

2040

8

13

Copper
Butte

2152

200

17

Walpaloosie
Camp

Walpaloosie
Mtn.

15

2030

13

065

12

13

Jungle
Hill

16

Jungle Hill
Camp

Hwy. 20

Columbia
Mtn.

13

82

To
Hwy. 20

To
KETTLE FALLS

To
REPUBLIC

Sherman Pass

R. 34 E.

N
20°

TRUE

MAGNETIC

1-Mile

BOULDER-DEER CREEK SUMMIT TRAIL 13S

Trail Length: 16 Miles
Elevation: 4600 - 5600 Feet
Difficulty: Moderate
Open: May - October
Usage: Medium
Nearest Town: Curlew or Republic
Nearest Horse Camp: Old Stage Road or Walpaloosie
Connecting Trails: 75, 71, 47, 1, 15, 16, 82.
Facilities at Trailhead: Loading ramp, hitch rails, toilets at camp
    ground just north of the trailhead, 5 campsites

DIRECTIONS

TO THE TRAILHEAD

This Trail Guide describes Trail 13 when riding south toward
Highway 20. You can reach the trailhead from Republic by taking
Highway 21 north to Curlew and then County Road 602 about 11
miles east to the Boulder-Deer Creek Summit.

Coming west from Kettle Falls, follow Highway 395 north about
22 miles to the Boulder-Deer Creek Road 61. Turn west onto Road 61
and go approximately 11 miles to the summit and the trailhead located
in Section 20, T.39N., R.35E.

Parking: Large area adequate for several rigs. Caution, be aware
of the limited visibility on the highway as you cross from the campground to the trailhead and parking.

Comments: The feature of this trailhead is the access to the other
trails along Trail 13 to the south, three horse camps and the Sherman
Pass Summit trailhead. See the Kettle Crest Trail 13 Trail Guide for
more information.

Note, this is the place to camp if you plan to ride south on Trail 13
from Sherman Pass across Highway 20.

JUNGLE HILL TRAIL 16

Trail Length: 2.5 Miles
Elevation: 4300 - 6500 Feet
Difficulty: Most Difficult
Open: May - October
Usage: Medium
Nearest Town: Kettle Falls
Nearest Horse Camp: Jungle Hill
Connecting Trails: 13N, 82
Facilities at Trailhead: Creek for horse water, loading ramp, hitch rails, 5 pull-through campsite, toilet, high posts installed to hold picket lines, (when we used it the rings were too high to reach without standing on a bucket or tieing your horse and then dismounting!) This camp is open to all users.

DIRECTIONS

TO THE TRAILHEAD

Access from Kettle Falls is by taking Highway 395 west 3 miles to Highway 20. Turn left and follow Highway 20 west for approximately 19 miles to the junction with the Albian Hill Road 2030. This is about 3 miles before you reach the top of Sherman Pass. Turn north on 2030 (right if coming from Kettle Falls) and go about 0.5 mile to the trail sign at the edge of the gravel pit site. The trailhead is 0.2 mile west across the meadow located in Section 8, T.36N., R.35E.

From Republic, take Highway 20 east about 20 miles and turn north (left) onto Road 2030 the Albian Hill Road.

Parking: Large lot with space for 6-10 trailers and a loop drive.

Comments: The trail climbs steeply for the 2.5 miles under a forest canopy with a few open areas. It begins near a stream and ends with a sweeping view to the east. Caution: An area that appears to be a good watering spot should be approached with care due to boggy conditions. This is located at a small pond along Trail 13 as you ride south after the junction of Trails 16 and 13. Riders walk their horses to this water spot or avoid it.

Note: This is the place to camp if you plan to ride south on Trail 13 from Sherman Pass across Highway 20, as this is an access trail to the Kettle Crest Trail 13. Road also 2030 offers a good opportunity for a loop ride if used with Trails 16, 13 and 15.

KETTLE CREST TRAIL 13

Trail Length: 30.2 Miles
Elevation: 4600 - 5600 Feet
Difficulty: Moderate
Open: May - October
Usage: Medium
Nearest Town: Kettle Falls or Republic
Nearest Horse Camp: Jungle Hill
Connecting Trails: 13 South and over 15 other trails that can be reached from Roads 2030 or 2020 off Highway 20 or by Highway 21 north of Republic
Facilities at Trailhead: Information signs, loading ramp, hitch rails, toilet, stock water

DIRECTIONS

TO THE TRAILHEAD

From Republic follow Highway 20 east for approximately 17 miles to the summit of Sherman Pass. The Sherman Pass Trailhead described here is on the north side of the highway. If riding south, the trail starts across the highway and the sign is partially hidden by brush. Remember, this is a very busy highway! (See Trail Guide for the Kettle Crest Trail 13S). Sherman Pass Summit, which is the midpoint of this 30 mile trail, is west of Kettle Falls approximately 25 miles in Section 19, T.36N., R.35E. The north end of this trail can be reached by taking Highway 21 north from Republic to Curlew and then going east on County Road 602. Follow 602 about 11 miles to the Boulder-Deer Creek Summit.

Parking: Large area is adequate for 6-8 trailer rigs and has a loop drive.

Comments: The adjacent campground to the Sherman Pass Trailhead does not permit horses into the camping area but hitch rails are nearby. The three campsites have tables and fire rings with cooking grills. A sign reads, "13 North" and "13 South."

The Kettle Crest Trail described here reaches from the Colville Indian Reservation Boundary on the south to the Boulder-Deer Creek Summit on the north. There are two segments to the trail. One segment, Kettle Crest Trail 13S is about 13 miles long and goes south from Highway 20 at Sherman Pass. The other is the Boulder-Deer Creek Summit Trail 13S segment that is over 16 miles long and goes south from the Boulder-Deer Creek Summit to Sherman Pass.

The Kettle Crest Trail is one of the most popular on the Colville National Forest. Features include open meadows, rock outcrops and large talus slopes. There are several steep pitches along the trail route. It is used by endurance riders to condition horses.

LAMBERT TRAIL 47

Trail Length: 1.6 Miles
Elevation: 5000 - 6100 Feet
Difficulty: Moderate
Open: May - October
Usage: Medium
Nearest Town: Republic
Nearest Horse Camp: Lambert Creek (west) or Old Stage Road (east)
Connecting Trails: 1, 13, 75
Facilities at Trailhead: Hitch rails, loading ramp, tables, fire ring, stock water at the creek, toilet. Trailhead is shared with Old Stage Road Trail 1

DIRECTIONS

TO THE TRAILHEAD

From Republic travel west on Highway 20 for 3 miles then go north on Highway 21 for about 8 miles to the Lambert Creek Road 546 and turn east. This becomes Road 2165. Travel on 2165 about 6 miles to where the road ends at the trailhead located in Section 4, T.37N., R.34E.

Recent forest fire damage has impacted the area of this campground and trailhead. Check with the Forest Service District Ranger's office in Republic for current trailhead and camp status information.

Parking: Ample for trailer rigs.

Comments: This trail is another short access to the Kettle Crest and Trail 13. It climbs steadily through meadows and open stands of timber and some of the area impacted by the forest fire.

There is spring and stock water through half the distance to the crest. Both campgrounds are designed for stock but are open to all users.

MARCUS TRAIL 8

Trail Length: 3.5 Miles
Elevation: 4800 - 6600 Feet
Difficulty: Moderate
Open: May - October
Usage: Medium
Nearest Town: Republic
Nearest Horse Camp: Walpaloosie
Connecting Trails: 13N
Facilities at Trailhead: None

DIRECTIONS

TO THE TRAILHEAD

From Republic take Highway 20 east about 12 miles to Road 2040. Turn north (left) for about 10 miles to Road 250. Follow Road 250 for 1.5 miles to the trailhead located in Section 21, T.37N., R.34E.

There is also road access from Republic north about 2.5 miles from Highway 20. Turn east onto Road 284 which becomes Road 2152 and connects with Road 2040. Follow 2040 to Road 250 and the trailhead. See the Trail Guide for the Timber Ridge Trail 17.

Parking: Limited at trailhead. A 200 foot parking area was started several years ago with planned room for 4 to 5 rigs.

Comments: The trailhead has a restricted campsite. The trail climbs steadily to the crest with the last half of the distance having views of the valley and mountains. The trail ride follows an old jeep trail for 1.5 miles then the trail turns into standard trail tread.

OLD STAGE ROAD TRAILS 75 and 1

Trail Length: 75, 1.8 Miles and 1, 5.8 Miles
Elevation: 5500 - 3900 Feet
Difficulty: Moderate
Open: May - October
Usage: Medium
Nearest Town: Republic and Kettle Falls
Nearest Horse Camp: Lambert Creek Campground
Connecting Trails: 13, 1, 75, 47
Facilities at Trailhead: This Trail Guide covers two trailheads at opposite ends of the Old Stage Road Trail. The trailhead at Trail 75 has stock water, 2 hitch rails, tables and 2 fire rings. The trailhead at Trail 1 at Lambert Creek on Road 2165 has hitch rails, loading ramp, tables, fire rings and toilet. Check with the Republic District Ranger Station for status due to forest fire damage. These camps are open to all users.

DIRECTIONS

TO THE TRAILHEAD

Trailhead for Trail 75: From Kettle Falls follow Highway 395 west 3 miles to Highway 20. Take Highway 20 west for approximately 19 miles to the junction with Road 2030 (Albian Hill). Travel Road 2030 for approximately 7 miles north to the trailhead located in Section 13, T.37N., R.34E.

Trailhead for Trail 1: From Republic take Highway 20 east about 3 miles then take Highway 21 north about 8 miles to Road 546 (Lambert Creek) which becomes Road 2156. It is about 5 miles on Road 2156 to the trailhead located in Section 4, T.37N., R.34E. This trailhead was involved in a recent forest fire and there was considerable damage at the trailhead.

Parking: Each trailhead has adequate parking for 4-6 large trailer rigs and both have a loop drive and pull-through sites.

Comments: The Old Stage Road Trail built in 1892 is the only remaining segment of the first Washington State Highway and is still open to wagons. From the east on Trail 75 it is a short distance to connect with Trail 13 and access to Copper Butte the highest point in Ferry County. From the west on Trail 1 it is about 5.8 miles to the junction with Trail 13. A 9 mile loop is possible with the Midnight Ridge Trail 47. There are several interpretive sites along the trail. One stop is historic Lust Springs. Water is available from small streams.

STICK PIN TRAIL 71

Trail Length: 2.6 Miles
Elevation: 4250 - 6250 Feet
Difficulty: Moderate
Open: June - October
Usage: Light to Medium
Nearest Town: Republic
Nearest Horse Camp: Walpaloosie
Connecting Trails: 13, 30
Facilities at Trailhead: Three drive-through sites, 4-hitch rails, stock
    water at creek

DIRECTIONS

TO THE TRAILHEAD

From Kettle Falls, take Highway 395 north about 22 miles and turn west onto the Boulder Creek Road 61. Follow Road 61 for 2 miles to the junction of Road 6110 (South Boulder Road). Take 6110 for about 13 miles to the junction with Albian Hill Road 2030. Now follow 2030 for 0.8 mile to Spur Road 2030-910 and the trailhead located in Section 30, T.38N., R.35E. The spur road is not on all current Forest Service maps.

The availability of access by Highway 20 and on Road 2030 between Kettle Falls and Republic should be checked with the Republic District Ranger Station office to see if that way is open to the trailhead.

Parking: Small lot adequate for 2-3 trailer rigs and it has a loop drive.

Comments: This trail is used to access Kettle Crest Trail 13 and the best views on the ride are near the last leg of the 2.6 mile timbered trail. The trail follows a stream for most of its length and does cross some boggy areas. It is also an access to other trails for more extended rides.

TAYLOR RIDGE TRAIL 74

Trail Length: 9.5 Miles
Elevation: 2350 - 5900 Feet
Difficulty: Moderate
Open: May - October
Usage: Light to Medium
Nearest Town: Kettle Falls
Nearest Horse Camp: Walpaloosie
Connecting Trails: 13
Facilities at Trailhead: Loading ramp

DIRECTIONS

TO THE TRAILHEAD

To reach this trailhead from Kettle Falls follow Highway 395 north about 22 miles to Boulder-Deer Creek Road 61. Turn left (west) onto 61 for 2 miles to the junction with Road 6110. Again turn left and follow 6110 for 2.8 miles to the trailhead in Section 16, T.38N., R.36E.

Parking: Small area but adequate to turn longer rigs. There is room to park 3-4 larger trailer rigs at the trailhead and more on the road.

Comments: The trailhead has 3 pull-in campsites with fire rings but no toilets or potable water. Horse water is available at the creek along Road 6110.

The trail climbs from the valley floor to ridge tops with several panoramic views. Trail vistas include Alligator and Thompson Ridges, Copper, US, Lambert, Twin Sisters and Stick Pin Mountains.

It crosses numerous small streams and passes several trail-side springs. You will find two dispersed campsites along the trail. The trail may also be reached mid-way by using Road 6113. Some segments of the trail may be relocated west of Road 6113 due to logging activity in beetle killed timber.

TIMBER RIDGE TRAIL 17

Trail Length: 3.2 Miles
Elevation: 4800 - 6200 Feet
Difficulty: Moderate
Open: May - October
Usage: Medium
Nearest Town: Republic
Nearest Horse Camp: Walpaloosie
Connecting Trails: 13N
Facilities at Trailhead: None

DIRECTIONS

TO THE TRAILHEAD

From Republic take Highway 20 east for about 3 miles to the junction with Highway 21 then go north 2.5 miles on Highway 21 to the Fish Hatchery Road 284. Take 284 east about 4 miles until it becomes Road 2152. Continue on 2152 to the junction with Spur Road 200. This is a low maintenance road so it is better to ride, not drive Road 200 to the trailhead located in Section 27, T.37N., R.34E.

Parking: Roadside only at the junction of Roads 2152 and 200.

Comments: This is an Adoptive Trail and receives very little maintenance. You should call the Republic District Ranger Station to be sure the trail is open.

It begins as an old road for 2 miles through wooded and meadow areas. The climb is gradual until it becomes an actual trail leading to the Kettle Crest Trail 13 then the last mile is a steep ride through the woods.

WALPALOOSIE TRAIL 15

Trail Length: 2.5 Miles
Elevation: 5000 - 6900 Feet
Difficulty: Easy to Moderate
Open: May - October
Usage: Light to Medium
Nearest Town: Kettle Falls
Nearest Horse Camp: Walpaloosie (open to all users)
Connecting Trails: 13N
Facilities at Trailhead: Toilet, stock water, loading ramp, tables, fire
    pits, high-line, heavy log feeder-tie stall combination for 6 horses,
    4 hitch rails

DIRECTIONS

TO THE TRAILHEAD

Out of Kettle Falls, reach the trail by taking Highway 395 west
approximately 3 miles to Highway 20. Follow Highway 20 for about
19 miles and make a right turn onto Road 2030 (Albian Road). Head
north about 3.8 miles to the trailhead and the camp on your left, located in Section 31, T.37N., R.35E.

From Republic, take Highway 20 east about 20 miles and turn
north onto Road 2030.

Parking: Area is large enough for 4-6 trailers and it has a loop
drive.

Comments: This is an access trail to the Kettle Crest Trail 13 and
it wanders through semi-open lodgepole stands with views of Graves
and Mack Mountains. The grade is moderate with a few steep sections.
Near the summit, the trail crosses a meadow on Walpaloosie Mountain
and then joins Trail 13. This is a good steep ride with great views to
the east.

Map 2

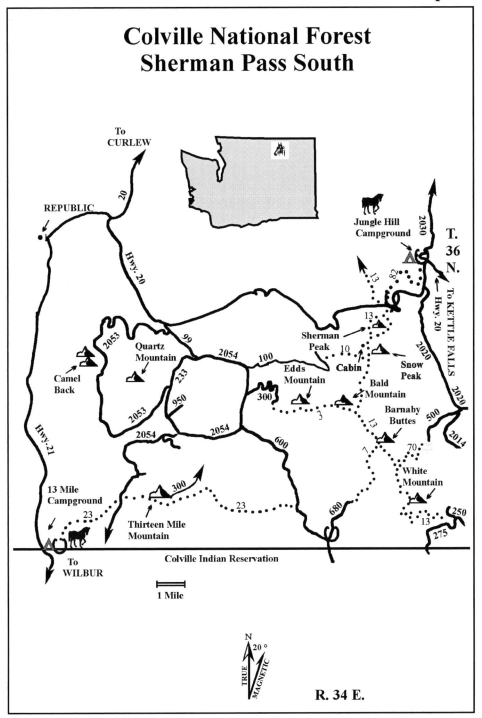

Colville National Forest
Sherman Pass South

To
CURLEW

REPUBLIC

20

Hwy. 20

Jungle Hill
Campground

2030

T.
36
N.

To KETTLE FALLS

Hwy. 20

13

82

13

2053

Quartz
Mountain

Camel
Back

99

2053

950

233

2054

100

Sherman
Peak

10

Cabin

Snow
Peak

2020

Edds
Mountain

300

Bald
Mountain

3

2054

2054

600

2014

500

Barnaby
Buttes

13

7

70

White
Mountain

680

13

250

275

2020

13 Mile
Campground

23

300

23

Thirteen Mile
Mountain

Hwy. 21

To
WILBUR

Colville Indian Reservation

1 Mile

N
20°

TRUE

MAGNETIC

R. 34 E.

BARNABY BUTTE TRAIL 7

Trail Length: 7.0 Miles
Elevation: 3400 - 6300 Feet
Difficulty: Easy
Open: May - October
Usage: Light
Nearest Town: Republic
Nearest Horse Camp: 13 Mile Campground (open to all users)
Connecting Trails: 23, 13, 70 (south on 13 one mile)
Facilities at Trailhead: Toilet, fire rings, tables, loading ramp, hitch
    rail

DIRECTIONS

TO THE TRAILHEAD

From Republic take Highway 20 east about 7 miles to Hall Creek
Road 99. Follow Road 99 south about 5 miles to Road 2054-600. Road
600 is long, fairly steep and rough for trailers.

You can also reach the trail by taking Highway 21 south 12 miles
to the 13 Mile Campground and trailhead. Ride Trail 23 to the junction
with Trail 7 on Road 600 and follow it south 2 miles to the junction
with Road 680. Follow 680 north about 3 miles to Trail 7 in Section
26, T.35N., R. 34E. This jeep-type trail (Road 680) is considered part
of Trail 7.

Note, there is also a trail called Barnaby Butte 70 at the north end
of Trail 7 and about one mile further south on Trail 13. Trail 70 is a
moderate grade and was the access to the old Barnaby Lookout. Road
access on Road 2020 to reach Trail 70 is not recommended due to
large water bars.

Parking: Very limited for trailer rigs at the Road 600 Trailhead.
Better parking exists about 0.8 mile before that trailhead at a dispersed
campsite near the creek. Unload and park there. Ample parking is only
available at the popular 13 Mile Trailhead and campground off Highway 21, the west access to Trail 7.

Comments: The Barnaby Butte Trail 7 follows a closed jeep road for about 3 miles. Several campsites with water nearby are along the way. The trail crosses many streams in the first 5 miles and goes through a variety of forest types from warm lower lands to cool crests. Stream vegetation contrasts with the 1988 White Mountain fire regrowth vegetation. Wildlife may include grouse, deer, bear and beaver.

KETTLE CREST TRAIL 13S

Trail Length: 13.3 Miles
Elevation: 5200 - 6500 Feet
Difficulty: Moderate
Open: May - October
Usage: Light to Medium
Nearest Town: Republic
Nearest Horse Camp: Jungle Hill (open to all users)
Connecting Trails: 3, 7, 10
Facilities at Trailhead: Toilets, information sign, loading ramp, hitch rails, stock water

DIRECTIONS

TO THE TRAILHEAD

The access from Republic is by following Highway 20 east for approximately 17 miles to Sherman Pass. The trailhead is on the north side of the highway in Section 25, T.36N., R.35E. If you are riding south, note the trail starts on the north side and crosses south over the highway. The sign can be partially hidden by brush. Remember this is a busy highway and traffic is high speed.

Caution: There is a difficult, steep, short drop to reach the trail as you cross south from the Sherman Pass Trailhead. The trail also splits and goes on each side of Sherman Peak. The easiest route is the west or right fork. They join together south in about 0.5 mile.

This Trail Guide describes Trail 13 when riding south from Sherman Pass. The Sherman Pass Summit Trailhead is approximately 25 miles west of Kettle Falls. Expect numerous blowdown of fire killed trees.

Parking: Large area at the Sherman Pass Trailhead with drive-through sites for 6 to 8 trailer rigs.

Comments: The Jungle Hill Campground and the Sherman Pass Trailhead both serve Trail 13 south and 13 north. Horses must be kept out of the adjacent Sherman Pass Campground, use the hitch rails and 3 campsites nearby. The 1988 White Mountain fire burned over this trail and shrub regrowth is abundant. There are numerous views of the Lake Roosevelt Valley (Columbia River) along the trail. Water can be found near to this trail between Snow Peak junction and Bell Mountain.

The first section of the trail forks and climbs Sherman Pass to an elevation of 6500 feet. Just under Snow Peak, the more difficult 2.7 mile Snow Peak Trail 10 joins Trail 13 and then Trail 10 takes off to the west through the 1988 White Mountain fire area. Snow Peak Cabin on this trail can be reserved for use. Further south, the junction of Trail 13 and Trail 3 (that also goes west) is just after Bald Mountain. Trail 13 continues on to Barnaby Buttes where it joins with Trail 7 leading to the southwest.

John and Bev Horn and authors at Snow Peak Cabin on Trail 13, Colville National Forest

—Photo by authors

THIRTEEN MILE TRAIL 23

Trail Length: 16.5 Miles
Elevation: 2000 - 4350 Feet
Difficulty: Easy
Open: May - October
Usage: Medium
Nearest Town: Republic
Nearest Horse Camp: 13 Mile Campground and Trailhead
Connecting Trails: 7
Facilities at Trailhead: Toilets, fire rings, 4 table areas, loading ramp,
  hitch rail

DIRECTIONS

TO THE TRAILHEAD

From Republic follow Highway 21 south approximately 12 miles
to the trailhead on the left (east). The location is Section 31, T.35N.,
R.32E. This is at the boundary of the Colville National Forest and the
Colville Indian Reservation.

Parking: The lot is large enough for 4-5 trailer rigs and has a loop
drive. There are campsites for five large rigs.

Comments: The higher trail (at Hall Creek end) passes through
several timber types, including old growth Ponderosa Pine, with many
great view points along the way. Side trip rides are possible to Fire
Mountain (5890 feet elevation) and to 13 Mile Mountain (4886 feet
elevation).

The lower trail (from 13 Mile Campground) winds through the
rock cliffs of the Sanpoil River. Southwest exposures and low elevation
make this trail available to users when others are still snowbound. This
part of the trail is at its best in late April or early May when eagles may
soar over the cliffs. Rattlesnakes have been seen in this area.

Trail 23 can be use as a connection to Trail 13 by taking Hall
Creek Road 99 to Road 2054-600 and then Road 680 (located in
Section 35, T.35N., R.34E.) at the east end of the trail and then follow-
ing Trail 7 to Barnaby Buttes and Trail 13.

Remember Road 600 is steep and rough for trailers. See the Trail
Guide for Barnaby Butte Trail 7 for information on Road 600 access.

Map 3

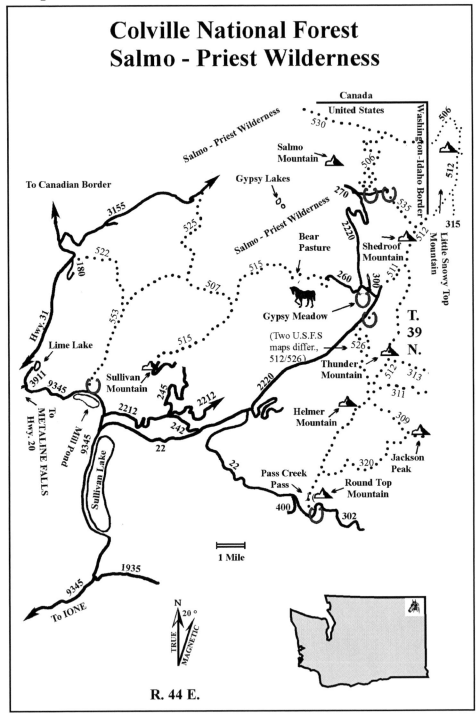

**Colville National Forest
Salmo - Priest Wilderness**

SALMO-PRIEST WILDERNESS
and SULLIVAN LAKE AREA

Nearest Town: Metaline Falls.

This remote area of NE Washington with access into NW Idaho is included because it offers a remoteness and the presence of both black bear and grizzly bear. Learn the safety measures essential to camp in grizzly bear habitat. See the book section on that subject.

The trails that are included provide access from Sullivan Lake into the Salmo-Priest Wilderness vicinity. The rider should always check with the local Forest Service office regarding trail conditions and bear situations.

Trails covered are the Salmo Loop Trails 506, 512 and 535 (an 18 mile loop), Shedroof Cutoff Trail 511 and Thunder Creek Trail 526. These additional trails offer loop opportunities that lead into Idaho and the Idaho Panhandle National Forest from the Colville National Forest, Trails 311, 312, 313 and 315.

REDBLUFF TRAIL 553

Trail Length: 5.2 Miles
Elevation: 2600 - 3600 Feet
Difficulty: Moderate
Open: May - October
Usage: Light
Nearest Town: Metaline Falls
Nearest Horse Camp: None
Connecting Trails: 522, 507
Facilities at Trailhead: Loading ramp, water, toilet at nearby Mill
    Pond Campground

DIRECTIONS

TO THE TRAILHEAD

To reach the Redbluff Trailhead, go north from Metaline Falls on Highway 31 for about 2 miles. Turn right and continue on Road 9345

for approximately 4 miles. The trail begins just beyond the entrance to the Mill Pond Campground in Section 30, T.39N., R.44E.

Parking: Graveled area.

Comments: This trail ends at the junction with Trail 507 near Crowell Mountain. It is a lowland, wooded trail with a highly variable grade and major climbs and descents. Near the 1 mile point you will have good views of Sullivan Lake, Hall Mountain and the surrounding country. There are two creek crossings, one at the 1 mile point and another at the 4 mile point where you also cross Trail 507. Trail 553 is often used for horse pack trips into the North Fork Drainage. Huckleberry picking is available in season so enjoy and watch for feeding bears.

SALMO LOOP TRAILS 506, 512 and 535

Trail Length: 18 Miles
Elevation: 4200 - 6400 Feet
Difficulty: Moderate to Difficult
Open: July - September
Usage: Medium
Nearest Town: Metaline Falls
Nearest Horse Camp: None
Connecting Trails: 511, 512, 315, 312, 313, 311, 349
Facilities at Trailhead: Toilets, creek water

DIRECTIONS

TO THE TRAILHEAD

Take Road 9345 east to Sullivan Lake (about 5 miles). At the north end of the lake take the Metaline Falls Road 22 (Nordman-Metaline Falls Road). It is about 6 miles on to the junction of Road 22 and 2220. Road 22 turns south. Continue north about 10 miles on Road 2220 past Gypsy Meadows to the end of the road. When meeting traffic on this road be prepared to use the one-lane turnouts. The trailhead is located in Section 22, T.40N., R.45E. on Road 2220 about 0.5 mile past the junction with Spur Road 270. The trailhead for this loop is the one for Trail 511.

Parking: Adequate at the trail junction with Road 220 and in the Gypsy Meadows dispersed camping area. The area will handle 3 or 4 two-horse rigs.

Comments: The Salmo Loop Trails are located within the Salmo-Priest Wilderness. You can travel either direction but the clockwise route is less strenuous on stock. The trail passes through stands of very large old growth cedar and hemlock. On Trail 506 a steep decline leads you down to the Salmo River which has pan sized trout. This area has the highest precipitation in Washington east of the Cascades so go prepared for rain and great huckleberry eating in season.

Trail 512 on the Shedroof Divide follows along the ridge with some views of Gypsy Peak, the Sullivan Creek drainage and a portion of upper Priest Lake. Also, in Idaho the trail goes to an open fire lookout on Little Snowy Top. This steep side trip is well worth the time and effort. The eastern part of 512 is high ridge country with spectacular views of the upper Priest drainage. There is almost no graze at the upper elevations and limited water along Trails 512 and 535. Pelletized feed is a must if your trip is over night.

One option to riding this area is to stop at the Shedroof Cutoff Trail 511 on Road 2220 about 13 miles from Sullivan Lake. Here you would camp at an area called Gypsy Meadows. Trail 511 begins about 0.5 mile beyond Gypsy Meadows. There is additional parking at this trailhead. Do not expect to find any grazing at Gypsy Meadows.

SHEDROOF CUTOFF TRAIL 511

Trail Length: 1.7 Miles
Elevation: 4400 - 6500 Feet
Difficulty: Moderate
Open: July - October
Usage: Light
Nearest Town: Metaline Falls
Nearest Horse Camp: None
Connecting Trails: 526, 512, 312
Facilities at Trailhead: None, stream for stock water

DIRECTIONS

TO THE TRAILHEAD

Reach this short trail by travelling the 5 miles from Metaline Falls to Sullivan Lake and then following Road 22 (Nordman-Metaline Falls Road) about 6 miles until it turns south at the junction with Road 2220. Follow 2220 another 7 miles to the 511 Trailhead. These are good roads. Be prepared to use one lane turn-outs to let traffic pass. Park at Gypsy Meadow which is located in Section 3, T.39N., R.45E.

Parking: A large dispersed camping area with room for 6-8 rigs. Use the trail junction with Road 2220 at Gypsy Meadows.

Comments: The Shedroof Cutoff Trail 511 from Gypsy Meadow follows a road for the first mile then leaves the road and enters the Salmo-Priest Wilderness about 0.1 mile above the road. It continues to climb up to a junction with the Shedroof Divide Trail 512. Expect to find this trail soft and muddy in to early July so horse use should be avoided up to that time. The climb is through a good huckleberry patch.

Camp at Gypsy Meadow which is about 0.5 mile before the trail meets Road 2220. This is a site used for dispersed camping and day rides into the area but the name does not relate to horse feed. You must bring your own. Grazing is extremely limited in this series of small meadows. Stock water is available at Gypsy Meadow and also just as you enter the Salmo-Priest Wilderness.

SHEDROOF DIVIDE TRAIL 512

Trail Length: 15.7 Miles
Elevation: 5400 - 5960 Feet
Difficulty: Easy to Most Difficult
Open: June - October
Usage: Light to Medium
Nearest Town: Metaline Falls
Nearest Horse Camp: None, (Gypsy Meadow, a dispersed camping area)

Connecting Trails: 320, 309, 526, 311, 312, 313, 315, 506, 535, 349
Facilities at Trailhead: Stock water in stream

DIRECTIONS

TO THE TRAILHEAD

From Sullivan Lake, travel east about 6 miles on Road 22 (also called the Nordman-Metaline Falls Road). At the junction of 22 and 2220, Road 22 turns south toward Round Top Mountain. Continue on Road 22, this is a good road. From the junction it is about 6 miles to Pass Creek Pass located in Section 17, T.38N., R.45E. where Trail 512 takes off about 0.3 mile beyond Pass Creek Pass. Note Spur Road 302.

Parking: The spur is a good road. There is parking for 3-4 two-horse trailers or two larger rigs.

Comments: Trail 512 is a National Recreation Area (NRA) Trail about 22 miles long all of which is located in the Salmo-Priest Wilderness. The 6 mile section of the trail that is part of the Salmo Loop Trail (comprised of Trails 506, 512 and 535 noted elsewhere) is more scenic than this 15.7 mile segment. This trail goes through semi-open timber stands as it flanks each mountain (Round Top, Thunder, Helmer and Shedroof). The old lookout trails to the top of these mountains are no longer maintained and may be a challenge to follow.

Many of the connecting trails lead into Idaho and the Idaho Panhandle National Forest. Check with the local Forest office as to these trails status. Some are due for closure near Grizzly Bear habitat. Consider this as bear country when setting up your camp. See the book section on tips for camping in Bear Country.

THUNDER CREEK TRAIL 526:

Trail Length: 2.9 Miles
Elevation: 4700 - 5500 Feet
Difficulty: Moderate
Open: June - October
Usage: Light

Nearest Town: Metaline Falls
Nearest Horse Camp: None
Connecting Trails: 512
Facilities at Trailhead: None

DIRECTIONS

TO THE TRAILHEAD

NOTE: The Forest Service Recreation Map for the Colville Forest dated 1992 apparently has Trail 526 incorrectly marked as Trail 512. The Salmo-Priest Wilderness Map correctly shows Trail 526.

This error was verified with a Sullivan Ranger District Trail Coordinator. However, these travel directions apply. You also may want to verify this trail number discrepancy.

From Sullivan Lake take Road 22 for 6 miles to where 22 turns south and 2220 continues north. Follow 2220 to Thunder Creek Road 345. (Not shown on all Forest Service Recreation maps). The junction is well signed. Turn right on the Thunder Creek Road and park near the gate located in Section 10, T.39N., R.45E. Motorized use beyond the gate is prohibited to preserve wildlife habitat.

Parking: Roadside for 2 or 3 rigs.

Comments: This trail is located in an area of old growth timber within the wilderness. Wet soils, thick brush and moss covered logs make it seem more like a coastal forest.

Gypsy Meadows just off Road 2220 is used for dispersed camping. Water is available for the first 1.5 miles up the trail.

Authors and Bev Horn at Snow Peak Lookout, Salmo-Priest Wilderness
—Photo by John Horn

Map 4

Gifford Pinchot National Forest
Walupt Lake

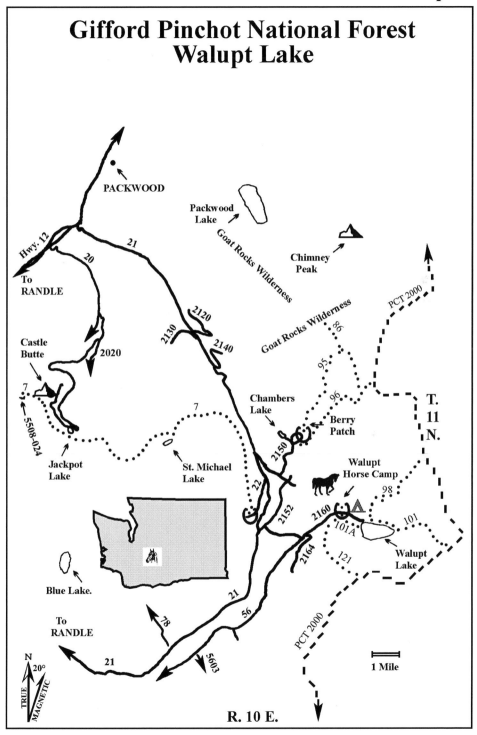

PACKWOOD

Packwood
Lake

Goat Rocks Wilderness

Chimney
Peak

Hwy. 12

To
RANDLE

21

20

2120

2130

2140

Goat Rocks Wilderness

PCT 2000

86

95

T.
11
N.

Castle
Butte

2020

96

7

5508-024

7

Chambers
Lake

2150

Berry
Patch

Jackpot
Lake

St. Michael
Lake

0

Walupt
Horse Camp

98

22

2152

2160

101

101A

Blue Lake.

2164

121

Walupt
Lake

To
RANDLE

21

56

78

PCT 2000

N
20°
TRUE
MAGNETIC

5603

1 Mile

R. 10 E.

COLEMAN WEEDPATCH TRAIL 121

Trail Length: 3.0 Miles
Elevation: 3900 - 5200 Feet
Difficulty: Moderate
Open: July - October
Usage: Medium
Nearest Town: Packwood
Nearest Horse Camp: Walupt
Connecting Trails: 2000
Facilities at Trailhead: Loading ramp, hitch rail, campsites

DIRECTIONS

TO THE TRAILHEAD

Coleman Weedpatch Trail can be reached by going south from Packwood on Highway 12 for about 2 miles to the junction with Road 21 to the left (south). Follow 21 for about 14 miles to the junction with Road 2160 to the left. Drive about 3 miles to the horse camp. This trail starts on Road 2160 less than a mile before the horse camp on Road 2160 into Walupt Lake.

Parking: Ample at the horse camp.

Comments: This short trail heads south from Road 2160 through second growth timber and ends when it reaches the Pacific Crest National Scenic Trail 2000.

KLICKITAT TRAIL 7

Trail Length: 17.7 Miles
Elevation: 4400 - 5500 Feet
Difficulty: Moderate
Open: July - October
Usage: Light
Nearest Town: Randle or Packwood
Nearest Horse Camp: Walupt
Connecting Trails: 128
Facilities at Trailhead: None at east or west end

DIRECTIONS
TO THE TRAILHEAD

The west end of this trail can be reached from Highway 12 by taking Road 23 south out of Randle for 5 miles to the intersection with Road 55. Follow 55 for 7 miles to the junction with Road 5508 and Spur Road 5508-024 to the left. Follow 024 1 mile to its end and the start of the trail.

To reach the trail's east end take Road 21 south about 2 miles before Packwood. Follow 21 for approximately 12 miles to the junction with Road 22. Take 22 about 2 miles to the trailhead.

Call the local Forest office for information on these road conditions. Also, see access by Road 20 below under Parking.

Parking: Limited trailhead space at the end of Road 22, a single rig can block the trail sign. Some riders go to a spur that is past the trail sign.

Better parking is at Jackpot Lake where old logging landing sites are available. To reach Jackpot Lake take Road 20 south from Highway 12. Road 20 is just before you reach Road 21 west of Packwood. Jackpot Lake is located off Road 20 in Section 4, T.11N., R.9E. near the west end of Trail 7. A short connector trail follows a spur road to reach Trail 7. The parking at the west end is at the end of the road.

Comments: The Klickitat trail is a good ridgetop trail to ride with panoramic views but may be hard to identify. It extends from Kilborne Creek on the Randle Ranger District to Elk Peak on the Packwood Ranger District. This trail proceeds eastward along a rolling, timbered ridgeline that offers scenic views until reaching the Randle District boundary near Castle Butte. It continues along the ridge to the Packwood District for another 16 miles passing by Jackpot Lake. Much of the trail is believed to have been an original Indian trail through the Cascades.

NANNIE RIDGE TRAIL 98

Trail Length: 4.5 Miles
Elevation: 3900 - 6100 Feet
Difficulty: Moderate
Open: July - October
Usage: Medium
Nearest Town: Packwood
Nearest Horse Camp: Walupt
Connecting Trails: 101, 2000
Facilities at Trailhead: Loading ramp, hitch rails, campsites

DIRECTIONS

TO THE TRAILHEAD

It can be reached by going south from Packwood on Highway 12 for about 2 miles to the junction with Road 21 to the left (south). Follow 21 for about 14 miles to the junction with Road 2160 to the left. Drive about 3 miles to the horse camp. This trail starts at the Walupt Lake Horse Camp about 1 mile down (east) the trail that parallels the paved road.

Parking: Ample at the horse camp.

Comments: Nannie Ridge Trail starts at the trailhead within the Walupt Campground. It branches off Trail 101 a short distance from the campground then takes a steep climb to the northeast onto an open ridgetop. The trail ends on the Pacific Crest National Scenic Trail 2000 near Sheep Lake.

With planning Trail 98 can be combined with Trail 96 and Trail 2000 for a day ride. Camp at Chambers Lake and with an early start, ride Trail 96 to the Walupt Lake Horse Camp. This is a good ride along ridges and at the Yakima Indian Reservation Boundary there are good photo opportunities.

A loop ride from Chambers Lake using Trails 95, 86 and 96 is well worth the trip while in the area. This is recommended for experienced horse and rider.

WALUPT LAKE TRAIL 101

Trail Length: 4.4 Miles
Elevation: 3800 - 5200 Feet
Difficulty: Moderate
Open: July - October
Usage: Heavy near the lake; Medium beyond
Nearest Town: Packwood
Nearest Horse Camp: Walupt
Connecting Trails: 2000
Facilities at Trailhead: Loading ramp, tie area, campsites

DIRECTIONS

TO THE TRAILHEAD

The Walupt Lake Trail can be reached by going south from Packwood on Highway 12 for about 2 miles to the junction with Road 21 to the left (south). Follow Road 21 for about 14 miles to the junction with Road 2160 to the left. Drive about 3 miles further to the horse camp. This trail starts at the Walupt Lake Horse Camp and parallels the paved road going east on the way to join Trail 2000.

Parking: Ample for large rigs at the horse camp.

Comments: The trail follows the lake shore to Walupt Creek. There it climbs into an open alpine area at Short Trail Camp before turning southeast to end at the Pacific Crest National Scenic Trail 2000. The area features high elevation vegetation.

Map 5

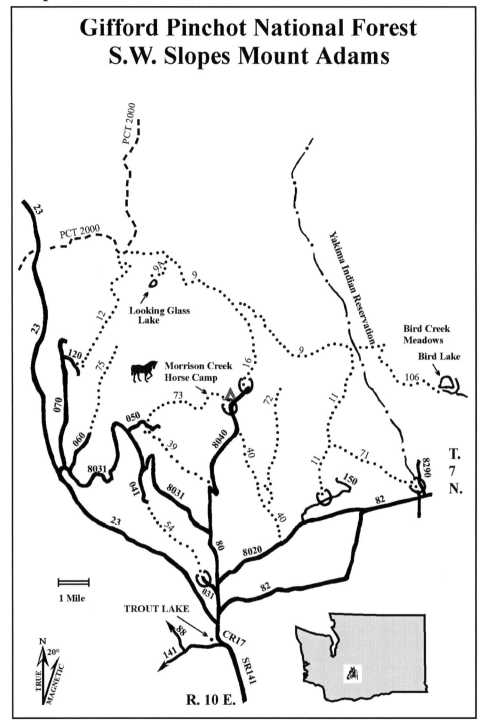

**Gifford Pinchot National Forest
S.W. Slopes Mount Adams**

PCT 2000

23

PCT 2000

9A
9

Looking Glass
Lake

12

23

75

120

Morrison Creek
Horse Camp

16

Yakima Indian Reservation

Bird Creek
Meadows
Bird Lake

106

070

060

050

73

9

72

11

8031

039

8040

40

11

71

8290

041

8031

150

T. 7 N.

23

54

40

82

1 Mile

80

8020

031

82

TROUT LAKE

88

CR17

N
20°
TRUE
MAGNETIC

141

SR141

R. 10 E.

AROUND THE MOUNTAIN TRAIL 9

Trail Length: 8.3 Miles
Elevation: 5900 - 6300 Feet
Difficulty: Moderate
Open: July - October
Usage: Heavy
Nearest Town: Trout Lake
Nearest Horse Camp: Morrison Creek
Connecting Trails: 11, 16, 100, 2000
Facilities at Trailhead: None

DIRECTIONS

TO THE TRAILHEAD

From Trout Lake take County Road 17 north for 2 miles then continue on Road 80 for 3 miles to the Road 8040 junction. Take Road 8040 6 miles to the camp. Access this trail from the Pacific Crest Trail 2000 or by riding Trail 16 off Road 8040 north of the horse camp or by Trail 11 off Roads 8020 and 150.

Carving at Morrison
Creek Camp
—*Photo by authors*

Parking: Park at the Morrison Creek Horse Camp where there are toilets, trailer space, horse ramp and campsites.

Comments: Wilderness permits are required for this trail and stock use restrictions apply. Group size is limited to 12 heartbeats, you and the horse both count. The west end of this trail is at the Pacific Crest Trail 2000 near Horseshoe Meadows in Section 16, T.8N, R.10E. Stagman Ridge Trail 12 is just west of this junction. Looking Glass Lake Trail 9A is 1 mile from the beginning of the trail. The terrain is rolling hills and scattered trees. Although the trail travels along the southwest base of Mount Adams it does not go all the way around the mountain as its' name might imply. The trail stays mainly just below timberline but has some great views of the glaciers above.

The majority of the trail is within the Gifford Pinchot National Forest except for the east end which is on the Yakima Indian Reservation. Horse use is not permitted past the junction of Trail 100 about 1 mile into the Yakima Indian Reservation at Crooked Creek Falls.

Recreation permits are required on the reservation and may be available for a small fee near Bird Creek Meadows. The wild flowers in bloom at Bird Creek Meadows are a special sight! Don't miss this area.

BUCK CREEK TRAIL 54

Trail Length: 2.4 miles
Elevation: 2720 - 3200 Feet
Difficulty: Moderate
Open: May - October
Usage: Light
Nearest Town: Trout Lake
Nearest Horse Camp: Morrison Creek
Connecting Trails: None
Facilities at Trailhead: Toilet

DIRECTIONS

TO THE TRAILHEAD

Take County Road 17 north from Trout Lake about 3.5 miles and turn left onto Road 031 soon after entering the National Forest. The trailhead is at the end of this short road. The trailhead is located in Section 34, T.7N., R.10E.

Note: There is also another Road 8031 about 2 miles further on Road 80.

Parking: Adequate for several rigs with trailers.

Comments: This trail travels through wooded areas above the

Salmon River Gorge. There are several creek crossings which can be muddy early in the season. Though the change in elevation of the trail is not great there are many ups and downs. You may find several other trails in this area that are not well marked. Don't forget your map and compass instructions in this book.

CROFTON RIDGE TRAIL 73

Trail Length: 2.7 Miles
Elevation: 4240 - 4600 Feet
Difficulty: Moderate
Open: July - October
Usage: Medium
Nearest Town: Trout Lake
Nearest Horse Camp: Morrison Creek
Connecting Trails: None
Facilities at Trailhead: Morrison Creek Horse Camp

DIRECTIONS

TO THE TRAILHEAD

From Trout Lake take County Road 17 north for 2 miles then continue on Road 80 for 3 miles to the Road 8040 junction. Take Road 8040 6 miles to the camp. The trailhead is off a short road just north of the horse camp located in Section 2, T.7N., R.10E.

Parking: Park at the horse camp where there is space for 4-5 rigs.

Comments: This trail climbs Crofton Ridge where there is a good view and then it levels out the rest of the way to the west end at Road 8031-050. Most of the trail riding is in timber.

PINE WAY TRAIL 71

Trail Length: 2.7 Miles
Elevation: 4250 - 4800 Feet
Difficulty: Difficult
Open: June - October
Usage: Light

Nearest Town: Trout Lake
Nearest Horse Camp: Morrison Creek
Connecting Trails: 11
Facilities at Trailhead: None

DIRECTIONS

TO THE TRAILHEAD

Take Road 17 north from Trout Lake for 1.5 miles and turn right onto the Mount Adams Recreation Area Road which turns into Road 82. Follow Road 82 about 8 miles to Road 8290 and turn left. This is near the National Forest and Yakima Indian Reservation boundary. The trailhead is 1.5 miles north (left) on Road 8290. The trailhead is located in Section 9, T.7N., R.11E.

Parking: Adequate for 4-5 rigs.

Comments: The trail begins as an old road and goes through second growth timber. It is rocky and rutted after the first 0.5 mile and is used as a stock route which is grazed during the summer months. There are a few small meadows with wild flowers in early July. Later in the summer it can be very dusty.

SHORTHORN TRAIL 16

Trail Length: 2.8 Miles
Elevation: 4720 - 6120 Feet
Difficulty: Difficult
Open: August - October
Usage: Light
Nearest Town: Trout Lake
Nearest Horse Camp: Morrison Creek
Connecting Trails: 9
Facilities at Trailhead: Campsites at Morrison Creek Campground, no horses allowed, use Morrison Creek Horse Camp

DIRECTIONS

TO THE TRAILHEAD

From Trout Lake take County Road 17 north for 2 miles then continue on Road 80 for 3 miles to the Road 8040 junction. Take Road 8040 6 miles to the camp. The trailhead is 0.3 mile north of Morrison Creek Horse Camp on Road 8040. The location is in Section 2, T.7N., R.10E.

Parking: Limited and very possibly a difficult turnaround because of lack of parking area and the heavy hiker car traffic. Ride from the horse camp.

Comments: This rocky trail follows an old stock road for the first part and then opens to views of the mountain. Creek crossings in this area can be deep on hot days because of snow melt. Expect steep, rough sections on this trail.

SNIPES MOUNTAIN TRAIL 11

Trail Length: 5.6 Miles
Elevation: 3800 - 6280 Feet
Difficulty: Moderate
Open: July - October
Usage: Light
Nearest Town: Trout Lake
Nearest Horse Camp: Morrison Creek
Connecting Trails: 9, 71
Facilities at Trailhead: None

DIRECTIONS

TO THE TRAILHEAD

From Trout Lake go north on County Road 17 which turns into Road 80. Follow Road 80 about 3 miles to Road 8020. Turn right on Road 8020 and follow it about 4 miles to Road 150 then turn left to the trailhead. Do not drive past the trailhead because the road becomes worse. Rigs with trailers can make it to the trailhead but the going is slow. You could ride the road for about one mile from the Gotchen Creek Trailhead which is about 3 miles on Road 8020 from Road 80. There are old corrals at the Trail 40 trailhead. The trailhead for the Snipes Mountain is in Section 18, T.7N., R.11E.

Parking: Limited for trailer rigs.

Comments: This is a steep and sometimes very rocky trail although there are some beautiful meadows in the northern section. Early in the season these meadow areas can be boggy so use caution. The meadows bloom with wild flowers until mid to late July.

Map 6

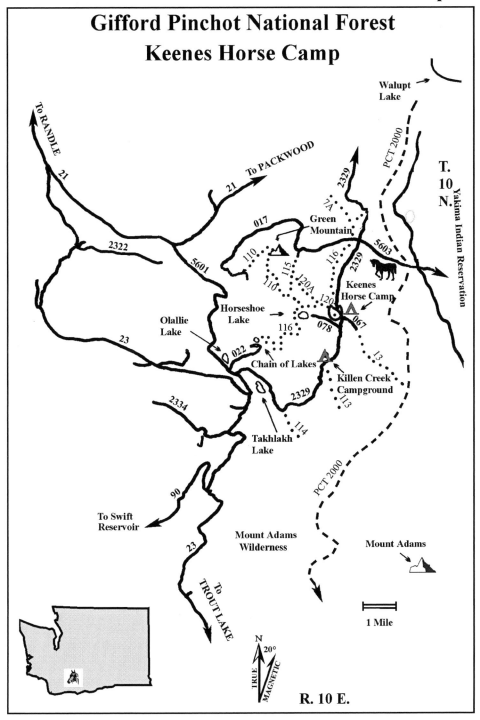

Gifford Pinchot National Forest
Keenes Horse Camp

Walupt Lake

PCT 2000

To RANDLE

21

To PACKWOOD

21

2329

T. 10 N.

Yakima Indian Reservation

017

7A

Green Mountain

5601

2322

110

116

2329

5603

115

110

120A

120

Keenes Horse Camp

Olallie Lake

Horseshoe Lake

116

120

067

116

078

13

022

Chain of Lakes

Killen Creek Campground

23

2329

113

2334

114

90

Takhlakh Lake

To Swift Reservoir

23

PCT 2000

Mount Adams Wilderness

Mount Adams

To TROUT LAKE

1 Mile

N 20°
TRUE
MAGNETIC

R. 10 E.

GREEN MOUNTAIN TRAIL 110

Trail Length: 4.5 Miles
Elevation: 2600 - 5100 Feet
Difficulty: Moderate
Open: July - October
Usage: Medium
Nearest Town: Randle or Trout Lake
Nearest Horse Camp: Keenes
Connecting Trails: 115
Facilities at Trailhead: None, see Keenes Horse Camp

DIRECTIONS

TO THE TRAILHEAD

Keenes Horse Camp is the trailhead for this trail. It can be reached by taking Road 23 North from Trout Lake or by Road 90 east from Swift Reservoir. Road 90 ends at Road 23. Turn right off Road 23 onto Road 2329. The camp is 6 miles further on Road 2329. Keenes Horse Camp is located in Section 34, T.10N., R.10E. This trail is reached from the horse camp by riding Trail 120 northwest a little over a mile to where it connnects with Trail 115. You pass the junction with Trail 116 to reach Horseshoe Lake. Turn left (south) on 115 for less than 0.1 mile to Trail 110. Trail 120 to Green Mountain is on the right (west). Other access routes from spur roads are also apparent on the Mount Adams Wilderness Map.

Parking: Ample at the horse camp.

Comments: This trail includes all users so expect to see motorized bikes and bicycles. The trail passes through mixed conifer stands in the climb to the summit of Green Mountain located in Section 20, T.10N., R.10E. There are panoramic views as you near the top. The ride is through some harvest units so expect to see views of Mount St. Helens, Mount Adams and Mt. Rainier. From the summit the trail descends to join with Spring Creek Trail 115. This ride is in huckleberry country. The trail continues from the summit, west to Road 5601-017.

HIGH LAKES TRAIL 116

Trail Length: 9.0 Miles
Elevation: 3800 - 4400 Feet
Difficulty: Easy
Open: June - October
Usage: Moderate
Nearest Town: Randle or Trout Lake
Nearest Horse Camp: Keenes
Connecting Trails: 115, 120, 7A
Facilities at Trailhead: None, see Keenes Horse Camp

DIRECTIONS

TO THE TRAILHEAD

Keenes Horse Camp is the trailhead for this trail. It can be reached by taking Road 23 north from Trout Lake or by Road 90 east from Swift Reservoir. Road 90 ends at Road 23. Turn right off Road 23 onto Road 2329. The camp is 6 miles down Road 2329. Keenes Horse Camp is located in Section 34, T.10N., R.10E.

This trail is reached from the horse camp by riding Trail 120 northwest about 0.6 miles to the junction with Trail 116 that goes south to Horseshoe Lake and Chain of Lakes.

The High Lakes Trail also begins near Olallie Lake off Spur Road 022 that connects to 2329, the road to the horse camp. Trail 116 travels north from Trail 120 for 4 miles then crosses Road 5603 and ends at Trail 7A.

Parking: Ample at the horse camp.

Comments: This trail goes through open forests, past an old lava flow from Mount Adams and on to the Chain of Lakes area. There are three stream crossings but no bridges.

KEENES TRAIL 120

Trail Length: 0.6 Miles
Elevation: 3450 - 3750 Feet
Difficulty: Easy
Open: July - October
Usage: Heavy
Nearest Town: Randle or Trout Lake
Nearest Horse Camp: Keenes
Connecting Trails: 115, 116, 13 (2.7 miles to Trail 2000)
Facilities at Trailhead: Horse campsites, loading ramps, corrals, high-lines, water trough, toilet, hitch rails in some of 14 camp units

DIRECTIONS

TO THE TRAILHEAD

Keenes Horse Camp is the trailhead for this trail. It can be reached by taking Road 23 north from Trout Lake or Road 90 east from Swift Reservoir. Road 90 ends at Road 23. Turn right off Road 23 onto Road 2329. The camp, renovated in 1997 by BCHW, is 6 miles down Road 2329 in Section 34, T.10N., R.10E.

Parking: Ample at horse camp.

Comments: This short trail begins at the horse camp and provides access to other longer trails in the area. It passes through semi-open forests and meadows before it joins the other trails. Trail 13 to the east is a 2.7 mile access to the Pacific Crest Trail. It is in the Mount Adams Wilderness and so all Wilderness Regulations and group size limits are in effect. This is now a "pack out manure" camp.

SPRING CREEK TRAIL 115

Trail Length: 2.9 Miles
Elevation: 3800 - 4100 Feet
Difficulty: Moderate
Open: July - October
Usage: Medium

Nearest Town: Randle or Trout Lake
Nearest Horse Camp: Keenes
Connecting Trails: 110, 116, 120
Facilities at Trailhead: None, see Keenes Horse Camp

DIRECTIONS

TO THE TRAILHEAD

Keenes Horse Camp is the trailhead for this trail. It can be reached by taking Road 23 north from Trout Lake or by Road 90 east from Swift Reservoir. Road 90 ends at Road 23. Turn right off Road 23 onto Road 2329. The camp is 6 miles down Road 2329. Keenes Horse Camp is located in Section 34, T.10N., R.10E.

From the horse camp ride Trail 120 northwest to the Trail 116 junction with Trail 120A. Trail 115 will be joined at mid length. It is also reached by taking Trail 120 for 0.6 mile to the intersection with Trail 116. Follow Trail 116 about 0.5 mile to the junction with Trail 115 to the north.

Another access from Spur Road 5603-042 to the north is apparent on the Gifford Pinchot National Forest and Mount Adams Wilderness maps.

Parking: Ample at the horse camp.

Comments: The trail is open to all users which means trail riders may encounter motorbikes. There are views of Mount Adams as the trail goes through an open forest with semi-open meadows and stands of peeled cedar.

This trail is thought to have been an Indian route between berry picking camps at Horseshoe Lake and fishing sites along the Cispus River. Look for the peeled cedar trees at the trailhead. Rectangular scars on the bark are evidence that bark was used to make berry picking baskets. Small ponds provide horse water along the route.

Map 7

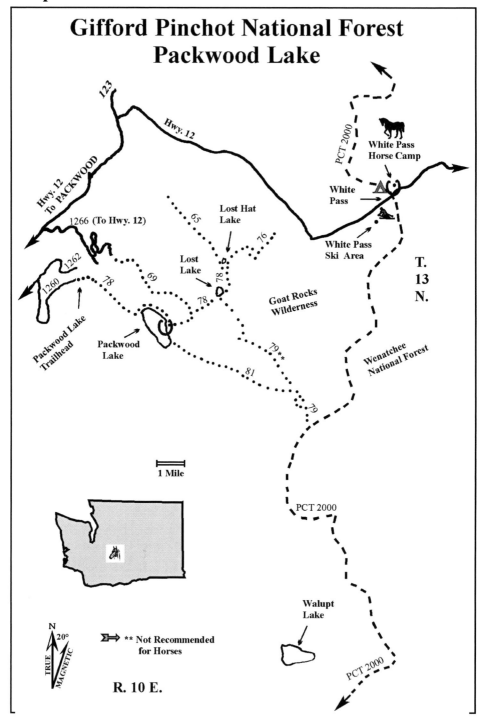

Gifford Pinchot National Forest
Packwood Lake

123

Hwy. 12

Hwy. 12
To PACKWOOD

PCT 2000

White Pass
Horse Camp

1266 (To Hwy. 12)

White
Pass

65

Lost Hat
Lake

76

White Pass
Ski Area

T.
13
N.

1262

1260

78

69

Lost
Lake

78

78

78

Goat Rocks
Wilderness

Packwood Lake
Trailhead

Packwood
Lake

79**

Wenatchee
National Forest

81

79

1 Mile

PCT 2000

Walupt
Lake

N
20°
TRUE
MAGNETIC

** Not Recommended
for Horses

PCT 2000

R. 10 E.

PACKWOOD LAKE TRAIL 78

Trail Length: 9.6 Miles
Elevation: 2800 - 6000 Feet
Difficulty: Difficult
Open: July - October
Usage: Extra Heavy to Packwood Lake and Medium beyond
Nearest Town: Packwood
Nearest Horse Camp: Walupt
Connecting Trails: 65, 76, 81, 69, 79 (note horse closure)
Facilities at Trailhead: Camp units, tie area, loading ramp

DIRECTIONS

TO THE TRAILHEAD

Take Road 1260 to the right (south) out of Packwood. It is 6 miles to the Packwood Lake Trailhead.

Parking: Large parking lot.

Comments: Most of this trail is in the Goat Rocks Wilderness. It starts at the end of Road 1260 and climbs easily through old-growth forests past two small harvest areas within the first mile. This gives a good view of Mt. Rainier before the trail enters the Goat Rocks Wilderness and continues toward Packwood Lake.

Near the lake the trail leaves the wilderness and descends to a developed area along the lake's north side and past a Forest Service Guard Station. (Trail 81 continues along the lake shore.) Trail 78 continues to Mosquito Lake and Lost Lake passing the junction with Trails 69 and Trail 79 (horses not permitted). It then continues north on an open ridgeline to end at the junction with Trails 65 and 76 beyond Lost Lake in Section 24, T.13N., R.10E.

This trailhead is shared with motorbikes but there are separate trails that parallel each other. You cross a steep rocky section just before the Trail 78 junction with Trails 65 and 76. This junction is beyond Lost Lake.

UPPER LAKE CREEK TRAIL 81

Trail Length: 7.4 Miles
Elevation: 2800 - 5600 Feet
Difficulty: Moderate
Open: July - October
Usage: Extra Heavy along Packwood Lake, Medium beyond
Nearest Town: Packwood
Nearest Horse Camp: Walupt
Connecting Trails: 78, 79 (open, not recommended for horses south of junction with Trail 81 in order to reach Trail 2000, also not recommended for horses between Trail 2000 and the junction with Trail 78)
Facilities at Trailhead: None

DIRECTIONS

TO THE TRAILHEAD

Take Road 1260 to the right (south) off Highway 12 out of Packwood. It is 6 miles to the Packwood Lake Trailhead. Trail 81 begins on Trail 78 at Packwood Lake in Section 21, T.13N., R.10E. and follows the northeast lake shore until it comes to Upper Lake Creek.

Parking: There is parking at the end of Road 1260.

Comments: Trail 81 leaves Packwood Lake and follows Upper Lake Creek through dense forest for approximately 4 miles. The trail climbs very steeply to join Trail 79 at Packwood Saddle. There is large old growth cedar and panoramic views on this trail. Horses can continue on Trail 79 south to reach Trail 2000 but the conditions are difficult. Trails in this area become increasingly more difficult for horses.

Map 8

Gifford Pinchot National Forest
Indian Heaven Wilderness

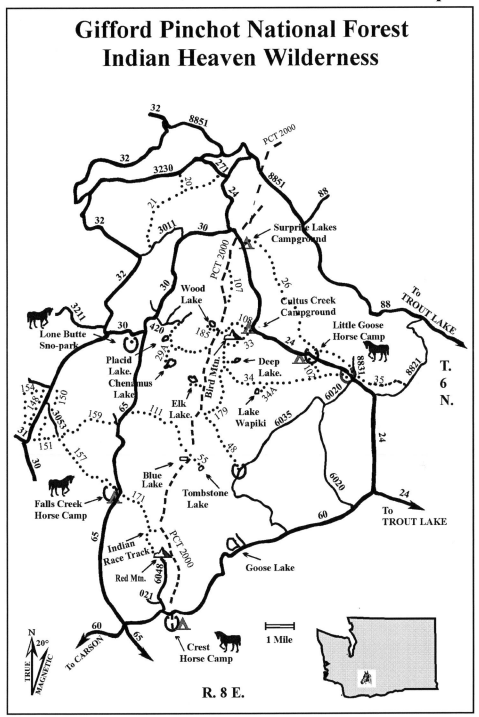

FILLOON TRAIL 102

Trail Length: 1.1 Miles
Elevation: 3900 - 4280 Feet
Difficulty: Moderate
Open: August - October
Usage: Medium
Nearest Town: Trout Lake
Nearest Horse Camp: Little Goose
Connecting Trails: 34
Facilities at Trailhead: Toilets, drinking water, stock water

DIRECTIONS

TO THE TRAILHEAD

The Filloon Trail begins at Little Goose Horse Camp. The trailhead location is Section 5, T.6N., R.9E. Coming from Trout Lake follow Highway 141 which turns into Road 24 at the Forest boundary. From this point follow Road 24 for 10 miles to the campground.

Parking: Ample.

Comments: This short trail begins at the south end of Little Goose Horse Camp off the circular drive at the camping area for horses. Take care not to block the driveway with a trailer. Trail 102 travels through huckleberry patches, beargrass and second growth timber and is the best access to Lemei Trail 34.

LEMEI LAKE TRAIL 179

Trail Length: 1.9 Miles
Elevation: 4680 - 5160 Feet
Difficulty: Moderate
Open: August - October
Usage: Medium
Nearest Town: Trout Lake
Nearest Horse Camp: Falls Creek or Little Goose
Connecting Trails: 2000, 33
Facilities at Trailhead: None

DIRECTIONS

TO THE TRAILHEAD

Little Goose Horse Camp is located in Section 5, T.6N., R.9E. and is northeast of Indian Heaven Wilderness on Road 24. From Trout Lake take Road 141 which turns into Road 24 at the Forest boundary. Follow Road 24 for 10 miles to the campground. Ride the trails from the horse camp to access the Lemei Lake Trail, either Trail 33 or Trail 2000 from the south. The southern end of Trail 179 is located in Section 15, T.6N., R.8E.

Parking: Use the Little Goose Horse Camp Trailhead.

Comments: The south end of the Lemei Lake Trail is at Trail 2000 just north of Junction Lake in Section 15. The north end is at Trail 33 near Clear Lake. The trail goes through open meadows and sparse timber.

Crest Horse Camp, Gifford Pinchot National Forest
—*Photo by authors*

LEMEI TRAIL 34

Trail Length: 5.3 Miles
Elevation: 3680 - 5160 Feet
Difficulty: Difficult
Open: August - October
Usage: Medium
Nearest Town: Trout Lake
Nearest Horse Camp: Little Goose
Connecting Trails: 33, 34A (to Waplid Lake), 102 (out of horse camp)
Facilities at Trailhead: None

DIRECTIONS

TO THE TRAILHEAD

The trailhead is near Smokey Creek Campground on Road 24 about 1.8 miles southeast toward Trout Lake from the Little Goose Horse Camp. It is located in Section 9, T.6N., R.9E. From Trout Lake take Highway 141 which becomes Road 24 at the Forest boundary. It is 10 miles on Road 24 to the camp.

Parking: Limited parking on the road at the trailhead but additional space at the trailhead for Trail 102 that goes out of the horse camp to Trail 34.

Comments: The best access to this trail is by the Filloon Trail 102 from Little Goose Horse Camp. This ride cuts off some of the elevation gain and provides better parking at the trailhead. The old access trail used by Indians is steep and rutted from years of use. It climbs nearly 1,500 feet in about 3 miles. It is now dusty and hot in the summer and can be slick early in the season. The views of Mount Adams, Goat Rocks and Mt. Rainier make the ride worthwhile. The view of Wapiki Lake (off Trail 34A) from above is one not soon forgotten.

MCCLELLAN MEADOWS TRAIL 157

Trail Length: 3.1 Miles
Elevation: 2900 - 3500 Feet
Difficulty: Easy
Open: July - November
Usage: Heavy
Nearest Town: Carson
Nearest Horse Camp: Falls Creek
Connecting Trails: 159
Facilities at Trailhead: None

DIRECTIONS

TO THE TRAILHEAD

From Carson take the Wind River Highway which becomes Road 30. Travel north 20 miles and turn right onto Road 3053. The trailhead is at the end of this road in Section 24, T.6N., R.7E.

Falls Creek Horse Camp, Gifford Pinchot National Forest
—Photo by authors

Parking: Limited at the trailhead and space to turn rigs around could be blocked. You might choose to ride Road 3053 to the trail or park at the horse camp on Road 65.

Comments: Trail 157 is mostly wooded with several creek crossings and bridges that are not always safe to cross. Watch for trails that lead to safer crossings. When in the area of McClellan Meadows it is essential to stay out of them as they are very sensitive to damage and very boggy to the point of being dangerous. Elk frequent the area in the fall of the year.

The trail ends at Road 65 just north of the Falls Creek Horse Camp. See the information on Trail 159 for making a loop ride using Road 65 but expect to meet trucks on the road.

SKI LOOP-WEST 148

Trail Length: 7.4 Miles
Elevation: 2800 - 3040 Feet
Difficulty: Moderate
Open: July - November
Usage: Medium
Nearest Town: Carson or Trout Lake
Nearest Horse Camp: Falls Creek
Connecting Trails: Hard Time Loop includes Trail 148A, 1.6 miles; Trail 148B, 0.3 mile; Trail 148C, 1.4 miles; Trail 148D, 1.4 miles
Facilities at Trailhead: Toilets

DIRECTIONS

TO THE TRAILHEAD

From Carson take the Wind River Highway (it becomes Road 30) and travel north 20 miles to the Oldman Pass area. The Road 3050 junction with Road 30 is in Section 9, T.6N., R.7E.

Parking: Ample at the Sno-Park.

Comments: This well maintained trail is west of Road 30 and leaves the Oldman Sno-Park area heading north. The northern section of the trail is moderately steep but its entire length is fairly easy. There are no particular views along the trail, just a nice easy ride through woods with clearcuts and small meadows. Use Trail 150 on the east side of Road 30 to make a loop ride.

Oldman Pass Area west of the Indian Heaven Wilderness, is also known as the Upper Wind River Sport Area. During snow season these trails are used for cross country skiing. Watch for small stumps left in the trail tread. Ski trails often do not have the same tread found on horse and hiker trails. The ski trails marked by blue diamonds higher on trees than most trail markers, are easy to follow, tend to be wide but low stumps are occasionally left to be covered by snow. Bridges may be of a different form which means horses must cross through the streams.

The Sno-Parks provide ample parking space and trailheads are usually well marked. Please remove manure from the parking asphalt. Horses should be tethered to high-line pickets or rope corrals.

SKI LOOP-EAST 150

Trail Length: 2.4 Miles
Elevation: 2800 - 3040 Feet
Difficulty: Moderate
Open: July - November
Usage: Medium
Nearest Town: Carson or Trout Lake
Nearest Horse Camp: Falls Creek
Connecting Trails: Hard Time Loop, 148
Facilities at Trailhead: Toilets

DIRECTIONS

TO THE TRAILHEAD

From Carson take the Wind River Highway which becomes Road 30 and travel north 20 miles to the Sno-Park areas in Section 23, T.6N., R.7E.

Parking: Ample at the Sno-Parks.

Comments: This trail begins on the east side of Road 30 across from the Oldman Sno-Park. It is the first trail to the left and parallels

Road 30. There are several loop ride opportunities so look over the maps for combinations.

There are no particular views along the trail, just a ride through woods, clearcuts and small meadows. Use Trail 148 on the west side of Road 30 to make a loop ride.

TERMINATOR TRAIL 159

Trail Length: 3.8 Miles
Elevation: 3000 - 4000 Feet
Difficulty: Moderate
Open: July - November
Usage: Medium
Nearest Town: Carson
Nearest Horse Camp: Falls Creek
Connecting Trails: 157
Facilities at Trailhead: None

DIRECTIONS

TO THE TRAILHEAD

From Carson take the Wind River Highway (which becomes Road 30) and travel north approximately 20 miles and turn right onto Road 3053. The trailhead is at the end of this spur road in Section 24, T.6N., R.7E.

Parking: Limited at the trailhead. The space needed to turn rigs around could be blocked by cars. You might choose to ride Road 3053 to the trail from McClellan Meadows Sno-Park.

Comments: The trail heads southeast towards Road 65 along a clearcut and then back into timber with several streams to cross. The last fraction of a mile the trail seems to disappear in a clearcut but look for a snow trail blue diamond marker straight ahead. From there watch for the blue markers to Road 65. To make a loop, follow Road 65 south for 2.5 miles and take Trail 157 back to where you started. The loop ride is about 11 miles long and can take most of the day. Expect to meet trucks when using the road.

PACIFIC CREST TRAIL 2000

Trail Length: 16.5 Miles
Elevation: 3400 - 5700 Feet
Difficulty: Easy to Difficult
Open: August - October
Usage: Heavy
Nearest Town: Trout Lake
Nearest Horse Camp: Falls Creek, Little Goose or Crest
Connecting Trails: 29, 33, 48, 55, 107, 108, 111, 171 (to Indian Race Track), 176 (to Elk Lake), 179, 185 (to Wood Lake)
Facilities at Trailhead: Crest Horse Camp, 3 camp units, hitch rail, toilet, no stock or drinking water

DIRECTIONS

TO THE TRAILHEAD

The trailhead is the Crest Horse Camp for this section of the Trail 2000. The trailhead is located in Section 21, T.5N., R.8E.

Parking: Ample at Crest Camp (southern end of trail) and at Surprise Lakes Indian Camp (northern end of trail).

Comments: This 18 mile section of the Pacific Crest Trail has taken on a new look in the last few years. Parts have been relocated to take traffic away from fragile meadow lands. In most cases the trail has been relocated to give more scenic vistas of the surrounding mountains. The trail is now more varied in its steepness and stays nearer the crest of the mountains but still accesses many lakes and ponds stocked with fish.

The old Pacific Crest Trail is blocked with brush at its junction with the new trail so use the new trail segment. Some sections are flat and easy while other sections rate as difficult. Because of the diversity of the trail conditions, more time than expected may be needed to reach your destination; allow time to visit lakes along the way.

From the Crest Horse Camp on Road 60 it is 1.8 miles north to the wilderness boundary and a total of 16.5 miles to where Trail 2000 crosses Road 24. Hikers frequent this trail so take time to be courteous and aware of their safety.

Little Goose Horse Camp, Gifford Pinchot National Forest
—*Photo by authors*

Map 9

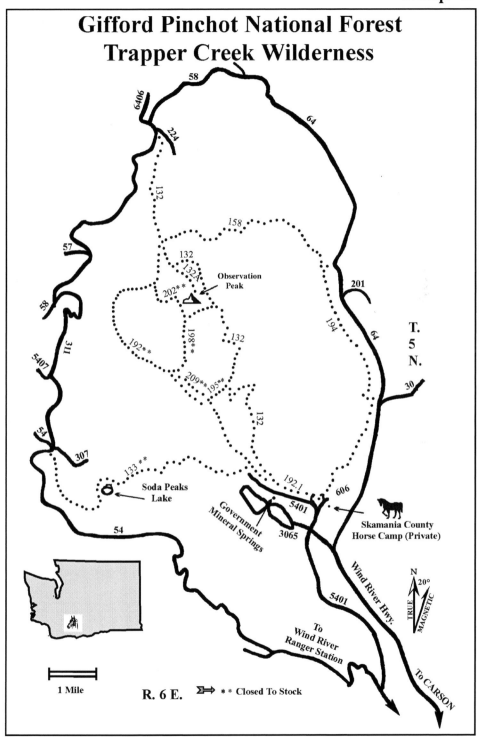

Gifford Pinchot National Forest
Trapper Creek Wilderness

58

6406

224

64

132

57

158

58

311

132

132A

Observation Peak

202**

201

5407

192**

198**

132

194

64

T.
5
N.

54

209** 195**

132

30

307

133 **

Soda Peaks Lake

192.1

606

5401

Government Mineral Springs

3065

Skamania County
Horse Camp (Private)

54

5401

Wind River Hwy.

N
20°
TRUE MAGNETIC

1 Mile

R. 6 E. ⇒ ** Closed To Stock

To
Wind River
Ranger Station

5401

To CARSON

BIG HOLLOW TRAIL 158

Trail Length: 3.2 Miles
Elevation: 1400 - 3800 Feet
Difficulty: Most Difficult
Open: June - October
Usage: Light
Nearest Town: Carson
Nearest Horse Camp: Skamania County (private)
Connecting Trails: 132, 194
Facilities at Trailhead: None

DIRECTIONS

TO THE TRAILHEAD

From Carson take the Wind River Highway (County Road 30) north about 14.6 miles and go left on Mineral Springs Road. After 0.5 mile turn right on Road 5401. After another 0.5 mile you will see the trailhead signs and parking area for trailers. The trailhead is located in Section 31, T.5N., R.7E. Access this trail by riding Trail 132 or Trail 194 from the trailhead for Trail 192.

Parking: Ample at trailhead for Trail 194. There is no trailer parking space on Road 64 near the east end of this trail in Section 18, T.5N., R.7E.

Comments: From the intersection with Trail 132, Trail 158 heads downhill and crosses Big Hollow Creek after about a mile. The stream current can be swift and up to 2 feet deep so keep this in mind if riding a green broke horse. From here the trail continues downhill to the intersection of Trail 194 near Road 64.

DRY CREEK TRAIL 194

Trail Length: 4.0 Miles
Elevation: 1200 - 1400 Feet
Difficulty: Easy
Open: May - November
Usage: Light

Nearest Town: Carson
Nearest Horse Camp: Skamania County (private)
Connecting Trails: 158
Facilities at Trailhead: None

DIRECTIONS

TO THE TRAILHEAD

From Carson take the Wind River Highway Road 30 north about 14.6 miles and go left on Mineral Springs Road. After 0.5 mile turn right onto Road 5401. After another 0.5 mile you will see the trailhead sign and parking for trailers. The trailhead is located in Section 31, T.5N., R.7E. Trail 194 intersects Trail 192 at the start of 192 just off Road 606.

Parking: Ample.

Comments: This trail runs parallel to Dry Creek. It is an easy cool ride along the creek in the summer. There is one good sized creek crossing at the northern end before reaching Trail 158 in Section 18, T.5N., R.7E.

TRAPPER TRAIL 192

Trail Length: 1.2 Mile
Elevation: 1200 - 1400 Feet
Difficulty: Easy
Open: May - November
Usage: Heavy
Nearest Town: Carson
Nearest Horse Camp: Skamania County (private)
Connecting Trails: 132
Facilities at Trailhead: None

DIRECTIONS

TO THE TRAILHEAD

From Carson take the Wind River Highway (County Road 30) north about 14.6 miles and go left on Mineral Springs Road. After 0.5

mile turn right on Road 5401. After another 0.5 mile you will see the trailhead signs and parking area for trailers. The trailhead is located in Section 31, T.5N., R.7E.

Parking: Ample.

Comments: This trail (called 192.1) is used to access Trail 132. Horses must continue on Trail 132 because the remainder of Trail 192 (called 192.2) is closed to horses. From the trailhead the ride is through old growth forest and a climb to the junction of Trail 132 in about 1 mile.

Falls Creek Horse Camp

—Photo by authors

Map 10

Gifford Pinchot National Forest
Siouxon Area

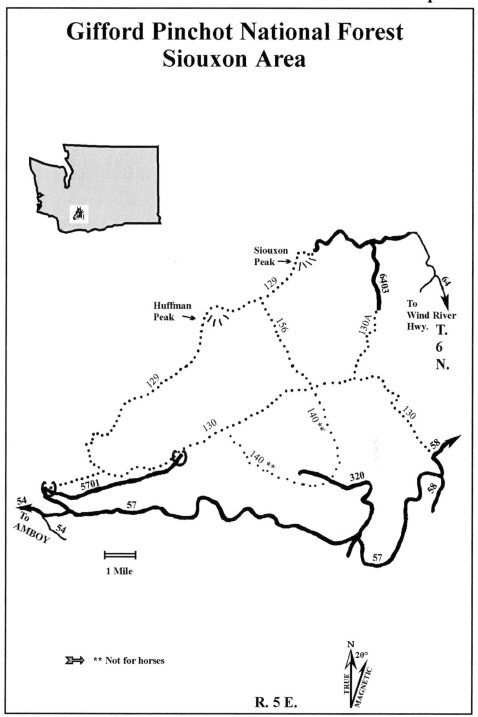

Siouxon Peak →

Huffman Peak →

129

156

6403

64

To Wind River Hwy. **T. 6 N.**

130A

129

130

140 **

140 **

130

58

58

5701

54

To AMBOY

57

320

57

54

1 Mile

⊃⇒ ** Not for horses

N 20°
TRUE MAGNETIC

R. 5 E.

HUFFMAN PEAK TRAIL 129

Trail Length: 10.0 Miles
Elevation: 1800 - 4000 Feet
Difficulty: Moderate
Open: July - October
Usage: Light
Nearest Town: Amboy
Nearest Horse Camp: None
Connecting Trails: 130, 156
Facilities at Trailhead: None

DIRECTIONS

TO THE TRAILHEAD

Take Highway 503 from Vancouver to Amboy and then take Highway 503 east to Chelatchie. Turn right onto N.E. Healy Road which becomes Road 54. Go 8 miles and turn left onto Road 57. After 0.8 mile turn left onto Road 5701. The trailhead is at the end of this road in Section 3, T.5N., R.5E. Access this trail from Trail 130 or by riding Trail 156.

Parking: See Trail Guide for Siouxon Trail 130 as they share a trailhead.

Comments: This trail leaves Trail 130 near the west end and travels steeply downhill toward Siouxon Creek. There is a good crossing as long as the water is not high. This is a good place to check cinches before crossing because the next 4 miles are steep. Allow plenty of time because the switchbacks go on forever. Near the top, the trail comes close to the edge of the ridgetop. The view is wonderful and is a place to stop for lunch. The trail continues for another 1.5 miles to the end at Road 6403.

SIOUXON TRAIL 130

Trail Length: 9.2 Miles
Elevation: 1200 - 2320 Feet
Difficulty: Moderate to Most Difficult
Open: June - November
Usage: Heavy
Nearest Town: Amboy and Chelatchie
Nearest Horse Camp: None
Connecting Trails: 129, 130A, 140, 156
Facilities at Trailhead: None

DIRECTIONS

TO THE TRAILHEAD

Take Highway 503 from Vancouver to Amboy, then take Highway 503 east to Chelatchie. Turn right onto N.E. Healy Road which becomes Road 54. Go 8 miles and turn left onto Road 57. After 0.8 mile turn left onto Road 5701. The trailhead is at the end of this road in Section 3, T.5N., R.5E.

Parking: Limited to several vehicles. There is space to park at the hairpin turn about 3 miles before the trailhead and ride the rest of the distance. If cars are parked at the trailhead, turn around before you get there. It is not easy to turn a trailer rig around on this road, but you can use the passing lane pull-outs.

Comments: Trail 130 parallels Siouxon Creek for about 3 miles and most of its length is in the shade. This makes the trail particularly nice on a hot day. The waterfalls on this creek form green pools with fern covered banks giving this area a rain forest look. The creek itself can be swift and deep early in the year. Crossing it should be done with caution for horse, rider and dogs. This trail is heavily used by hikers and mountain bikers. It gains 1,900 feet in the final 3 miles with switchbacks and rocky ground. Return can be even more difficult.

Access Trail 129 and Trail 156 to make a loop ride. This will be a long day ride because of the steepness and difficulty of the trails once you leave Trail 130. This trail system loop made up of Trails 130, 129 and 156 is not for beginning riders or horses. Trails are steep, narrow and at times are on the cliff edge. There is no room for mistakes.

WILDCAT TRAIL 156

Trail Length: 2.5 Miles
Elevation: 1300 - 3600 Feet
Difficulty: Most Difficult
Open: June - October
Usage: Light
Nearest Town: Amboy
Nearest Horse Camp: None
Connecting Trails: 129, 130
Facilities at Trailhead: None

DIRECTIONS

TO THE TRAILHEAD

Take Highway 503 from Vancouver to Amboy, then take Highway 503 east to Chelatchie. Turn right onto N.E. Healy Road. It becomes Road 54. Go 8 miles and turn left onto Road 57. After 0.8 mile turn left onto Road 5701. The trailhead is at the end of the road in Section 3, T.5N., R.5E. You can access this trail from Trail 130 or Trail 129.

Parking: Use the access from Trail 130 or from 129 at either end.

Comments: Wildcat Trail 156 is a great trail but only for experienced horses and riders. It is extremely rocky and rutted and not much real estate is wasted on the switchbacks. This trail is not for those that are afraid of heights or horses that are not stable of mind and body.

The view of Wildcat Falls from the top is great. The falls cascade 75 feet and are well worth the sight if you are prepared to accept the challenge of getting there. The trail above the falls goes out on a ledge above the canyon where you can hear the falls below. Some like the view from here while others just try to get on down the trail away from it. You can make a loop ride using Trail 130 and Trail 156 but note it will take longer than you would expect.

Map 11

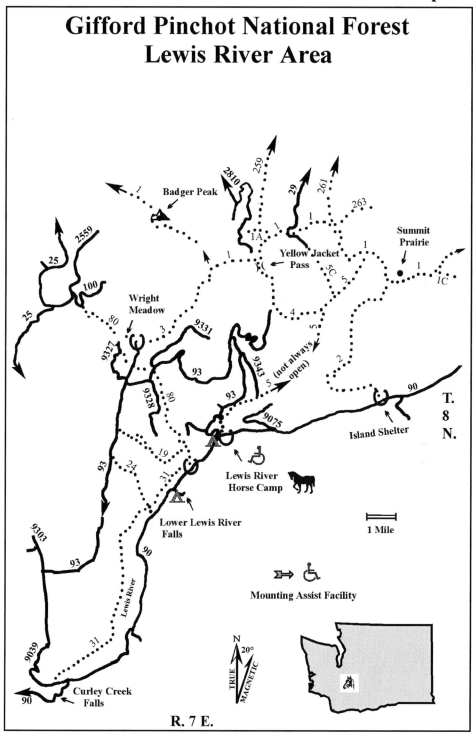

Gifford Pinchot National Forest
Lewis River Area

Badger Peak

2810

259

29

261

263

Summit Prairie

1A

Yellow Jacket Pass

5C

5

1

1

1C

2559

25

100

25

Wright Meadow

80

9327

3

9331

9343

5 (not always open)

5

4

2

90

Island Shelter

T. 8 N.

93

93

9328

80

19

93

9075

24

31

Lewis River Horse Camp

9303

93

90

9039

31

Lower Lewis River Falls

Lewis River

1 Mile

Mounting Assist Facility

N
TRUE
20°
MAGNETIC

90

Curley Creek Falls

R. 7 E.

This trail is not recommended for horse use as it was designed as a hiker trail. It is not for beginners, horse or rider. Children should not ride this trail and dogs may increase the risk as passing space can be limited.

CRAGGY PEAK TRAIL 3

Trail Length: 4.4 Miles
Elevation: 3400 - 6200 Feet
Difficulty: Moderate
Open: July - October
Usage: Medium
Nearest Town: Cougar
Nearest Horse Camp: Lewis River
Connecting Trails: 80, 1, 17
Facilities at Trailhead: None, old hunting camp site

DIRECTIONS

TO THE TRAILHEAD

Take I-5 Exit 21 at Woodland to Highway 503 and follow 503 northeast to Swift Reservoir. Continue past the junction with Road 25 at the east end of Swift Reservoir where Highway 503 becomes Road 90. Follow 90 about 5 miles to Curly Creek Falls. Turn left onto Road 9039 and continue north across the Lewis River about 4.5 miles to the intersection with Roads 9039 and 93. Follow Road 93 north about 9 miles to Road 9327-040 (a spur road) in Section 34, T.9N., R.7E. This is the south end of the trail in Wright Meadow.

Parking: Along the road.

Comments: This trail is located on the east side of Mount St. Helens National Volcanic Monument. It follows along a ridge in a Pacific Silver Fir and Noble Fir forest and through meadows of wild flowers. Features of this trail are views of Mt. Rainier and the rock formations along Shark Rock Ridge Scenic Area and Blue Lake. Craggy Peak Trail goes from Wright Meadow to Craggy Peak where it connects with Trail 1.

Water is scarce on this ride later in the year after the snow melts.

CUSSED HOLLOW TRAIL 19

Trail Length: 3.3 Miles
Elevation: 1400 - 3400 Feet
Difficulty: Most Difficult
Open: July - October
Usage: Medium
Nearest Town: Cougar
Nearest Horse Camp: Lewis River
Connecting Trails: 80
Facilities at Trailhead: None

DIRECTIONS

TO THE TRAILHEAD

Take I-5 Exit 21 to Highway 503. Follow 503 to Cougar and about 4 miles past the junction with Road 25 at the east end of Swift Reservoir where 503 becomes Road 90. Follow Road 90 to the junction of Roads 90 and 9039 then take 9039 for about 4.5 miles to the junction of Roads 93 and 9039. Proceed on 93 for approximately 7 miles and the trail will be on the right in Section 15, T.8N., R.7E.

This trail can also be reached by riding Trail 80 that is just beyond the Lewis River Campground on Road 90.

Parking: Along the roadside of Road 93.

Comments: This trail descends at a steep and steady rate. It follows the route of Cussed Hollow Creek and passes through the old burn near the junction of the Wright Meadow Trail. At this point you are only 0.8 mile from Road 90 on Trail 80.

LEWIS RIVER TRAIL 31

Trail Length: 13.6 Miles
Elevation: 1260 - 1800 Feet
Difficulty: Easy
Open: June - October

Usage: Heavy
Nearest Town: Cougar
Nearest Horse Camp: Lewis River
Connecting Trails: 19, 80, 24
Facilities at Trailhead: Stock water in creek

DIRECTIONS

TO THE TRAILHEAD

An 11 mile segment of this trail is reached from Highway 503. Take I-5 Exit 21 at Woodland and follow 503 to Cougar and to Swift Reservoir where Highway 503 turns into Road 90. Follow Road 90 to Curly Creek Falls which is one of the Lewis River Trail 31 access points on Road 9039 after crossing the Lewis River. This location is in Section 29, T.7N., R.7E.

Another access is at the Crab Creek bridge crossing of the Lewis River on Road 90 about 6 miles past Road 9039. You can also access this trail at Lower Falls Campground.

The shorter section of the trail is accessed at the Lower Lewis Campground and climbs above the river through a second growth Douglas-fir forest.

Parking: Along the roadside at a wide spot.

Comments: Trail 31 is located on the Southeast side of Mount St. Helens. It follows the Lewis River from Curly Creek Falls to the Lower Falls Campground. Features on this ride are Curly Creek Falls with a rock arch, Miller Creek Falls, Cascade Gorge and the historic Bolt Camp Shelter with rustic split cedar bunks built in 1931 by the Forest Service. The shorter section of the trail ends on Road 90 near Quartz Creek Trail 5.

SUMMIT PRAIRIE TRAIL 2

Trail Length: 9.0 Miles
Elevation: 2450 - 5240 Feet
Difficulty: Moderate
Open: July - October

Usage: Heavy
Nearest Town: Cougar
Nearest Horse Camp: Lewis River
Connecting Trails: 1
Facilities at Trailhead: None

DIRECTIONS

TO THE TRAILHEAD

Take I-5 Exit 21 at Woodland to Highway 503 and go northeast to Swift Reservoir where 503 becomes Road 90. Follow 90 approximately 19 miles east past Swift Reservoir where the trail will be on your left in Section 7, T.8N., R.9E.

Parking: Roadside only.

Comments: This trail allows motor bikes. It is a challenging uphill ride on the east side of Mount St. Helens for two miles along ridgetop, through alpine forests and across high country meadows. Distant views open up to show Juniper Peak, Dark Divide and the Shark Rock Scenic Area. Check out the Summit Prairie Lookout that was built in 1932.

WRIGHT TRAIL 80

Trail Length: 8.5 Miles
Elevation: 1750 - 3600 Feet
Difficulty: Moderate
Open: May - October
Usage: Heavy
Nearest Town: Cougar
Nearest Horse Camp: Lewis River
Connecting Trails: 3 (connects to Boundary Trail 1), 19
Facilities at Trailhead: None

DIRECTIONS

TO THE TRAILHEAD

From Cougar follow Highway 503 northeast past Swift Reservoir where 503 becomes Road 90. Follow Road 90 about 14 miles past the end of Swift Reservoir and the junction with Road 25. Trail 80 takes off to the north from Road 90 just beyond the Lewis River Campground in Section 2, T.8N., R.7-1/2E. (Note the partial Range of 7-1/2 that is due to survey adjustments.)

Parking: Along the roadside.

Comments: Wright Meadow Trail passes through a variety of forest conditions that includes mature forest, creek crossings, clear cuts and Wright Meadow. The meadow may offer some elk watching. Be prepared to meet mountain bikes and motor bikes as they also use this trail.

Little Goose Horse Camp

—*Photo by authors*

Map 12

Gifford Pinchot National Forest
Kalama Horse Camp - Mount St. Helens

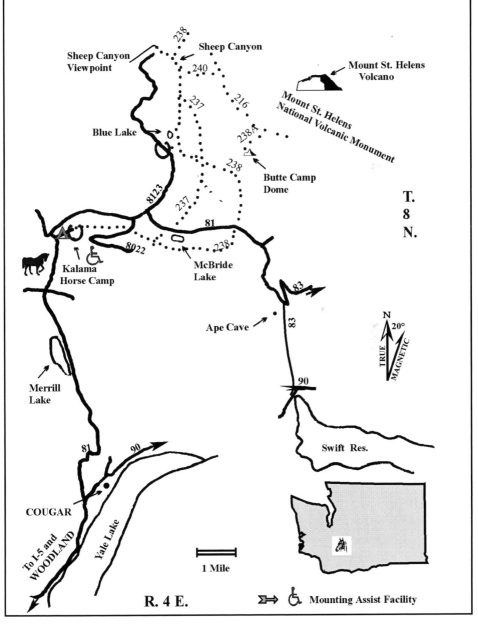

Sheep Canyon Viewpoint

Sheep Canyon

238

240

237

216

Mount St. Helens Volcano

Mount St. Helens National Volcanic Monument

Blue Lake

238A

238

Butte Camp Dome

8123

237

T. 8 N.

81

8022

238

Kalama Horse Camp

McBride Lake

Ape Cave

83

83

N 20°

TRUE

MAGNETIC

90

Merrill Lake

Swift Res.

81

90

COUGAR

Yale Lake

To I-5 and WOODLAND

1 Mile

R. 4 E.

Mounting Assist Facility

TOUTLE TRAIL 238

Trail Length: 14.2 Miles
Elevation: 3000 - 4100 Feet
Difficulty: More Difficult
Open: July - October
Usage: Medium
Nearest Town: Cougar
Nearest Horse Camp: Kalama
Connecting Trails: 237, 240 and 216 (both closed to stock)
Facilities at Trailhead: Kalama Horse Camp has extensive camping
and parking facilities. At other trailhead access points (Road 123 at
Toutle Trailhead, None; at Red Rock Pass trail crossing, None)

DIRECTIONS

TO THE TRAILHEAD

Access from the Kalama Horse Camp is by Highway 503 from
Woodland to Cougar. Take Road 8100 it is about 0.2 miles before you
enter Cougar. Follow 8100 (81) north for about 8 miles to Road 8100-
440, a spur road right into the horse camp.

Parking: There is extensive parking at the Kalama Horse Camp,
but at other accesses to Trail 238 parking is only along the road or at
Blue Lake Trailhead on Road 8123.

Comments: This trail is located on the south side of Mount St.
Helens in Section 28, T.8N., R.4E. The Kalama segment of Toutle
Trail 238 parallels the Kalama River through old growth forest and
past McBride Lake at 5.5 miles. This section of the trail ends at the
intersection with Road 8100. It crosses several apparent roads in this
stretch but is well marked. After crossing the road, the Toutle Trail
continues on from Red Rock Pass Trailhead, following the edge of a
regenerated harvest area. The trail enters a dense forest of Noble Fir
and continues to the South Fork of the Toutle River. Here the trail is
closed to stock use west of Sheep Canyon. Loop opportunities are
possible with Blue Lake Trail 238. Trail 240 is open to stock west to
the Sheep Canyon trailhead.

Map 13

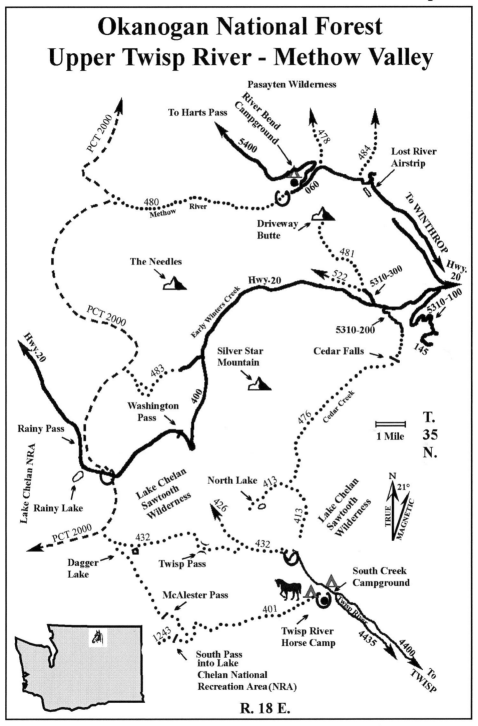

Okanogan National Forest
Upper Twisp River - Methow Valley

Pasayten Wilderness

River Bend Campground

To Harts Pass

PCT 2000

5400

478

484

Lost River Airstrip

060

To WINTHROP

480

Methow River

Driveway Butte

481

Hwy. 20

522

5310-300

Hwy. 20

The Needles

Early Winters Creek

5310-200

Cedar Falls

5310-100

145

PCT 2000

483

Silver Star Mountain

476

Cedar Creek

400

T. 35 N.

Hwy-20

1 Mile

Washington Pass

Rainy Pass

Lake Chelan NRA

Lake Chelan Sawtooth Wilderness

North Lake

413

N 21°

TRUE MAGNETIC

Rainy Lake

Lake Chelan Sawtooth Wilderness

426

PCT 2000

432

413

Dagger Lake

Twisp Pass

432

South Creek Campground

McAlester Pass

401

Twisp River

1243

South Pass into Lake Chelan National Recreation Area (NRA)

Twisp River Horse Camp

4435

4400

To TWISP

R. 18 E.

SOUTH CREEK TRAIL 401

Trail Length: 7.8 Miles
Elevation: 3000 - 6200 Feet
Difficulty: Moderate
Open: June - September
Usage: Heavy
Nearest Town: Twisp
Nearest Horse Camp: Twisp River
Connecting Trails: 428, 1243 (NRA Trail)
Facilities at Trailhead: Horse camp, corrals, 25 developed sites

DIRECTIONS

TO THE TRAILHEAD

From Twisp take Road 44 about 22.6 miles to the South Creek Campground, Road 44 becomes 4430 on the way. If you crossed over to the other road along the west side of the Twisp river, that road is Road 4435 after you passed Reynolds Creek. The horse camp is on the right side of Road 4435 before it ends. There is a sign that reads, "Horse Camp 3/10 mile". It is located in Section 19, T.34N., R.19E.

Parking: Ample at campsite.

Comments: This trail begins near the Twisp River Horse Camp at the end of Road 4435. A bridge over South Creek leads to the South Creek Trail. The trail climbs up to a ridge that divides the Twisp River and Lake Chelan National Recreation Area (NRA). Permits are required to camp in the NRA.

The junction with Trail 428 to Lewis Lake is two miles up Trail 401. Along the trail there is a lack of camping spots with water but you will find a hitch rail and horse camp area near the lake. Plan to carry pelletized horse feed if your trip is overnight.

WEST FORK METHOW RIVER TRAIL 480

Trail Length: 8.0 Miles
Elevation: 2800 - 4200 Feet
Difficulty: Easy
Open: Late June - September
Usage: Medium
Nearest Town: Winthrop
Nearest Horse Camp: Twisp River
Connecting Trails: 2000 and access to 756 and 755
Facilities at Trailhead: Loading ramp, stock water at river, 6 large
 pens, hitch rails, room for high-lines

DIRECTIONS

TO THE TRAILHEAD

Travel west from Winthrop on Highway 20 for 14 miles to the
Mazama turn-off. This follows the Methow River. Turn right to
Mazama then left at Mazama onto Harts Pass Road 1163. Follow 1163
for 7 miles and take Road 5400, 0.3 mile past Ballard Camp to a fork
in the road. A sign reads, "River Bend Campground" It is 0.8 mile to
the end of Road 060 (a good road) and a primitive camp located in
Section 2, T.36N., R.18E.

Parking: Large open area in a pine setting.

Comments: Here is a primitive site, suited for self contained
campers and is a good choice for a ride location. It is also an area
essential to help keep clean.

This is a scenic river bottom route, in mostly fir stands, that is
access to the Pacific Crest National Scenic Trail 2000. Old camp sites
may be available at about 2 mile intervals along the trail. A horse
camping area (Horse Heaven Camp) with feed and water is located 2
miles southwest of the trail end at Trail 2000. It has been described in
some Forest Service literature but is not shown on the maps. The camp
still exists and is available on a first come basis but the local Forest
Office staff may not know if it is occupied as reservations or permits
are not required.

PACIFIC CREST NATIONAL SCENIC TRAIL (PCT) 2000 (SOUTH)

Trail Length: 30 Miles (Rainy Pass to Harts Pass)
Elevation: 4900 - 7000 Feet
Difficulty: Moderate
Open: July - October
Usage: Medium
Nearest Town: Winthrop
Nearest Horse Camp: None
Connecting Trails: Numerous, use a PCT or Pasayten Wilderness map
Facilities at Trailhead: Rainy Pass parking lot (south end of trail) on Highway 20 has loading ramp, hitch rail, toilets, campsites; Hart Pass (north end of trail) on Road 5400 has loading ramp, hitch rail, toilets, campsite

DIRECTIONS

TO THE TRAILHEAD

To reach the Harts Pass Trailhead located in Section 1, T.37N., R.17E. Take Highway 20 from Winthrop for 14 miles to the Mazama turn-off. Turn right onto the Hart Pass Road which is County Road 1163. Follow this road for 18.5 miles to Harts Pass and turn right onto Road 600 toward Slate Peak. Check for current trailer access.

To reach the Rainy Pass Trailhead located in Section 21, T.35N., R.17E., take Highway 20 from Winthrop west to Rainy Pass. This is about 30 miles. Trail 2000 (PCT) starts in the parking lot.

Parking: Trailhead parking lots are adequate for horse rigs.

Comments: This section of the Trail 2000 (PCT) from Rainy Pass to Harts Pass follows sidehills and ridges of the Cascade Crest. Most of the trail is above timberline with wide vistas.

The trail is the major north-south route to the western part of the Pasayten Wilderness where many loop rides are possible. Camps are generally located about every 6-7 miles although in late summer finding water can be a problem in some stretches. There is fishing along the way.

Camps with horse feed are available at Porcupine Creek, Methow River, Glacier Pass (about mile 7 on this section). Reduce your impact by finding established camps away from the trail and carry pelletized feed. The trail between Methow and Glacier Pass sometimes has slides.

The Walker Hitch: it is easy to throw and it keeps the load off the side of the horse.

—*Photo by authors*

Map 14

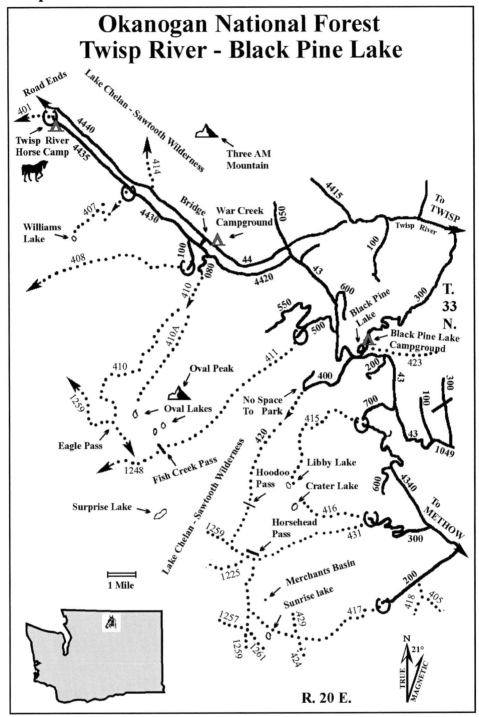

Okanogan National Forest
Twisp River - Black Pine Lake

Road Ends

Lake Chelan - Sawtooth Wilderness

401

4440

4435

Twisp River
Horse Camp

Three AM
Mountain

407

4430

Bridge

War Creek
Campground

414

4415

To
TWISP

Twisp River

050

100

Williams
Lake

408

100

080

44

4420

43

600

300

T.
33
N.

Black Pine
Lake

410

550

500

Black Pine Lake
Campground

410A

411

200

423

43

410

Oval Peak

400

No Space
To Park

700

300

100

1259

Oval Lakes

420

415

43

1049

Eagle Pass

1248

Fish Creek Pass

Libby Lake

Hoodoo
Pass

Crater Lake

600

4340

To
METHOW

Surprise Lake

416

Lake Chelan - Sawtooth Wilderness

1259

Horsehead
Pass

431

300

1 Mile

1225

Merchants Basin

200

418

405

Sunrise lake

1257

429

417

1259

1261

424

N
21°

TRUE
MAGNETIC

R. 20 E.

CRATER CREEK TRAIL 416

Trail Length: 3.2 Miles
Elevation: 3800 - 6800 Feet
Difficulty: Moderate
Open: June - September
Usage: Medium to Heavy
Nearest Town: Twisp
Nearest Horse Camp: Twisp River
Connecting Trails: 429, 431, with connections to 417
Facilities at Trailhead: Toilet, loading ramp, 5 hitch rails, stock water

DIRECTIONS

TO THE TRAILHEAD

You reach this trailhead by going south from Carlton for about 5 miles on Highway 153. The Libby Creek Road is at about 1.5 miles and the road to take is Road 1034 for 2 miles to Road 4340 along Gold Creek. Next take 4340 for about 6 miles to Road 300. Follow Road 300 to the end, about 4 miles of very steep travel. This route requires good brakes. The road is gravel and has many curves but there is a camp with great views at the end of the road located in Section 6, T.31N., R.21E.

Parking: Large with adequate turn-around area.

Comments: The junction to Trail 416 is a 0.8 mile ride up Trail 431 which goes to Eagle Lake. It is a moderately steep grade up to Crater Lake. There is a horse campsite below the lake.

This spot has great views and lots of riding opportunities and the trails are well maintained so expect many rigs during hunting season.

The hitching and tethering restrictions for overnight use require high-lines and the point of tie must be at least 8-feet from any tree to prevent root damage. These tethering restrictions keep stock from some tree shelter at night and is another reason to carry a light weight horse blanket like the ones described earlier in the book.

FOGGY DEW TRAIL 417

Trail Length: 7.6 Miles
Elevation: 2400 - 6200 Feet
Difficulty: Moderate
Open: June - September
Usage: Medium to Heavy
Nearest Town: Pateros and Twisp
Nearest Horse Camp: Twisp River
Connecting Trails: 429, 405, 417, 424, 431, 1259, 1257, 1225, 1255, 1260, 1261
Facilities at Trailhead: Loading ramp, 3 hitch rails, campsites

DIRECTIONS

TO THE TRAILHEAD

You reach this trailhead by going north from Pateros for 17 miles on Highway 153. Turn left (west) onto Road 4340 along Gold Creek. This is about 5 miles south of Carlton. Follow Road 4340 to the junction with Road 200. The Foggy Dew camp is at the junction of Roads 200 and 4340. Follow 200 past the camp for approximately 2 miles to a sharp hairpin turn. Just past this turn is the trail crossing of 405 that goes to Trail 418. There is very limited parking for trailer rigs at this site. Continue on Road 200 to the end of the road where horse facilities are located at the Trail 417 trailhead located in Section 19, T.31N., R.21E.

Parking: Large enough for 7-8 rigs and a good sized turn around area but not much flat ground for camping.

Comments: The first 4 trail miles are an easy grade then the ride becomes steep and rocky for the last 3.5 miles. Foggy Dew Falls is at 3 miles. When you reach Merchants Basin at 6 miles there is good grazing and some camping areas. The Basin also has some horse facilities and toilet. This area has good opportunities for loop trips and rides to lakes. Hitching or stock tying restrictions for overnight stays require high-line use, with the point of tie at least 8-feet from any tree.

You may meet motorbikes and bicycles for a ways as they are allowed to the junction with the Martin Creek Trail 429.

LIBBY CREEK TRAIL 415

Trail Length: 5.3 Miles
Elevation: 4400 - 7600 Feet
Difficulty: Moderate
Open: June - September
Usage: Medium
Nearest Town: Twisp
Nearest Horse Camp: Twisp River
Connecting Trails: None
Facilities at Trailhead: Toilet

DIRECTIONS

TO THE TRAILHEAD

From Twisp take Road 44 about 11 miles to the Buttermilk Creek Road 43 which crosses the Twisp River. A sign reads "Buttermilk Creek/Black Pine Lake". Follow Road 43 for about 11 miles to Road 4330. Take 4330 south along Buttermilk Creek. The pavement ends past the turn to Black Pine Lake. Continue past Road 400 that goes to Trail 420. (Not suited to horse rigs!) Pass Roads 220 and 700 (gate access closed). Take the next right on Road 740 where a sign reads, "Libby Creek No. 415". The location is Section 13, T.32N., R.20E.

You can also reach this trailhead by going south from Carlton for 1.5 miles on Highway 153. At the junction with the Libby Creek Road, turn right (west). Take this road to the junction with Road 740 and a sign to Trail 415.

Parking: Large area with space to turn around, adequate for up to 8 rigs.

Comments: This is a pretty spot with a good road into the location but the trail is steep, rocky and only goes to Libby Lake. It is recommended only for experienced stock users. The lake area is very rocky with limited campsites and there is no horse feed at or near the lake so pelletized feed must be carried for overnight trips to the area.

Be prepared to use caution when you cross the boulder field the last 0.5 mile to the lake. There are no suitable horse camps at the lake but there is a campsite about 1 mile before the lake.

WAR CREEK TRAIL 408

Trail Length: 9.3 Miles
Elevation: 2400 - 6000 Feet
Difficulty: Easy
Open: June - September
Usage: Medium
Nearest Town: Twisp
Nearest Horse: Twisp River
Connecting Trails: 409 (crossing War Creek may be hazardous)
Facilities at Trailhead: Toilet, loading ramp, hitch rail

DIRECTIONS

TO THE TRAILHEAD

From Twisp take Road 44 about 14 miles to the War Creek Campground. Go past the campground a short distance, turn left and take the bridge over the Twisp River to Road 4430. Turn right and go another short distance to Road 4430-100. Turn left onto 100. It is about 1 mile to the trailhead located in Section 13, T.33N., R.19E.

Parking: There is a turn around area with space for at least 3 rigs.

Comments: This trail is access to War Creek Pass and the Lake Chelan National Recreation Area (NRA). Permits are required to camp in the NRA. The ride on this trail takes you uphill through several forest types of vegetation zones. Grazing can be in short supply on this trail. Rattlesnakes are occasionally seen near the trailhead area.

WEST FORK BUTTERMILK TRAIL 411

Trail Length: 9.5 Miles
Elevation: 4000 - 7400 Feet
Difficulty: Moderate to Most Difficult
Open: June - September
Usage: Medium
Nearest Town: Twisp

Nearest Horse Camp: Twisp River
Connecting Trails: 1259
Facilities at Trailhead: Toilet, hitch rail, loading ramp, shelter just
below the parking area

DIRECTIONS

TO THE TRAILHEAD

From Twisp take Forest Road 44 about 11 miles to the Buttermilk
Creek Road 43 which crosses the Twisp River. A sign reads, "Buttermilk Creek / Black Pine Lake". Follow Road 43 for 4.5 miles to the
junction with Road 4300-500. Take 500 for 3.5 miles to the end of the
road and the trailhead located in Section 34, T.33N., R.20E.

Parking: Adequate with large turn around area.

Comments: This is a primitive trail to ride and it has limited
campsites. A sign at the trailhead warns the trail is very difficult and is
for experienced riders only. There is a stream crossing at 8 miles that is
considered dangerous for horses but you can find a better crossing 150
feet upstream from the trail.

As you ride you will notice the trail has not had maintenance for
the past several years. At 6 miles there is a large boggy section to pass
through.

WILLIAMS CREEK TRAIL 407

Trail Length: 7.5 Miles
Elevation: 3000 - 7000 Feet
Difficulty: Moderate
Open: June - September
Usage: Medium
Nearest Town: Twisp
Nearest Horse Camp: Twisp River
Connecting Trails: None
Facilities at Trailhead: Toilet, hitch rail

DIRECTIONS

TO THE TRAILHEAD

From Twisp take Road 44 about 14 miles to the War Creek Campground. Go past the campground a short distance, turn left and take the bridge over the Twisp River to Road 4430. Turn right and go about 3 miles on Road 4430.

This can also be reached by going about 18 miles on Road 44 from Twisp and crossing over to Road 4430 at Mystery Camp and turning left (back toward Twisp, 0.5 mile) to the Williams Lake Trailhead located in Section 34, T.34N., R.19E. There are trail signs at the road.

Parking: Small turn around area with space for 2 rigs if care is taken in parking.

Comments: This short trail into the Lake Chelan-Sawtooth Wilderness is access to Williams Lake. It has a modest grade on the uphill ride to the lake. During the last 3 miles you will pass through an old burn area. Water is in short supply on this trail.

Map 15

Okanogan National Forest
Pasayten Wilderness-Andrews Creek East

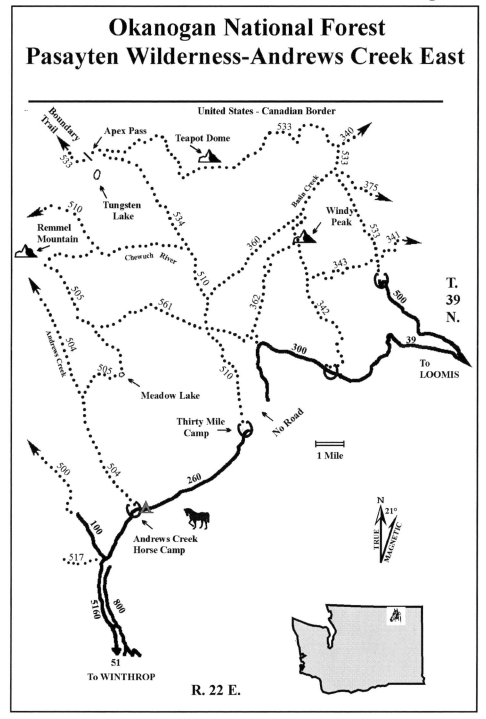

United States - Canadian Border

Boundary Trail

Apex Pass

Teapot Dome

533

340

533

533

375

341

Basin Creek

Windy Peak

510

Tungsten Lake

Remmel Mountain

534

Chewuch River

510

510

360

343

533

500

T. 39 N.

505

561

362

342

39

To LOOMIS

Andrews Creek

504

505

Meadow Lake

510

300

No Road

1 Mile

Thirty Mile Camp

500

504

260

N
21°
TRUE
MAGNETIC

100

Andrews Creek Horse Camp

517

5160

800

51
To WINTHROP

R. 22 E.

BASIN CREEK TRAIL 360

Trail Length: 6.0 Miles
Elevation: 4500 - 8100 Feet
Difficulty: Moderate
Open: July - September
Usage: Heavy
Nearest Town: Winthrop
Nearest Horse Camp: None
Connecting Trails: 510, 342 (access to 533 Boundary Trail)
Facilities at Trailhead: At trailhead for Trail 510, toilets, campsites, high-line, hitch rails, stock water

DIRECTIONS

TO THE TRAILHEAD

From Winthrop, go north for about 29 miles on the West Chewuch River Road. The pavement ends at the Andrews Creek Trailhead, about 21 of the 29 miles. Continue past on gravel Road 250 for about 8 miles. This is a good road that follows the river to the Thirty Mile Trailhead for Trail 510. After you enter the Forest the road numbers are 51 and 5160.

Ride Trail 510 from the trailhead for about 5.5 miles to reach the junction with Basin Creek Trail 360 located in Section 11, T.39N., R.22E.

Parking: The Thirty Mile Trailhead has a circle drive and room for 2-3 rigs.

Comments: This trailride is one of the accesses to Horseshoe Basin and Boundary Trail 533. Trail 360 climbs to the crest of the ridge and is primarily in Lodgepole stands that have a scattering of larch and fir near Topaz Mountain.

Ride this trail with care as it difficult because of steepness. Plan to do your camping at Basin Creek about 2 to 2.5 miles up the trail from the west end. You will pass the junction with the Windy Creek Trail 362 at about 4.5 mile.

BOUNDARY TRAIL 533

Trail Length: 73 Miles
Elevation: 5100 - 7200 Feet
Difficulty: Moderate
Open: July - September
Usage: Medium to Heavy
Nearest Town: Tonasket (east end of trail)
Nearest Horse Camp: None
Connecting Trails: From east to west; 341, 343, 342, 375, 534, 504, 510, 500, 506, 477, 478, 453, 495, 2000, 749
Facilities at Trailhead: East end has loading ramp, hitch rails, toilets

DIRECTIONS

TO THE TRAILHEAD

To reach the east end of Trail 533 into the Pasayten Wilderness, drive north on Highway 97 from Tonasket to Ellisforde. Turn left and cross the river to Road 9437. Follow 9437 to Road 9425 and continue to Loomis. Pass through Loomis and travel about 2.0 miles north then turn left onto Road 39. Follow 39 for 14 miles to the junction with the Iron Gate Road 500. Turn right (north) and follow Road 500 for 5.2 miles to the trailhead located in Section 1, T.39N., R.23E.

The Boundary Trail can also be reached from several trails that start north of Winthrop, Trails 500, 504 and 510 (see these Trail Guides) and from Trail 478 that start above Mazama at the north end of the Methow Valley (See the Trail Guide for Trail 478).

Parking: Ample at trailhead.

Comments: This main east-west trail crosses the Pasayten Wilderness and ties together other access trails. Therefore, Boundary Trail 533 is presented in the book in segments on each of the three Trail Maps that cover the Pasayten Wilderness. The route varies from timbered valleys to long sidehills and high ridge routes with much of the eastern portion of the trail above timberline.

Some Forest Service literature breaks the Boundary Trail into 2 sections. The mid point is Mile 36 at the Ashnola River and the junction of the Boundary Trail with Trail 500. The section from Iron gate to Ashnola River is Boundary Trail (east). The section from Ashnola River to the Trail 2000 (PCT) at Castle Pass located in Section 20, T.40N., R.17E. is the Boundary Trail (west). Each is about 36 miles in length.

The many trail connections along 533 make loop rides possible. The Horseshoe Basin, Remmel, Cathedral and Sheep Mountain areas are popular with riders because grazing is available. In addition, the trail passes near 8 lakes and a number of rivers.

WINDY PEAK TRAIL 342

Trail Length: 11.5 Miles
Elevation: 4500 - 8100 Feet
Difficulty: Difficult
Open: July - September
Usage: Heavy
Nearest Town: Tonasket
Nearest Horse Camp: None
Connecting Trails: 343, 360, 533 (Boundary Trail)
Facilities at Trailhead: Toilets, hitch rails, loading ramp

DIRECTIONS

TO THE TRAILHEAD

From Tonasket go north on Highway 97 and 20 to Ellisforde. Turn left and cross the Okanogan River to County Roads 9437 and 9425 to Loomis. Go through Loomis about 2 miles north and turn west (left) onto Road 39. This is the Toats Coulee Road. Take Road 39 for about 21 miles to Long Swamp Campground and the trailhead located in Section 21, T.39N., R.23E.

Parking: Ample for trailer rigs.

Comments: The ride on this high ridge wilderness trail varies between Lodgepole Pine stands and spruce or fir and the more open meadows with alpine areas of Windy Peak. The three connecting trails make a series of loop rides possible.

While this is a trail considered difficult because of the steep sidehills and some trail tread slippage you will find abundant horse feed. Near Windy Peak the snow melt will not be until late July. Meadow Camp is at about 9 miles on the trail.

CHEWUCH TRAIL AT THIRTY MILE CAMP TRAIL 510

Trail Length: 18.1 Miles
Elevation: 3500 - 7100 Feet
Difficulty: Moderate
Open: July - September
Usage: Heavy
Nearest Town: Winthrop
Nearest Horse Camp: None
Connecting Trails: 561, 534, 360, 362
Facilities at Trailhead: Toilets, campsites, high-line, hitch rails, stock water

DIRECTIONS

TO THE TRAILHEAD

From Winthrop, go north for about 29 miles on the West Chewuch River Road. The pavement ends at the Andrews Creek Trailhead, about 21 of the 29 miles. Continue past on gravel Road 250 for about 8 miles. This is a good road that follows the river to the Thirty Mile Trailhead. After you enter the Forest the road numbers became 51 and 5160.

You can also take Road 9137 north and cross over to the west side of the river at the bridge about 6 miles north of Winthrop. Turn right after you cross the bridge and continue north for about 14 miles on Roads 51, 5160 and 250 to the trailhead for Thirty Mile Camp located in Section 1, T.38N., R.22E.

Parking: The area has a circle drive and room for 2-3 rigs.

Comments: This is a scenic valley trail that follows the river grade and is in Lodgepole Pine stands except the last two miles that are meadow and subalpine areas.

Trail riders use this as a major stock route into the Remmel and Cathedral area. The trail is also used to access the Four Point Lake and Tungsten Mine area. You can reach the Horseshoe Basin by the Basin Creek Trail 360. There are many fishing areas along the route with Cutthroat Trout in Remmel and other lakes.

This area has heavy use. Campsites are worn down with damage to trees and ground so please avoid already trampled locations and walk the last quarter of a mile to the lakes.

Old cabin at tungsten mine in Pasayten Wilderness, Okonogan National Forest
—*Photo by authors*

Map 16

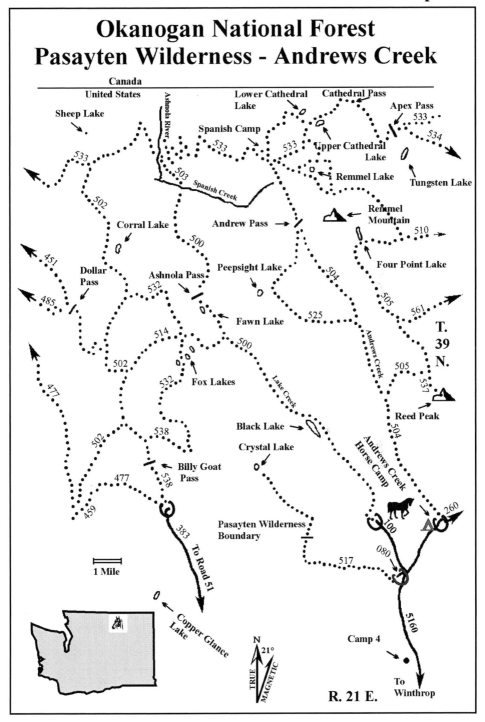

Okanogan National Forest
Pasayten Wilderness - Andrews Creek

Canada
United States
Sheep Lake
Ashnola River
Lower Cathedral Lake
Cathedral Pass
Apex Pass
533
534
Spanish Camp
533
533
Upper Cathedral Lake
Remmel Lake
Tungsten Lake
533
503
Spanish Creek
502
Corral Lake
Andrew Pass
Remmel Mountain
510
451
Dollar Pass
Ashnola Pass
Peepsight Lake
500
Four Point Lake
485
532
504
505
561
Fawn Lake
525
T. 39 N.
514
500
502
505
532
Fox Lakes
537
Reed Peak
477
Lake Creek
Andrews Creek
504
502
538
Black Lake
Andrews Creek Horse Camp
Crystal Lake
260
459
Billy Goat Pass
538
477
100
383
To Road 51
Pasayten Wilderness Boundary
080
517
1 Mile
5160
Copper Glance Lake
N
21°
Camp 4
TRUE
MAGNETIC
R. 21 E.
To Winthrop

ANDREWS CREEK TRAIL 504

Trail Length: 16.0 Miles
Elevation: 3000 - 6600 Feet
Difficulty: Easy
Open: June - September
Usage: Heavy
Nearest Town: Winthrop
Nearest Horse Camp: None
Connecting Trails: 533 (Boundary Trail), 505, 525, 510 537, also access to 561, 510
Facilities at Trailhead: Horse camp area on left side has 2 corrals, 5 hitch rails, sorting pen, pit toilets, fire pits, stock water at the creek, day-use on the right side has loading ramp, 2 hitch rails

DIRECTIONS

TO THE TRAILHEAD

From Winthrop, go north on the West Chewuch River Road (213) to the end of the pavement. It is about 23 miles to the trailhead. After you enter the National Forest the Road is 51.

Parking: The day use area has a large turn-around area and parking for 5-6 rigs. This area is not very wide and if full, turning a large rig may be awkward.

The horse camp area has a large area to park and will handle several large rigs. The map location is Section 20, T.38N., R.22E.

Comments: A sign at the horse camp reads, "Coleman Ridge 9 miles; Andrews Pass 12 miles, Boundary Trail 15 miles". This is a river bottom trail that goes through mature timber and enters rolling meadow country near a popular camping area, Spanish Camp. The views on the ride in are not great until you reach Andrews Pass and the Spanish Camp area, then there are miles of open country to ride.

The camp is very popular with horse riders because of good grass and many possible side trips. Try fishing Remmel and Upper and Lower Cathedral lakes as well as Andrews Creek.

CRYSTAL LAKE TRAIL 517

Trail Length: 9.2 Miles
Elevation: 2500 - 7400 Feet
Difficulty: Moderate
Open: July - September
Usage: Medium
Nearest Town: Winthrop
Nearest Horse Camp: Twisp River
Connecting Trails: None
Facilities at Trailhead: Toilets, stock water, loading ramp, hitch rail

DIRECTIONS

TO THE TRAILHEAD

From Winthrop, take the West Chewuch River Road about 18.5 miles to the trailhead located in Section 30, T.38N., R.22E. The road becomes 51 at the Forest boundary. You will pass Camp 4 and cross Buck Creek where the road becomes 5160. After you cross the Dodd Creek bridge, take narrow Road 080 to the left 0.2 mile to the camp area.

Parking: There is a large area to turn around.

Comments: This is a long sidehill and valley trail and it is not maintained on a yearly basis. The trail goes along Farewell Creek and over the ridge to Disaster Creek to a very nice alpine lake. There is no trail access to other lakes in the vicinity but the trail does offer good views of the Chewuch River and the Mt. Harney area. There are Cutthroat and Rainbow trout in the lake.

At about 5 miles on the ride you cross Wilderness Boundary Pass. There is a ridge between Crystal Lake and nearby Kidney Lake.

This country has small meadow areas and bare rocky ridges.

The camping around the lake has caused overuse and horses should be kept away from the lake with camping at other off-trail locations. You will need to carry pelletized feed if this is an overnight trip.

LAKE CREEK TRAIL TO BLACK LAKE TRAIL 500

Trail Length: 18.9 Miles
Elevation: 3200 - 6300 Feet
Difficulty: Easy to lake, Most Difficult beyond
Open: July - September
Usage: Medium to Heavy to Black Lake
Nearest Town: Winthrop
Nearest Horse Camp: None
Connecting Trails: 514, 533
Facilities at Trailhead: Toilets, stock water at creek, loading ramp, hitch rail, fire pit, 3 corrals (2 are large), campsites

DIRECTIONS

TO THE TRAILHEAD

From Winthrop, take the West Chewuch River Road about 19 miles to a bridge over Lake Creek. The road becomes 51 at the Forest Boundary. Just past the bridge, turn left onto Road 5160-100 and drive two miles to the trailhead located in Section 24, T.38N., R.21E. You will pass Camp 4 and cross Buck Creek where the road becomes 5160. After you cross the Dodd Creek Bridge continue on 5160 a short distance to a sign that reads, "To Trail 500 Lake Creek". Take dirt Road 100 to the left for two miles to the trailhead.

Parking: A large turn-around area and 5 back-in sites.

Comments: This 18.9 mile ride includes 4.2 miles to Black Lake and about 14 beyond the lake to reach Trail 503 that connects to Trail 533.

The sign at the trailhead reads, "Black Lake 5-miles, Ashnola Pass 12 miles and Ashnola River 19 miles". This is a large mountain valley lake and horse grazing restrictions apply to this as with all lakes. You should bring pelletized feed for this location.

Some stream crossings may be difficult in the spring. The trail beyond the lake is not recommended for horses due to hazardous conditions.

This is a popular day ride and hiking area to the lake for trout fishing. The camp at the north end of the lake has a hitch rail and may be used by parties with stock. Please camp at least a quarter of a mile from Black Lake because of over-use and select off-trail locations. This country has small meadow areas and bare rocky ridges. Trail 500 continues north toward the Canadian border and connects with Trail 503 that goes to the Boundary Trail.

LARCH CREEK TRAIL 502

Trail Length: 16.2 Miles
Elevation: 4700 - 7640 Feet
Difficulty: Difficult
Open: July - September
Usage: Heavy
Nearest Town: Winthrop
Nearest Horse Camp: None
Connecting Trails: 477, 514, 506, 533, 451
Facilities at Trailhead: Billy Goat Trailhead has loading ramp, hitch rail, toilets

DIRECTIONS

TO THE TRAILHEAD

To reach this trail drive north from Winthrop about 9 miles on the West Chewuch Road 51. When you reach the Eightmile Creek Road 5130, turn left and travel about 18 miles on Roads 5130 and 383 to the Billy Goat Trailhead at the end of Road 383.

Ride the Hidden Lake Trail 477 about 4 miles to Drake Creek and the junction with the Larch Mountain Trail 502. This junction is located in Section 8, T.38N., R.20E.

You can also access this trail by using several other trailheads off Road 51 from Winthrop.

Parking: Ample at Billy Goat Trailhead.

Comments: This heavily traveled trail is in the Pasayten Wilderness. It is primarily a ridge and sidehill trail into one of the more popular horse use areas. The trail reaches some high country, with the highest being McCall-Timber Wolf Divide at 7640 feet elevation. The ride offers excellent views of the Pasayten from several angles as you cross four passes on the way to Sheep Mountain. They are, Billy Goat Pass, 3 Fools Pass, Larch Pass and McCall-Timberline Pass.

Try the fishing in these lakes, Corral, Crow, Quartz, Sheep and Ramon. They are all in the Sheep Mountain area. When you get beyond Larch Pass the country is mostly open rolling meadows that are above timberline. A number of excellent side trip rides are possible to lakes and high basins or connecting trails.

This is country to be extra aware of the impact of our horses around lake shores and streams when watering.

High country in the Pasayten Wilderness
—*Photo by authors*

Map 17

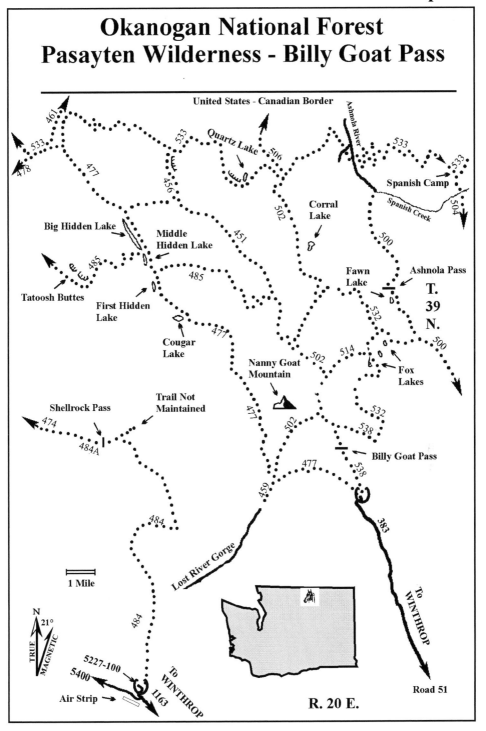

EAST FORK PASAYTEN 451

Trail Length: 10.5 Miles
Elevation: 4500 - 7000 Feet
Difficulty: Moderate to Most Difficult
Open: July - September
Usage: Medium
Nearest Town: Winthrop
Nearest Horse Camp: None
Connecting Trails: 456, 485, 502
Facilities at Trailhead: Billy Goat Trailhead has loading ramp, hitch
　　rail, toilets

DIRECTIONS

TO THE TRAILHEAD

To reach this trail drive north from Winthrop about 9 miles on the
West Chewuch Road 51. When you reach the Eightmile Creek Road
5130 turn left and travel about 18 miles to the Billy Goat Trailhead.
Ride Trail 502 for about 5 miles to the junction with Trail 451. This
junction is located in Section 20, T.39N., R.20E.

You can also take Trail 477 north to the Hidden Lakes. Trail 451
will connect with 477 between First and Middle Hidden Lakes.

Parking: Ample at trailhead.

Comments: This trail is in the Pasayten Wilderness. It is a valley
bottom ride up the East Fork of Pasayten River and then turns to the
McCall Creek drainage when coming from the Hidden Lakes area.
From this direction the timber stands are Lodgepole and become alpine
meadows.

This trail has the advantage of making large loop rides possible
between Sheep Mountain and the Hidden Lakes all from the same
trailhead. Hidden Lakes are the lower elevation part of this trail.

Trail riders need to be aware of some narrow right-of-ways and
plan to follow the pack string passing guidelines. Also, expect several
difficult stream crossings when water levels are high.

HIDDEN LAKES TRAIL 477

Trail Length: 22.7 Miles
Elevation: 3900 - 5700 Feet
Difficulty: Difficult
Open: June - September
Usage: Heavy
Nearest Town: Winthrop
Nearest Horse Camp: Twisp River
Connecting Trails: 459, 502, 484, 456, 458, 485, 451, 533
Facilities at Trailhead: Toilets, hitch rails, loading ramp, creek for
   stock water

DIRECTIONS

TO THE TRAILHEAD

This trail to the Hidden Lakes in the Pasayten Wilderness starts at the end of Road 383 up Eight Mile Creek in Section 14, T.20N., R.38E. From Winthrop, take Road 9137 north about 6 miles to the bridge that crosses over the Chewuch River. Turn right and continue north on Road 51. At about 2.5 miles past the bridge take Road 5130 left at the "Y". Follow 5130 to the end of the pavement where it becomes Road 383. The camp is at the end of 383. This is about 15 miles from Road 51.

You will pass the Copper Glance Trail 519 on Road 383. It goes to Copper Glance Lake but there are no horse facilities and there is inadequate parking on the road for horse rigs.

Parking: Ample for horse trailers.

Comments: This is a heavily traveled route into a string of popular fishing lakes. The trail ride follows open hillsides with views for about the first 5 miles. From then on the ride is in timber and the valley bottom on to the lakes and past. At about 16 miles you pass the junction of Trail 485 going to the east and at about 17 miles you pass the 485 trail junction to the Tatoosh Buttes to the west.

There is no graze at Hidden Lakes so carry pelletized feed if you plan to visit. There is a pass between Middle and Big Hidden Lakes. Big Hidden Lake drains to the north and the others drain south to Lost River and the Methow River. Lost River is about 100 yards south of Diamond Creek. This reaches scenic meadows and sand bars along the river where a limited amount of horse feed may be available. Loop rides are possible to the Sheep Mountain area.

MONUMENT CREEK TRAIL 484

Trail Length: 25.0 Miles
Elevation: 2200 - 7500 Feet
Difficulty: Moderate
Open: July - September
Usage: Medium
Nearest Town: Winthrop
Nearest Horse Camp: Twisp River
Connecting Trails: 474, 477, 484A (see Comments)
Facilities at Trailhead: Loading ramp, hitch rails, fire pit, toilets

DIRECTIONS

TO THE TRAILHEAD

Travel west from Winthrop on Highway 20 for 14 miles to the Mazama turn-off. This follows the Methow River. Turn right to Mazama then left at Mazama onto Harts Pass Road 1163. Follow 1163 for 7 miles. Take a right at the next "Y" onto Road 5227-100. Road 5400 continues to the left. Cross a small bridge, pass the wilderness information sign then take the first dirt road to the right.

The trailhead for the Pasayten Wilderness is 1 mile up a very narrow road located in Section 5, T.36N., R.19E.

Parking: Use the junction with Road 5227-100 as the place to park and turn around large rigs. There is space for 2-4 large rigs. The trailhead has a circle drive.

Comments: The section of the trail from Butte Pass on to Hidden Lakes has not been maintained in recent years and has lots of downfall. Also, in the late 1980's a fire went over part of the Monument Creek Trail. It has not been maintained in recent years.

Published Forest Service Recreation Guide information list Trail 484-A as continuing over Shellrock Pass and past Fred's and Doris Lakes. However, Forest Maps now show that this is Trail 474 and that 484 goes north into the Pasayten Wilderness toward Big Hidden Lake but that trail has not had maintenance in about 10 years. Trail 484 mostly follows ridges and sidehills and it continues over Shellrock Pass (18 miles) and past Fred's and Doris Lakes (23 miles). Be prepared to sort out this difference.

The following relates to Trail 484 before it reaches Shellrock Pass: Trail 484 is seldom used beyond the Eureka Creek bridge. Signs at the trailhead read, "Abandoned Trail Eureka Creek (4 miles)" and also warn of rattlesnakes in this area. This trail may be difficult to follow as it passes through the 1986 Eureka fire between Lost River and Pistol Pass. Beyond Eureka Creek Bridge this trail is not recommended for stock due to hazardous sections and slides. The upper Monument Valley is isolated country with impressive views. A loop is possible with this trail and the Robinson Creek Trail 478.

A windy ridge view of the North Cascades from Pasayten Wilderness
—*Photo by authors*

Map 18

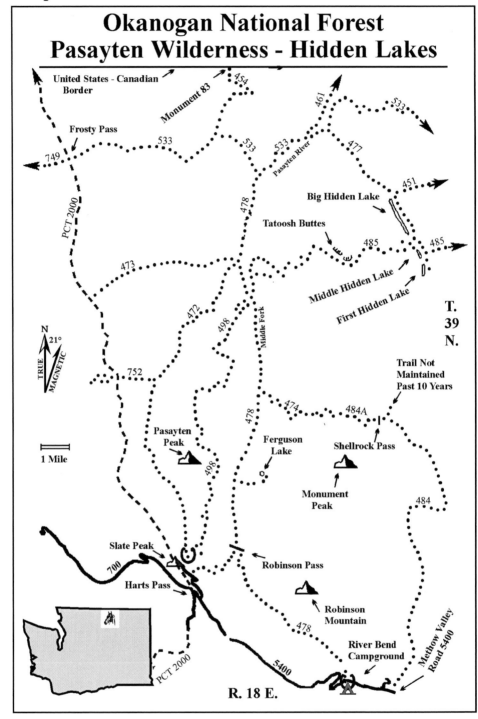

Okanogan National Forest
Pasayten Wilderness - Hidden Lakes

United States - Canadian Border

Monument 83

454

461

533

Frosty Pass

533

533

533

Pasayten River

477

749

PCT 2000

478

451

Big Hidden Lake

Tatoosh Buttes

485

485

473

Middle Hidden Lake

First Hidden Lake

T. 39 N.

472

498

Middle Fork

N 21°
TRUE
MAGNETIC

752

Trail Not Maintained Past 10 Years

1 Mile

474

484A

478

Pasayten Peak

Ferguson Lake

Shellrock Pass

498

Monument Peak

484

Slate Peak

700

Robinson Pass

Harts Pass

Robinson Mountain

478

River Bend Campground

Methow Valley Road 5400

PCT 2000

5400

R. 18 E.

PACIFIC CREST NATIONAL SCENIC TRAIL (PCT) 2000 (NORTH)

Trail Length: 33 Miles (Harts Pass to Canadian Border)
Elevation: 4500 - 7100 Feet
Difficulty: Moderate
Open: July - October
Usage: Medium
Nearest Town: Winthrop
Nearest Horse Camp: None
Connecting Trails: Numerous, including Boundary Trail 533; use either Pacific Crest National Scenic Trail map or Pasayten Wilderness map
Facilities at Trailhead: Harts Pass (south end of 33 miles) has loading ramp, hitch rail, toilets but limited campsites

DIRECTIONS

TO THE TRAILHEAD

To reach the Harts Pass trailhead located in Section 1, T.37N., R.17E., take Highway 20 from Winthrop for 14 miles to the Mazama turn-off. Turn right onto the Harts Pass road which is Road 1163. Follow this road for 18.5 miles to Harts Pass and turn right onto Road 600 towards Slate Peak. Trailers are not allowed at the trailhead. See the Trail Guide for Trail 478 and details of where to stop.

Parking: Trailhead parking lots are adequate for horse rigs.

Comments: This section of Trail 2000 follows sidehills and ridges of the Cascade Crest. Most of the trail is above timberline with wide vistas.

The trail is the major north-south route to the western part of the Pasayten Wilderness with many loop rides possible. Camps are generally located about every 6-7 miles although in late summer finding water can be a problem in some stretches. There is fishing along the way.

Camps with horse feed are available at Windy Pass, Goat Lakes

Basin, Mountain Home, Hopkins Pass (below Hopkins Lake) and Castle Pass about 3 miles from the Canadian border. Reduce your impact from stock by finding camps away from the trail.

Lakeview Ridge between Rock and Woody Pass may not melt open until late July or early August.

ROBINSON CREEK TRAIL 478

Trail Length: 27.4 Miles
Elevation: 2300 - 6000 Feet
Difficulty: Moderate
Open: June - September
Usage: Medium
Nearest Town: Winthrop
Nearest Horse Camp: Twisp River
Connecting Trails: 498, 474, 471, 473 (connects with 2000), 472, 485, 498
Facilities at Trailhead: Toilets, loading ramp, stock water at the creek, large day use area, 5 hitch rails, primitive campsites

DIRECTIONS

TO THE TRAILHEAD

To reach the trailhead, travel west from Winthrop along the Methow River on Highway 20 for 14 miles to the Mazama turn-off. Turn right across the river to Mazama then left at Mazama onto Harts Pass Road 1163. Follow 1163 for 7 miles and take Road 5400. One mile past the trail turn off for Road 484 there is a sign that reads, "No trailers beyond this point June 1 - December 31." When you pass over Robinson Creek the trailhead is immediately there. It is located in Section 36, T.37N., R.18E. The signs are clear. The distance is just over 9 miles after you turned onto Road 116.

Parking: There are 4 back-in spaces.

Comments: This trail is mostly in big timbered river bottoms with open views as you pass the meadow areas created from avalanche chutes. Near Robinson Pass there are good views.

Many of the connecting trails have not had maintenance or been logged out for several years and access to them should be determined by contacting the Winthrop District Ranger Station. New trail closures or abandonments are always possible.

The trail is access to good fishing lakes and the central part of the Pasayten Wilderness. Side trips are possible to Ferguson, Fred's and Doris Lakes for Cutthroat and Rainbow trout. These trails offer trips with good views, Tatoosh Butte 485, Ft. Defiance 471 and Buckskin Ridge 498.

You have to ford Robinson Creek at about 5.5 miles. There are also at least three bridges to cross in the first 5 miles of the trail.

TATOOSH BUTTES TRAIL 485

Trail Length: 10.6 Miles
Elevation: 4400 - 7100 Feet
Difficulty: Most Difficult
Open: July - September
Usage: Medium
Nearest Town: Winthrop
Nearest Horse Camp: None
Connecting Trails: 478, 477 (Hidden Lakes area)
Facilities at Trailhead: Trailhead for 478 on Road 5400 has stock water, day use area, 5 hitch rails, primitive campsites, Trailhead for 478 on Road 5400 has toilets, loading ramp, hitch rail, stock water, primitive campsites, day use area

DIRECTIONS

TO THE TRAILHEAD

This trail can be reached from the Robinson Creek Trailhead by going on Trail 478. Their junction (and also Trail 471) in the wilderness is located in Section 9, T.39N., R.18E. To reach the trailhead, travel west from Winthrop along the Methow River on Highway 20 for about 14 miles to the Mazama turn-off. Turn right across the river to Mazama then left at Mazama onto Harts Pass Road 1163. Follow 1163 for 7 miles and take Road 5400. One mile past the turn off for Trail 484 there is a sign that reads, "No trailers beyond this point June 1 - December 31."

When you pass over Robinson Creek the trailhead is immediately there. It is located in Section 36, T.37N., R.18E. The signs are clear. The distance is just over 9 miles after you turned onto Road 1163.

Parking: There are four back-in spaces at the trailhead for Trail 478.

Comments: Trail 485 begins in big timber if ridden from the Hidden Lakes area west. If ridden from the junction with Trail 471, which is reached by Trail 478, it climbs from the Pasayten drainage through timber up to open meadows. The Tatoosh Buttes contain extensive wild flower filled meadows and offer the rider broad panoramic views of ridges that can be visited. A short ride will also take you to several fishing lakes.

This area is worth considering because of good graze and lower use than the Hidden Lakes. Some literature shows that the trail junction between access Trail 478 and the Tatoosh Butte Trail 485 is with Trail 470 but Forest Service Maps show it is Trail 471. Contact the Winthrop District Ranger Station for new trail status information.

Map 19

Olympic National Forest
LeBar Horse Camp - Skokomish River

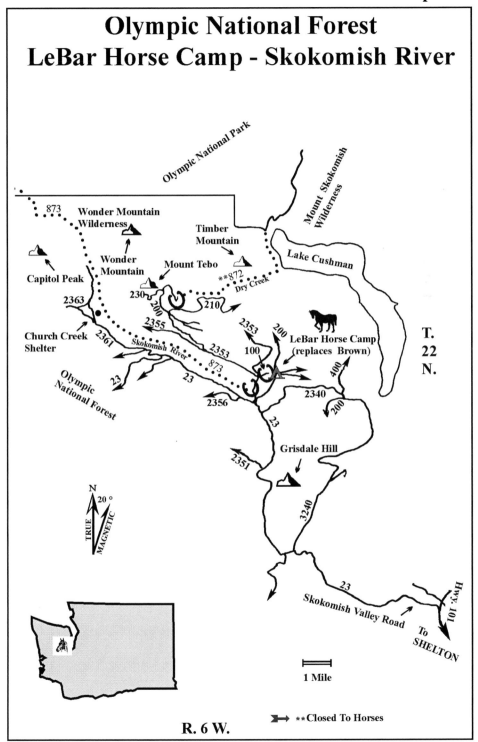

Olympic National Park

Wonder Mountain Wilderness

873

Mount Skokomish Wilderness

Capitol Peak

Wonder Mountain

Wonder Mountain

Mount Tebo

Timber Mountain

Lake Cushman

**872
Dry Creek

2363

230

200

210

2355

2353

200

LeBar Horse Camp (replaces Brown)

T. 22 N.

Church Creek Shelter

2361

Skokomish River

2353

100

873

400

Olympic National Forest

23

23

2356

2340

200

23

Grisdale Hill

2351

3240

N
20°
TRUE
MAGNETIC

23
Skokomish Valley Road

Hwy. 101

To SHELTON

1 Mile

**Closed To Horses

R. 6 W.

LOWER SOUTH FORK SKOKOMISH 873

Trail Length: 13.1 Miles
Elevation: 800 - 1250 Feet
Difficulty: Moderate
Open: May - October
Usage: Medium
Nearest Town: Shelton or Hoodsport
Nearest Horse Camp: LeBar in 1998 (will replace Brown)
Connecting Trails: None
Facilities at Trailhead: Toilets, potable water, horse camp

DIRECTIONS

TO THE TRAILHEAD

This trail is located 22 miles northwest of Shelton in the Skokomish River Recreation Area. Reach this trailhead by taking Highway 101 about 6 miles north of Shelton to the Skokomish Valley Road. This is also 7 miles south of Hoodsport. Turn west onto the Valley Road and travel about 5 miles to Road 23. Follow 23 for 9 miles to the junction with Road 2353. Turn right onto 2353 and drive 1 mile to the trailhead on Spur Road 100 located in Section 4, T.22N., R.5W.

Parking: Available for about 7 vehicles at the trailhead but use the horse camp near the trailhead.

Comments: This trailhead offers day ride and stock pack trip opportunities into areas with wildlife and camping. The trail receives yearly maintenance and is available for use year around throughout the length. The trail goes through ancient forest and follows the South Fork of the Skokomish River. You will find as points of interest, the old LeBar Claim, Church Creek Shelter and Harps Shelter. Expect to see Olympic Elk (Roosevelt) in the river basin if riding quietly. The trail connects to Road 2361 and the Upper South Fork Trailhead.

Map 20

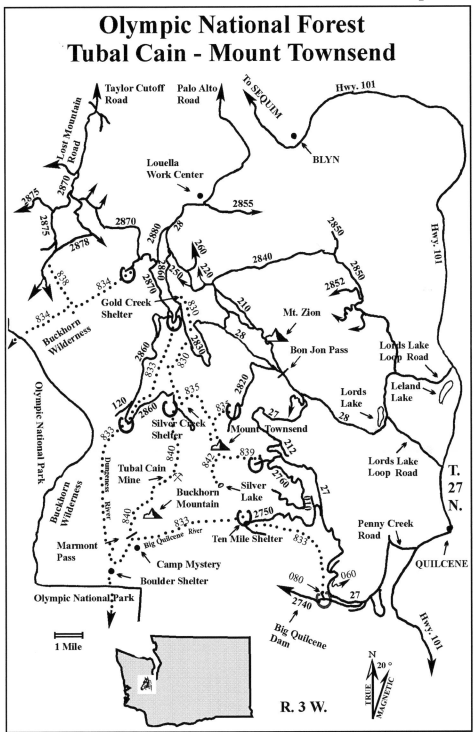

Olympic National Forest
Tubal Cain - Mount Townsend

Taylor Cutoff Road

Palo Alto Road

To SEQUIM

Hwy. 101

Lost Mountain Road

2870

BLYN

2875

2875

Louella Work Center

2855

2870

2878

2880

28

2850

2840

2850

Hwy. 101

2852

260

250

220

2860

834

Gold Creek Shelter

2870

830

210

Mt. Zion

838

834

Buckhorn Wilderness

830

2830

28

Bon Jon Pass

Lords Lake Loop Road

2860

833

830

820

Leland Lake

Olympic National Park

120

835

835

Lords Lake

28

2860

Silver Creek Shelter

835

Mount Townsend

27

Lords Lake Loop Road

833

840

842

839

212

Buckhorn Wilderness

Dungeness River

Tubal Cain Mine

Buckhorn Mountain

Silver Lake

2760

27

T. 27 N.

840

833

2750

Penny Creek Road

Marmont Pass

833

Big Quilcene River

Ten Mile Shelter

833

QUILCENE

Camp Mystery

080

060

Boulder Shelter

Olympic National Park

2740

27

Hwy. 101

1 Mile

Big Quilcene Dam

N
20°
TRUE
MAGNETIC

R. 3 W.

BIG QUILCENE TRAIL - UPPER PORTION OF TRAIL 833

Trail Length: 5.3 Miles
Elevation: 2500 - 6000 Feet
Difficulty: Moderate
Open: June - November
Usage: Medium
Nearest Town: Quilcene
Nearest Horse Camp: None
Connecting Trails: Dungeness segment of 833, 840
Facilities at trailhead: None

DIRECTIONS

TO THE TRAILHEAD

The Big Quilcene trail has two segments. This is the upper access. Where the trail is in the Buckhorn Wilderness, Wilderness Regulations are in effect. To reach the trailhead take Highway 101 south of Quilcene 1 mile to Penny Creek Road. Follow it about 1 mile to Road 27. Continue on 27 for 11 miles to the intersection with Road 2750. Take 2750 for 5 miles to the Big Quilcene Trailhead located in Section 15, T.27N., R.3W. Wet Weather Creek and Ten Mile Shelter are at the parking area.

Parking: Ample parking area.

Comments: You can camp either at Ten Mile Shelter, Shelter Rock Camp in 2.6 miles, or Camp Mystery at 4.6 miles. There are also several areas along the river. Observe stock requirements near water and when possible use existing camp areas. The trail follows the river and then goes into the backcountry through sub-alpine forests, rocky meadows and silver fir and western hemlock stands. This is an area to visit in late spring when rhododendron and wild flowers are in bloom. The views are spectacular in the Marmot Pass area.

The trail intersects with Trail 840 at Camp Mystery and connects with the Dungeness Trail (also 833) at 5.3 miles. A loop ride may be possible with some riding on Road 2860 and by using Trail 840. Water may be scarce in the higher elevations.

DUNGENESS PORTION OF TRAIL 833

Trail Length: 8.1 Miles
Elevation: 2500 - 6000 Feet
Difficulty: Moderate
Open: May - October
Usage: Medium
Nearest Town: Sequim
Nearest Horse Camp: None
Connecting Trails: 840 and Big Quilcene portion of 833
Facilities at Trailhead: Toilet

DIRECTIONS

TO THE TRAILHEAD

The Dungeness portion of Trail 833 starts approximately 21 miles south of Sequim on Road 2860 in Section 36, T.28N., R.4W. To access the trail, take the Palo Alto Road that is 2.0 miles north of Sequim Bay State Park on Highway 101 for about 6 miles to Road 28. Continue on Road 28 for about 1 mile to Road 2860. Follow 2860 for 11 miles to the trailhead.

Parking: There is a large parking lot at the trailhead.

Comments: Trail 833 enters the Buckhorn Wilderness at the 1 mile point and Wilderness Regulations are in effect for the trail. It follows the Dungeness River for about the first 3.5 miles to Camp Hardy. At this point the trail climbs steadily to the intersection with the Home Lake Trail into Olympic National Park. Here, Trail 833 swings back toward the north and the Marmot Pass junction with the Big Quilcene Trail 833 at Camp Mystery.

With a return on Trail 840 a loop ride is nearly possible back to Road 2860. Check your map. This means a ride of 3.5 miles on Road 2860 back to the Dungeness Trailhead. You will pass the hiker-only Trail 832 into the National Park at the 1 mile point.

GRAY WOLF TRAIL 834

Trail Length: 7.7 Miles
Elevation: 1250 - 2000 Feet
Difficulty: Moderate
Open: May to October
Usage: Medium
Nearest Town: Sequim
Nearest Horse Camp: None
Connecting Trails: 838
Facilities at Trailhead: None

DIRECTIONS

TO THE TRAILHEAD

This trail starts 13 miles southwest of Sequim on Road 2870 in Section 33, T.29N., R.3W. Temporary closure of this trail to stock has resulted from 1997 slides. Check with the local Forest Office for current status.

Reach the trailhead by going 2.5 miles west of Sequim on Highway 101. Take the Taylor Cut Off Road south about 3 miles to the junction of the Lost Mountain Road. Watch the signs at this intersection. Proceed to the intersection with Road 2870, it is the left hand fork of this intersection. Follow Road 2870 about 5 miles to the trailhead on the west side of the bridge at the parking area.

Parking: Large area.

Comments: The Forest Service Trail Regulation Information Sheet for this trail shows 100 foot limit from water. Note, this is closer than the 200 feet for most water sources.

The trail is along the Gray Wolf River and offers some fishing access. There is a log stringer hiker bridge at 4.2 miles and Camp Tony is at about 6 miles where it is necessary to ford the river in order to connect with 838, the Slab Camp Trail. You can ride to the Olympic Park Boundary but horses are not permitted in the park on this trail so it is necessary to return by the same route or arrange for someone to pick you up off Road 2875.

This trail is in the Olympic Penninsula rain shadow and the scenery is outstanding. Wilderness Regulations for stock use are in effect.

LOWER BIG QUILCENE SEGMENT OF TRAIL 833

Trail Length: 6.2 Miles
Elevation: 1200 - 2500 Feet
Difficulty: Easy
Open: May - October
Usage: Medium
Nearest Town: Quilcene
Nearest Horse Camp: None
Connecting Trails: Big Quilcene Trail segment of 833
Facilities at Trailhead: Tables, fire pits, toilet, tent sites but no horse
    facilities

DIRECTIONS

TO THE TRAILHEAD

The Lower Big Quilcene Trail 833 starts 7.0 miles south of Quilcene on Road 2700-080 in Section 31, T.27N., R.2W.

The Big Quilcene has two segments and this is the lower access. Take Highway 101 south of Quilcene 1 mile to Penny Creek Road on the right. Follow Penny Creek Road 1 mile to Road 27 (Big Quilcene River Road), turn left and continue about 5 miles to the intersection with Road 2700-080 on the left. The trailhead is at the old Big Quilcene Campground and Road 080 ends there.

Mountain bikes and motorized bikes use this portion of Trail 833.

Parking: There is ample parking.

Comments: Additional areas for camping can be found at the end of this trail. The entire length of the trail is typical northwest forests and fishing opportunities exist along the way.

At about 2.5 miles you pass the Bark Shanty and reach Camp

Jolley at 4.5 miles. The Ten Mile Shelter is at 6 miles on the border of the Buckhorn Wilderness. This is also the start of the Big Quilcene Trail 833.

A loop ride is not possible back to your rig but a pick up could be made at the Big Quilcene Trailhead (Ten Mile Shelter and Road 2750).

LITTLE QUILCENE TRAIL 835

Trail Length: 4.2 Miles
Elevation: 4200 - 3400 Feet
Difficulty: Moderate
Open: April - September
Usage: Medium
Nearest Town: Quilcene
Nearest Horse Camp: None
Connecting Trails: 842
Facilities at Trailhead: None

DIRECTIONS

TO THE TRAILHEAD

This trail starts 14 miles west of Quilcene on Road 2820. To reach the trailhead take the Lords Lake Road that is 2 miles north of Quilcene and turn left onto Road 28. Follow 28 over Bon Jon Pass to the intersection with Road 2820 that goes to the trailhead.

Parking: The parking area is small.

Comments: There are many areas available for camping but water is very scarce on this trail. When the weather allows, this trail offers open spaces, rhododrendron blooming in the spring, views of snow-capped peaks and even the Strait of Juan de Fuca.

Caution: You may meet a mountain bike on the road so use extreme caution on the steep grades that range from 15-20 percent to the Little River Summit. The trail descent to the trailhead on Road 2860 at 4.2 miles is extremely steep, 35-40 percent. The Little River Summit is reached in about 1 mile from the trailhead. At 2 miles you intersect with the Mt. Townsend Trail and at a little over 4 miles reach Road

2860. This is not a loop ride but the trail intersects with the Mt. Townsend Trail and a pick up could be made at the end of the Little Quilcene Trail on Road 2860.

MOUNT TOWNSEND TRAIL 839

Trail Length: 6.7 Miles
Elevation: 2850 - 5250 Feet
Difficulty: Moderate
Open: May to October
Usage: Medium
Nearest Town: Quilcene
Nearest Horse Camp: None
Connecting Trails: 842, 835
Facilities at Trailhead: None

DIRECTIONS

TO THE TRAILHEAD

Trail 839 starts 15 miles west of Quilcene on Road 2760. There are two routes to this trailhead that is located in Section 2, T.28N., R.3W.

(1) One mile south of Quilcene turn right onto Penny Creek Road to Road 27. Continue about 9 miles to Road 2760 and the trailhead. (2) Two miles north of Quilcene on Highway 101 take the Lords Lake Road. At Lords Lake turn left onto Road 28 and continue about 4 miles to the intersection with Road 27. Turn left over Skaar Pass and go about 4 miles to Road 2760. It is 0.8 mile to the parking area.

Parking: This is a small parking area and may be crowded with hikers' vehicles.

Comments: Views from 6200 foot Mount Townsend are some of the best in the Olympics. Wildflower viewing is outstanding mid-June through September. From the trailhead you reach Sink Lake at 0.5 mile, Camp Windy is at 3.5 miles and the Silver Lakes Trailhead and Trail 842 are at 4 miles. The top of Mount Townsend is at the 5 mile point.

From here you descend for a little over 1 mile to the intersection with the Little Quilcene Trail 835 that goes back to Road 2820.

This is not a loop ride so consider a return from the top of Mount Townsend rather than ride down to Trail 835 and back. Water may be scarce in the summer and stock will work on this trail. The grade to the summit is 20 percent while the summit grade is 8 percent. The summit is a long broad area. The trail is in the Buckhorn Wilderness and Wilderness Regulations are in effect.

TUBAL CAIN TRAIL 840

Trail Length: 8.6 Miles
Elevation: 3000 - 6000 Feet
Difficulty: Moderate
Open: May - October
Usage: Medium
Nearest Town: Quilcene
Nearest Horse Camp: None
Connecting Trails: 833 (Dungeness), 833 (Big Quilcene), 839
Facilities at Trailhead: None

DIRECTIONS

TO THE TRAILHEAD

This trail starts 25 miles south of Sequim on Road 2860. To reach the trailhead take the Palo Alto Road 2 miles north of Sequim Bay State Park on Highway 101. Go about 6 miles to Road 28 and continue 1.1 miles on Road 28 to the intersection of Road 2860. Take Road 2860 for 15 miles. You go past the Dungeness 833 Trailhead to reach the Tubal Cain Trailhead located in Section 29, T.28N., R.3W.

Parking: Parking is limited at this trailhead.

Comments: The Silver Creek Shelter is 400 feet from the trailhead. After you leave the shelter there are existing campsites along the trail that should be used rather than start a new one. Always use existing campsites when possible.

The remains of the historic Tubal Cain Mine are at about 3.5 miles and Tull City copper and manganese mines are visible along with views of the Olympic Mountains and Copper Creek Valley. This is not a loop trail but returning on a section of Trail 833 will allow a pick up at a different location if two rigs are used.

The Buckhorn Lake Cutoff is at 5.5 miles and Buckhorn Pass is at 7 miles. The junction with Big Quilcene Trail 833 at Marmot Pass is at about 8.8 miles. Tubal Cain Trail is in Buckhorn Wilderness so Wilderness Regulations apply.

Mount Adams in Giffford Pinchot National Forest
—Photo by authors

Map 21

Olympic National Forest
Mount Muller - Littleton Loop

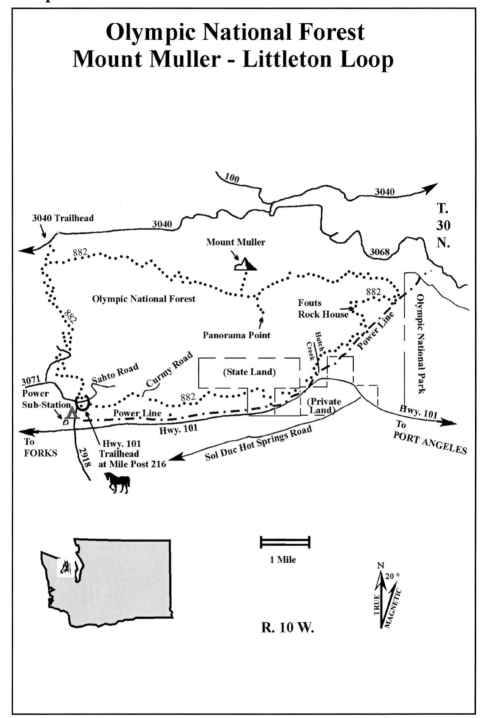

1 Mile

R. 10 W.

MOUNT MULLER - LITTLETON LOOP 882

Trail Length: 12.8 Miles
Elevation: 1000 - 3700 Feet
Difficulty: Easy to Moderate
Open: June - October
Usage: Medium
Nearest Town: Port Angeles
Nearest Horse Camp: None
Connecting Trails: None, this is a loop trail
Facilities at Trailhead: Creek water, toilet

DIRECTIONS

TO THE TRAILHEAD

The trailhead is 31 miles west of Port Angeles on Highway 101. You will pass Lake Crescent. The turn right (north) to the trailhead is at Mile Post 216 onto Road 3071. Drive 0.5 miles to the parking area located in Section 27, T.30N., R.10W. Trail number is 889 on some maps.

Parking: Large and adequate for trailer rigs.

Comments: This ride will test your horse's condition as it climbs 2200 feet in 3 miles from the 1000 foot elevation trailhead. The route is a mixture of spectacular views of Mt. Olympus, Lake Crescent and the Straits of Juan De Fuca. The trail has timber on the north and more open areas of meadows and rocky slopes on the south. The east end drops through a mixture of vine maple and large boulders but finishes in a valley of mossy overhangs and ferns.

This area is rich in history events including three major fires in the century, mining, a fire lookout on Mount Muller and Civilian Conservation Corps (CCC) construction work. A panorama viewpoint is near the side trail climb to Mount Muller, site of the 1917 fire lookout. It is about 7.5 miles to Mount Muller. Stock water is available at the trailhead and at the 10 mile point (Hutch Creek).

Caution: There have been cougar sightings on this loop. Check with the Soleduck Ranger District. If a cougar is seen, Forest Service literature recommends do not run, stand still, stay on the uphill trail side to appear larger, and gather small children in close.

Map 22

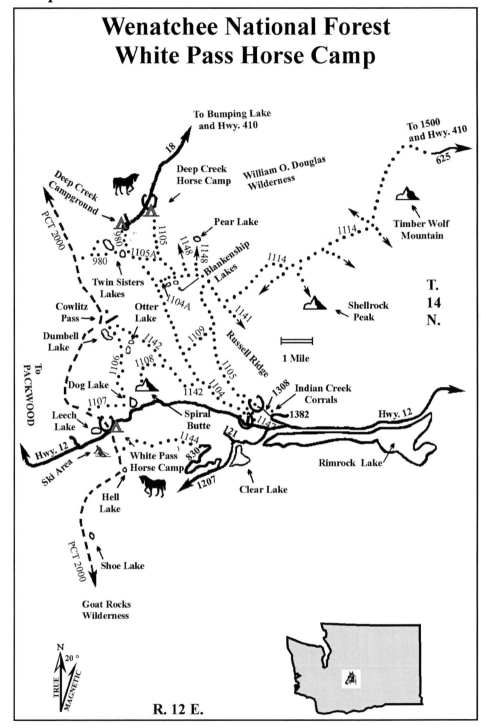

Wenatchee National Forest
White Pass Horse Camp

To Bumping Lake
and Hwy. 410

To 1500
and Hwy. 410

625

18

Deep Creek
Horse Camp

William O. Douglas
Wilderness

Deep Creek
Campground

Timber Wolf
Mountain

1114

PCT 2000

Pear Lake

1105

980

1105A

1148

1148

Blankenship
Lakes

1114

Shellrock
Peak

T.
14
N.

980

Twin Sisters
Lakes

1104A

Cowlitz
Pass

Otter
Lake

1141

1142

1109

Russell Ridge

1 Mile

Dumbell
Lake

1106

1108

1105

To
PACKWOOD

Dog Lake

1107

1142

1104

1142

1308

Indian Creek
Corrals

Hwy. 12

Leech
Lake

Spiral
Butte

1147

1382

Hwy. 12

Ski Area

1144

830

121

Rimrock Lake

White Pass
Horse Camp

1207

Clear Lake

Hell
Lake

PCT 2000

Shoe Lake

Goat Rocks
Wilderness

N
20°

TRUE

MAGNETIC

R. 12 E.

CRAMER LAKE TRAIL 1106

Trail Length: 5.4 Miles
Elevation: 4200 - 5040 Feet
Difficulty: Moderate
Open: June - October
Usage: Heavy
Nearest Town: Naches or Packwood
Nearest Horse Camp: White Pass
Connecting Trails: 1107, 2000
Facilities at Trailhead: None, horse camp has spring water, loading ramp, 8 hitch rails, 2 toilets, 6 dispersed campsites with 18 horse capacity

DIRECTIONS

TO THE TRAILHEAD

Take Highway 12 west from Naches (about 55 miles) to White Pass or go east from Packwood (about 18 miles) to White Pass. The trailhead is east of the pass about 2 miles at Dog Lake near the White Pass Horse Camp in Section 36, T.14N., R.11E.

Parking: None, use the nearby horse camp trailhead which has parking for trailer rigs.

Comments: This trail is heavily used by trail riders but does make a good loop ride. Remember no horses are allowed in the Dog Lake Campground so enter at the horse camp and ride the 1.7 miles on Trail 1107 to reach this trail. Horse feed is available early in the season and the trail is usually snow free by the first of July. Mosquitoes can be a problem here anytime for rider and horse. The horse camp is at Leech Lake.

INDIAN CREEK TRAIL 1105

Trail Length: 8.0 Miles
Elevation: 3400 - 5200 Feet
Difficulty: Easy
Open: June - October
Usage: Heavy
Nearest Town: Packwood
Nearest Horse Camp: White Pass
Connecting Trails: 1109, 1114, 1147, 1148, 1105A, 1104A, (1 mile trail that connects 1105 and 1104)
Facilities at Trailhead: Loading ramp, hitch rails, toilet at Highway 12 location

DIRECTIONS

TO THE TRAILHEAD

Take Highway 12 east from Packwood over White Pass about 8 miles. Rimrock Lake is south on your right. From Highway 12 take Road 1308 north about 2.5 miles to the Indian Creek Trailhead in Section 36, T.14N., R.12E.

Parking: There is space for 6 rigs at the trailhead and the 4 dispersed camping units.

Comments: This trail can be wet and marshy both early and late in the year but it does offer many loop ride opportunities. There is a spring for water south of the trailhead. This is a popular horse camping spot. The start of the trail follows an abandoned mining road but the ride out from Indian Creek Bridge is steep with switchbacks. When you reach the plateau there are acres of meadows and numerous lakes, all with mosquitoes.

See the Wenatchee National Forest; Norse Peak Wilderness - Bumping Lake Trail Map and Trail Guides for additional trailhead information from Highway 410 and Bumping Lake.

The Road from White Pass Highway to the Indian Creek Bridge is usually snow free by mid-June and the full length of the trail snow free by mid-July. However, as with many trails there usually will be blown down timber in the spring. Step off your horse and cut or move a log or two since horse riding is the primary use of this trail. It is a place to avoid during the wet spring conditions.

PEAR LOOP 1148

Trail Length: 3.4 Miles
Elevation: 4460 - 4960 Feet
Difficulty: Easy
Open: June - October
Usage: Heavy
Nearest Town: Packwood
Nearest Horse Camp: White Pass or Deep Creek
Connecting Trails: 1105, 1114, 979
Facilities at Trailhead: Loading ramp, hitch rails, toilet at Highway
12 location

DIRECTIONS

TO THE TRAILHEAD

Take Highway 12 east from Packwood to White Pass. Rimrock Lake is to the right or south. Trail 1148 access from Highway 12 is by the Indian Creek Trailhead that is over the pass about 8 miles. Take Road 1308 north about 2.5 miles off Highway 12. Ride Trail 1105 north about 5 miles to the junction with Trail 1148 located in Section 10, T.14N., R.12E. This is east of the Blankenship Lakes. See the Deep Creek Horse Camp on the Wenatchee National Forest; Norse Peak Wilderness-Bumping Lake Trail Map and the Trail Guides that follow the map for additional trailhead information.

Parking: There are 6 parking spaces and 4 dispersed campsites at the trailhead.

Comments: This well defined loop trail to Pear Lake leaves and returns to 1105. However, you need to watch for user made trails along the meadows before Pear Lake. They tend to lead you in the wrong direction to reach Pear Lake. Unique to the William O. Douglas Wilderness, Pear Lake is 128 feet deep and emerald green. Take a towel for a refreshing swim in Pear Lake but be prepared for mosquitoes.

SAND RIDGE TRAIL 1104

Trail Length: 8.5 Miles
Elevation: 3360 - 5500 Feet
Difficulty: Easy
Open: June - October
Usage: Medium
Nearest Town: Packwood
Nearest Horse Camp: White Pass
Connecting Trails: 1142, 1109, 1105-A, 980, 1104-A (1 mile trail that connects 1105 and 1104)
Facilities at Trailhead: Toilet

DIRECTIONS

TO THE TRAILHEAD

Take Highway 12 east from Packwood to White Pass. The Sand Ridge Trailhead on Highway 12 is over the Pass about 6 miles and before Indian Creek Campground in Section 1, T.13N., R.12E.

Parking: There are 8 parking spaces at the trailhead and 2 dispersed campsites.

Comments: Water is not available at the trailhead. This is a well defined trail that follows an old abandoned mining road. Expect bogs at the 4 and 6 mile points that remain boggy into late August. The beginning ride is steep but levels off out along the ridgetop and most of the trail is in forested areas. There are side trips to lakes and horse use is heavy in the summer and hunting seasons because of meadows and lakes. There is also access to the Pacific Crest National Scenic Trail 2000 by Trail 980 near Twin Sisters Lakes.

PACIFIC CREST NATIONAL SCENIC TRAIL (PCT) 2000

Trail Length: 11.3 Miles
Elevation: 4400 - 7930 Feet
Difficulty: Moderate
Open: June - October
Usage: Heavy
Nearest Town: Packwood
Nearest Horse Camp: White Pass South
Connecting Trails: 1144, 1117 and 1118
Facilities at Trailhead: White Pass Trailhead South, horse ramp,
    toilet, camp space for 4 rigs

DIRECTIONS

TO THE TRAILHEAD

Take Highway 12 east from Packwood about 18 miles to the White Pass Horse Camp located in Section 2, T.13N., R.11E. This segment of Trail 2000 is in the Goat Rocks Wilderness, south from Highway 12 and goes past the junction with Trail 1118 at Tieton Pass.

Parking: There are 6 parking spaces at this White Pass South Trailhead with 4 dispersed camping areas.

Comments: This 11 miles of Trail 2000 is from White Pass to Old Snowy Mountain, in Section 21, T.12N., R.11E., and can usually be found to be snow free by the end of July. At mile point 1 the trail enters the Goat Rocks Wilderness where there is no overnight camping at Shoe Lake. There is some camping, but without horse feed, down Trail 1117 about 0.2 mile. Pelletized feed is needed here on overnight trips. Trail 1117 is about 0.8 mile past Shoe Lake. Wilderness Regulations and permit requirements apply on this segment of Trail 2000 where hiking is the primary use.

PACIFIC CREST NATIONAL SCENIC TRAIL (PCT) 2000

Trail Length: 25.2 Miles
Elevation: 4800 - 6600 Feet
Difficulty: Moderate
Open: June - October
Usage: Medium
Nearest Town: Packwood
Nearest Horse Camp: White Pass
Connecting Trails: 958, 971, 980, 956, 953 all north of White Pass on Highway 12
Facilities at Trailhead: Loading ramp, hitch rails, toilets, 6 dispersed campsites with a capacity of 18 horses

DIRECTIONS

TO THE TRAILHEAD

Take Highway 12 east from Packwood about 18 miles over White Pass to Leech Lake and the horse camp. You can access Trail 2000 from Leech Lake (horse camp) located in Section 2, T.13N., R.11E. You can also reach the north end of this segment of the Trail 2000 (PCT) by going from Pomeroy east on Highway 410 to Chinook Pass or by taking Highway 410 from Naches to Chinook Pass where Trail 2000 crosses the highway.

Parking: Horse camp has space for horse trailer rigs.

Comments: This segment of Trail 2000 goes north from White Pass to Dewey Lake. Another 2.6 mile section of Trail 2000 continues on from Dewey Lake north to Highway 410 at Chinook Pass. Although hikers are the primary users of the trail it is open to horses. Expect to find snow on the trail up to the end of July.

Map 23

Wenatchee National Forest
Norse Peak Wilderness - Bumping Lake

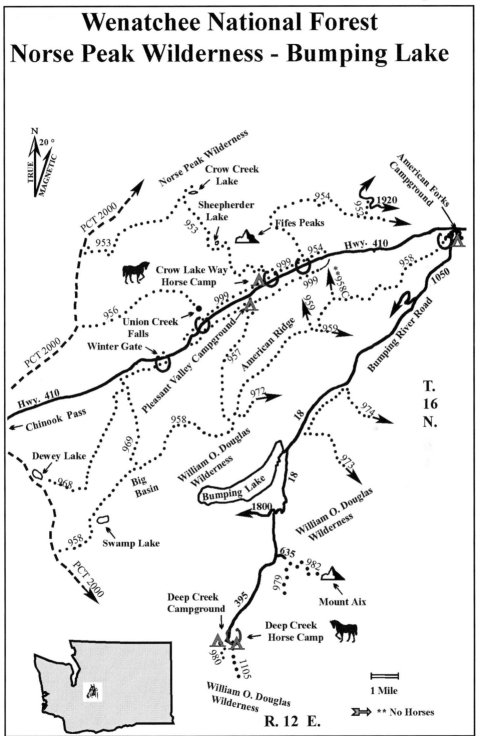

AMERICAN RIDGE TRAIL 958

Trail Length: 26.7 Miles
Elevation: 2800 - 6700 Feet
Difficulty: Difficult to Most Difficult near Trail 969
Open: May - October
Usage: Light
Nearest Town: Yakima
Nearest Horse Camp: Crow Lake Way
Connecting Trails: 2000, 957, 970, 972, 969 (closed by 1996 flood, check at the Naches Ranger Station for trail status)
Facilities at Trailhead: None

DIRECTIONS

TO THE TRAILHEAD

Take Highway 410 northwest from Yakima to Naches past the junction with Highway 12. Continue to follow 410 when it turns west at the junction with the 19 Road (1900). It is about 3.5 miles to the

William O. Douglas Wilderness Meadow

—Photo by authors

American Forks Campground. Take Road 2000 (Bumping Lake Road). The trailhead is about 0.8 mile off Highway 410 in Section 12, T.17N., R.13E.

Parking: Limited at this trailhead, but 2-3 trailer rigs can park. There is a gravel area at the bulletin board. However, some choose to park at either Goat Creek or Goose Prairie Trailheads even though there are no horse facilities there.

Comments: This trail, south of Highway 410 is used very little yet it offers some of the more spectacular views on the Naches District. Goat Peak is the spot for solitude. The trail does lack water except for a few isolated springs that may be difficult to locate. Horse feed is limited until you get to the Big Basin and Trail 957 junction. Beyond the junction with Trail 970, water and horse feed are available. Trail 958C is closed to horses.

CROW LAKE WAY TRAIL 953

Trail Length: 12.7 Miles
Elevation: 3400 - 6400 Feet
Difficulty: Most Difficult
Open: June - October
Usage: Heavy
Nearest Town: Yakima
Nearest Horse Camp: Crow Lake Way
Connecting Trails: 2000, 951, 999
Facilities at Trailhead: Toilets, hitch rails, loading ramp, water available through August at Miners Creek, 6 dispersed campsites

DIRECTIONS

TO THE TRAILHEAD

Take Highway 410 northeast from Yakima to Naches and past the junction with Highway 12. Continue to follow 410 when it turns west at the junction with the 19 (1900) Road. It is about 10 miles from that junction to the trailhead located in Section 14, T.17N., R.12E. If you reach the Pleasant Valley Campground you have gone too far.

Crow Lake Way
Trail 953 into
the Norse Peak
Wilderness; Fifes
Peak
—*Photo by authors*

Parking: Space for 12 units at this trailhead. A road 150 feet east of the Crow Lake Way entrance provides access to a good overflow camp area across the creek. This will accommodate 2-3 additional rigs.

Comments: This trail climbs quickly and goes north from Highway 410 and provides access to Trail 2000. It has a variety of terrain that includes steep side slopes. The high alpine meadows on Grassy Saddle have wildflowers and wildlife.

Horse riders and hikers are the primary users of this trail and there is adequate camping along the trail at the ridgetop and water is plentiful after Grassy Saddle. There is horse feed at the ridge past the 3 mile point, at the 6 mile point and at several large meadows before reaching Trail 2000 (PCT). There are camp spots in the timber when you reach the larger meadows. The views of Fifes Ridge and Mt. Rainier are excellent. These trails are usually snow free by the end of July. You enter the Norse Peak Wilderness within 0.2 mile. This trailhead is also a viewpoint for Fife Peaks.

DEWEY LAKE TRAIL 968

Trail Length: 6.9 Miles
Elevation: 3600 - 5200 Feet
Difficulty: Moderate
Open: June - October
Usage: Heavy
Nearest Town: Yakima
Nearest Horse Camp: Crow Lake Way
Connecting Trails: 969, 2000 from Chinook Pass Summit
Facilities at Trailhead: Toilets, loading ramp

DIRECTIONS

TO THE TRAILHEAD

Trail 968 is reached from the trailhead for Trail 969. Take Highway 410 northwest from Yakima to Naches past the junction with Highway 12. Continue to follow Highway 410 when it turns west at the junction with the 19 Road (1900). It is about 16 miles to the Mesatchee Creek Trailhead for Trail 969 located in Section 34, T.17N., R.11E.

Parking: There are 15 parking spaces. See the Mesatchee Creek 969 Trail Guide.

Comments: Use Trail 969 as the trail access at Mesatchee Creek. Ride Trail 969 south about 1 mile to access Trail 968 to Dewey Lake in the William O. Douglas Wilderness. At Dewey Lake there is a campfire closure within a quarter of a mile of the lake, also avoid the sites that are under repair from overuse. There are camping restrictions within 100 feet of the lake edge.

From the junction with Trail 969, Trail 968 is flat for about 4 miles through old river beds. It then goes through an old forest fire area and some old growth timber. The Mesatchee Creek crossing at 4 miles can be dangerous for horses so use the upstream crossing. After crossing the river there is a 3 mile climb to the lake with the last 0.5 mile steep, expect this area to have snow late into July. Horse riding and hiking are the primary uses of this trail. You will find horse feed 0.5 mile below Dewey Lake.

FIFES RIDGE TRAIL 954

Trail Length: 8.8 Miles
Elevation: 3600 - 6300 Feet
Difficulty: Moderate
Open: June - October
Usage: Medium
Nearest Town: Yakima
Nearest Horse Camp: Crow Lake Way
Connecting Trails: 952, 999
Facilities at Trailhead: None

DIRECTIONS

TO THE TRAILHEAD

Take Highway 410 northwest from Yakima to Naches and past the junction with Highway 12. Continue to follow 410 when it turns west at the junction with the 19 Road (1900). It is about 9 miles to the trailhead in Section 13, T.17N., R.12E. There is a sign for the trail along the north side of the road. A bumpy road down to the trailhead crosses Trail 999 on the way in and you will see the bulletin board for the trail.

Parking: Park near the bulletin board. The narrow bumpy road is passable in spite of the brush. It leads to a small dispersed camping area with parking for 2 rigs.

Comments: There is stock water to the east of the trailhead during most of the summer. This trail follows Wash Creek into the Norse Peak Wilderness with a gentle grade to begin with and changes to a steady climb up to the ridge. The views are good on top of the ridge and this trail is usually snow free by mid-June. There is water but very little horse feed and camping sites are limited. Connecting Trail 952 outside the wilderness also has good views but is used by motorbike riders. Trail 999 along the Highway connects this trailhead to the Crow Lake Way Trailhead.

KETTLE CREEK TRAIL 957

Trail Length: 6.2 Miles
Elevation: 3600 - 5600 Feet
Difficulty: Most Difficult
Open: June - October
Usage: Medium
Nearest Town: Yakima
Nearest Horse Camp: Crow Lake Way
Connecting Trails: 958, 999
Facilities at Trailhead: None, toilets at Pleasant Valley Campground
(horses not permitted, hiker access only)

DIRECTIONS

TO THE TRAILHEAD

Take Highway 410 northwest from Yakima to Naches and past the junction with Highway 12. Continue to follow 410 when it turns west at the junction with the 19 Road. It is about 11 miles from that junction to the trail which leaves from the Pleasant Valley Campground. Hikers only access the trail from the campground. Access to this trail is by Trail 999, a horse use trailhead is at Crow Lake Way Trail 953.

Parking: There are only 6 small spaces so horse rigs should park at the Trail 953 Trailhead and ride Trail 999 to reach Trail 957. Use the river ford 0.3 mile west of the Pleasant Valley Campground. New signs may now be in place.

Comments: This trail leaves the campground south and climbs into the William O. Douglas Wilderness and meets the American Ridge Trail 958 in Section 16, T.16N., R.12E. There are several camping sites along the way with plenty of water. Kettle Lake is only a small pond and not a destination type lake. The ride is a steady climb up to a flat about half way to the ridge. Horse riders are the primary users of this trail but the trail is not recommended for horses early in the season when wet. It is usually not snow free to the ridge until after mid-July.

MESATCHEE CREEK TRAIL 969

Trail Length: 5.3 Miles
Elevation: 3600 - 5800 Feet
Difficulty: Moderate
Open: June - October
Usage: Medium
Nearest Town: Yakima
Nearest Horse Camp: Crow Lake Way
Connecting Trails: 958, 968
Facilities at Trailhead: Toilets, loading ramp, dispersed campsites, stock water at creek

DIRECTIONS

TO THE TRAILHEAD

Take Highway 410 northwest from Yakima to Naches past the junction with Highway 12. Continue to follow 410 when it turns west at the junction with the 19 Road (1900). It is about 16 miles from that junction to the Mesatchee Creek Trailhead for Trail 969 located in Section 34, T.17N., R.11E.

The trailhead sign is at highway mile post 74. Avoid the road 0.5 mile west of the trailhead entrance that appears to be a place to park closer to the trailhead. It is not adequate for trucks with trailers.

Parking: There are 15 parking spaces and a circle drive with pull-through spaces suitable for 4-horse rigs at the trailhead.

Comments: This trail is south of Highway 410 and goes into the William O. Douglas Wilderness and offers a place for solitude. The views of high open basin country and waterfalls and the ridgetop access make this a trail worth riding. The White Pine stand on the flat plateau is also worth seeing. Camp off the trail and away from the streams. Horse riding and hiking are the primary uses of this trail. A log bridge crosses Morse Creek.

PLEASANT VALLEY LOOP TRAIL 999

Trail Length: 16.5 Miles
Elevation: 3300 - 3400 Feet
Difficulty: Difficult
Open: June - October
Usage: Medium
Nearest Town: Naches
Nearest Horse Camp: Crow Lake Way
Connecting Trails: 957 (south of Highway 410), 953, 954 (north of Highway 410)
Facilities at Trailhead: None, toilets at Hells Crossing Campground

DIRECTIONS

TO THE TRAILHEAD

Take Highway 410 northwest from Yakima to Naches past the junction with Highway 12. Follow 410 when it turns west at the junction with the 19 Road (1900). It is about 8 miles to the Hells Crossing Campground which is the trailhead for this trail.

Parking: None at this trailhead for horse rigs. Trail riders should park at either the Union Creek (Trail 956) or Crow Lake Way Trailhead. The Goat Peak Trail 958C from the campground to American Ridge is closed to horses.

Comments: Access for horses to Trail 999 is from either of the horse access trailheads, (Trail 957 or Trail 953). The trailhead for 999 is at the Hells Crossing Campground located in Section 18, T.17N., R.13E. It serves to tie Trails 953, 954 and 957 trailheads together because there is inadequate parking for horse rigs at Trail 954.

Horse riding and hiking are the primary uses of this trail loop built by a hiking club. It provides access to the William O. Douglas Wilderness and the American Ridge area south of Highway 410 and to the Norse Peak Wilderness to the north. The trail is on both sides of the highway. Mountain bikes are permitted on the trail north of the highway. The area is usually snow free by late June.

UNION CREEK TRAIL 956

Trail Length: 7.1 Miles
Elevation: 3500 - 6000 Feet
Difficulty: Moderate
Open: June - October
Usage: Heavy
Nearest Town: Yakima
Nearest Horse Camp: Crow Lake Way
Connecting Trails: 2000, 987
Facilities at Trailhead: Dispersed campsites, no horse facilities or toilets

DIRECTIONS

TO THE TRAILHEAD

Take Highway 410 northeast from Yakima to Naches and past the junction with Highway 12. Continue to follow Highway 410 when it turns west at the junction with the 19 (1900) Road. It is about 13 miles further to the trailhead at Union Falls Creek where there is a paved entrance. This trail is north of Highway 410 and the trailhead is located in Section 25, T.17N., R 11E.

Parking: Space for 6 rigs at the trailhead, 2 are paved and suitable for 4-horse trailers. The overflow parking to this trailhead is a gravel area adjacent to the highway as you enter the area. It is east of the entrance and will hold 2 rigs. This trailhead is a bit awkward to get in and out of but 4-horse rigs use the parking.

Comments: Union Creek Trail provides access to the Pacific Crest National Scenic Trail 2000. It can be used in early season to provide access to Union Creek Falls which are just a quarter of a mile up the trail. From the falls the trail climbs for about a mile then levels off. It remains in heavy timber to Union Creek Basin. Some sections have steep side slopes and require caution when crossing. The Norse Peak Wilderness starts at 0.3 mile up the trail.

There is water along the trail to this point but carry drinking water when you continue up the ridge and on to Cement Basin or Lake Basin. Beyond the falls the trail is usually snow free by mid-July.

Trail riders need to be aware of rolling rocks at the gorge crossing at the 6.5 mile point. Horse riding and hiking are the primary uses of the trail. There is some horse feed at top of the ridge past the 3 mile point.

Above: Crystal Mountain Ski Area below PCT in Norse Peak
    Wilderness.
Below: White Pass Ski Area from Trail 1104 in William O.
    Douglas Wilderness.   —*Photos by authors*

Map 24

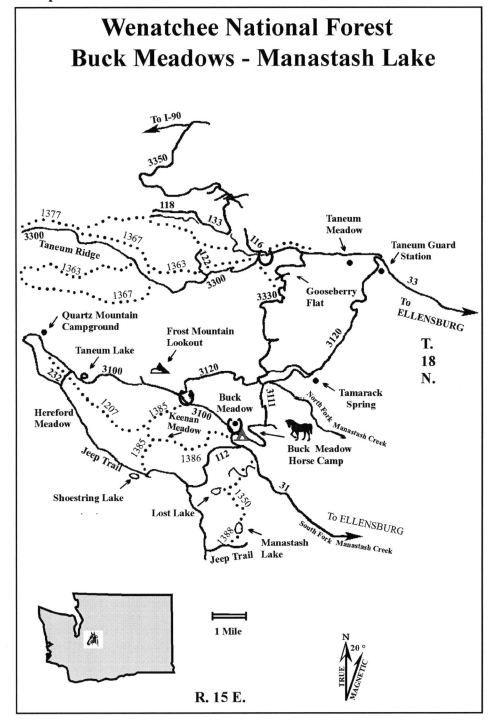

Wenatchee National Forest
Buck Meadows - Manastash Lake

To I-90

3350

1377

3300

Taneum Ridge

1367

1363

1367

118

133

116

122

1363

3300

3330

Taneum Meadow

Taneum Guard Station

33

Gooseberry Flat

To ELLENSBURG

Quartz Mountain Campground

Frost Mountain Lookout

Taneum Lake

232

3100

3120

3120

Buck Meadow

3111

Tamarack Spring

North Fork Manastash Creek

T. 18 N.

Hereford Meadow

1207

1385

3100

Keenan Meadow

1385

1386

112

Jeep Trail

Shoestring Lake

Lost Lake

1350

1388

Jeep Trail

Manastash Lake

31

Buck Meadow Horse Camp

To ELLENSBURG

South Fork Manastash Creek

1 Mile

N 20°

TRUE

MAGNETIC

R. 15 E.

HEREFORD MEADOW TRAIL 1207

Trail Length: 3.8 Miles
Elevation: 5100 - 5700 Feet
Difficulty: Moderate
Open: June - October
Usage: Heavy
Nearest Town: Cle Elum
Nearest Horse Camp: Buck Meadows
Connecting Trails: 1385
Facilities at Trailhead: None

DIRECTIONS

TO THE TRAILHEAD

From Ellensburg take Road 31 west (south side of I-90) about 22 miles to Buck Meadows and the junction of Roads 31 and 3111.

Follow 3100 for about 6 miles to Road 232 and Hereford Meadows. The Trail 1207 crosses Road 232 about 0.3 mile down the road in Section 11, T.18N., R.14E.

The trail can also be reached by Trail 1385 from Road 3100 less than two miles past the Buck Meadows junction of Roads 31, 3100 and 3111.

Parking: Roadside or at the Buck Meadows area.

Comments: This is a scenic trail to ride through meadows and along the South Fork of Manastash Creek but the trail is heavily used by motor bikes and All Terrain Vehicles (ATV).

KEENAN MEADOW TRAIL 1386

Trail Length: 3.1 Miles
Elevation: 4300 - 5100 Feet
Difficulty: Moderate
Open: June - October

Usage: Heavy
Nearest Town: Ellensburg or Cle Elum
Nearest Horse Camp: Buck Meadows
Connecting Trails: 1385, 1207
Facilities at Trailhead: Toilet, parking

DIRECTIONS

TO THE TRAILHEAD

There are two routes to consider in going to this trailhead at the Buck Meadows Camp: (1) From Ellensburg, take Road 31 west (south side of I-90) approximately 22 miles along Manastash Creek. The trailhead is on left; or (2) From the Taneum Guard Station, take Road 33 (3300) approximately 0.3 mile north to the junction with Road 3120. Follow 3120 south approximately 6 miles to Tamarack Springs and the junction of Roads 3120 and 3111. Follow 3111 approximately 7 miles to the junction with Road 31. Trail 1386 is across from the road junction. This is the Buck Meadows area.

Parking: Adequate parking at the horse camp and adjacent area.

Comments: Trail 1386 is expected to originate from the new campground planned to replace the old horse camp by the same name. Some portions of these trails are scheduled to be open to all users including motorized. The current Buck Meadows Horse Camp is to be available for several more years while a new camp area is built across the road. The new camp will accommodate many more people and better protect the wet areas in the vicinity. There will be a camp host in residence part of the season. As of 1997 the new area was waiting funding and the old horse camp was being used.

Trail 1386 is used in conjunction with the Shoestring Lake Trail 1385 that is about 1.7 miles to the right or north. The Keenan Meadow Trail 1386 trail passes through timber and the large Keenan Meadow area.

MANASTASH LAKE TRAIL 1350

Trail Length: 4.4 Miles
Elevation: 4100 - 5500 Feet
Difficulty: Moderate
Open: June - October
Usage: Heavy
Nearest Town: Ellensburg
Nearest Horse Camp: Buck Meadows
Connecting Trails: 1388
Facilities at Trailhead: None

DIRECTIONS

TO THE TRAILHEAD

From Ellensburg take Road 31 approximately 20 miles west along Manastash Creek. The trailhead is on your left in Section 23, T.18N., R.15E. This is about 1 mile before the junction of Roads 31, 3100 and 3111 and just past Spur Road 114.

Parking: Roadside parking spaces are available at the trailhead.

Comments: There is a large meadow about 0.2 mile west of the trailhead and a sign that reads: "Manastash Lake 4 mi. and Lost Lake 2 mi." This meadow is used as a dispersed campsite and staging area by trailriders. Parking here is an option although there is evidence of a muddy spot as you leave the main road. Remember to clean up your dispersed campsite and not clean out the trailer.

This trail, heavily used by motorbike and All Terrain Vehicles (ATV) riders, provides access to the extensive Manastash Ridge trail system that is a scenic ridgetop trail. It also gives access to the Quartz Mountain area, the Pacific Crest National Scenic Trail 2000 some 20 miles northwest of Manastash Lake as well as the Hereford Meadow Trail 1207 along South Fork Manastash Creek.

SHOESTRING LAKE TRAIL 1385

Trail Length: 3.6 Miles
Elevation: 4480 - 5600 Feet
Difficulty: Moderate
Open: June - October
Usage: Extra Heavy
Nearest Town: Ellensburg or Cle Elum
Nearest Horse Camp: Buck Meadows
Connecting Trails: 1207, 1386
Facilities at Trailhead: None

DIRECTIONS

TO THE TRAILHEAD

From Ellensburg, take Road 31 west (south side of I-90) approximately 24 miles to Buck Meadows Camp and the junction of Roads 31 and 3111. Trail 1385 is less than 2 miles further as you continue northwest on Road 3100. The trail crossing is on the left (south) in Section 16, T.18N. R.15E.

Parking: Roadside at the trailhead or in a new small parking lot that is large enough for 2-3 trailer rigs.

Comments: This is the trail to Shoestring Lake. It passes through timber on the way to the lake. An old road, crossed just before the lake, is used by four-wheel ATV riders. Four-wheel vehicle use is permitted from near the lake to the Manastash Ridge Trail.

TANEUM RIDGE TRAIL 1363

Trail Length: 11.8 Miles
Elevation: 2800 - 6000 Feet
Difficulty: Easy
Open: June - October
Usage: Extra Heavy

Nearest Town: Cle Elum or Ellensburg
Nearest Horse Camp: Buck Meadows
Connecting Trails: 1377, 1361, 1367
Facilities at Trailhead: Toilet

DIRECTIONS

TO THE TRAILHEAD

From Ellensburg take Cemetery Road to Road 33. These roads are along the south side of I-90 and you are travelling northwest. Continue about 15 miles from I-90 to the Taneum Guard Station and go past it about 4 miles on Road 33. When you reach the junction of Roads 33 and 3300 the trailhead is at that location on Road 3300. It is in Section 26, T.19N., R.15E.

Parking: There is parking at the trailhead but turning space is somewhat limited.

Comments: This trail has been rebuilt in recent years and the ride offers ridgetop views of surrounding country. There are connecting trails to many other areas of the Manastash Ridge country from this trail system.

Old trail shelter on the Pacific Crest Trail
—*Photo by authors*

Map 25

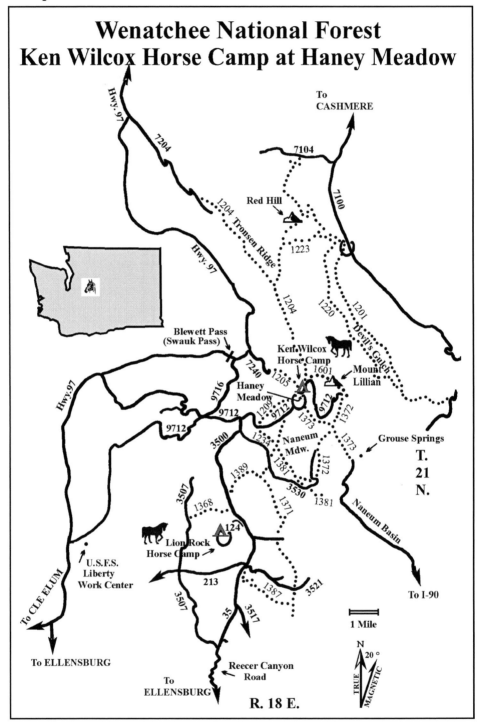

Wenatchee National Forest
Ken Wilcox Horse Camp at Haney Meadow

Hwy. 97

7204

To
CASHMERE

7104

7100

1204

Red Hill

Trousen Ridge

1223

Hwy. 97

1204

1220

1201

Devil's Gulch

Blewett Pass
(Swauk Pass)

Ken Wilcox
Horse Camp

Mount
Lillian

7240

1205

1601

9716

Haney
Meadow

Hwy. 97

9712

1209

9712

1373

1372

9712

3500

1234

Naneum
Mdw.

1373

Grouse Springs

T.
21
N.

1389

1381

1372

3530

1381

3507

1368

1371

Naneum Basin

124

Lion Rock
Horse Camp

U.S.F.S.
Liberty
Work Center

213

1387

3521

To I-90

3507

35

3517

1 Mile

To CLE ELUM

To ELLENSBURG

Reecer Canyon
Road

To
ELLENSBURG

N

20°

TRUE

MAGNETIC

R. 18 E.

DEVILS GULCH TRAIL 1220

Trail Length: 12.3 Miles
Elevation: 2400 - 4400 Feet
Difficulty: Moderate
Open: June - October
Usage: Heavy
Nearest Town: Cashmere
Nearest Horse Camp: Ken Wilcox at Haney Meadow
Connecting Trails: 1223, 1201
Facilities at Trailhead: Loading ramp, toilet, hitch rail, creek water

DIRECTIONS

TO THE TRAILHEAD

From Cashmere take Road 7100 south about 9 miles along Mission Creek to the trail access located in Section 18, T.22N., R.18E. The south end of this trail can also be reached by continuing on Road 7100 south to the Beehive Reservoir and then turning right (northwest) about 2 miles on Road 9712. This route should be checked out at the Leavenworth District Ranger Station.

Parking: Parking at the trailhead is adequate for trailer rigs. There are also areas that may be used to turn around.

Comments: Devils Gulch Trail has a good grade but there are potentially hazardous water crossings at the 4.5, 6.5 and 7 mile points. Horse feed is limited on trail. Motorbikes are the primary users of some of this trail.

MISSION RIDGE TRAIL 1201

Trail Length: 8.0 Miles
Elevation: 2400 - 4800 Feet
Difficulty: Most Difficult
Open: June - October
Usage: Medium
Nearest Town: Cashmere

Nearest Horse Camp: Ken Wilcox at Haney Meadow
Connecting Trails: 1220, 1223
Facilities at Trailhead: Loading ramp, hitch rail, toilets, creek water
for stock

DIRECTIONS

TO THE TRAILHEAD

From Cashmere take Road 7100 south along Mission Creek about
9 miles to the trailhead access. You pass the junction with Road 7104
about 2.5 miles before the trailhead that is located in Section 18,
T.22N., R.19E.

Parking: There are 20 spaces and 2 spaces on the roadside. The
area is an old logging landing.

Comments: This trail is steep in places. You will not find water on
this ridgetop trail but there is some horse feed available. Motor bikes
are the primary trail users. A loop ride is possible from the trailhead
using the Mission Ridge Trail 1201 to the junction with 1220 and
returning on Devils Gulch Trail 1220 if the trails are open. Check with
the local Forest Office for a current trail status.

NANEUM WILSON TRAIL 1371

Trail Length: 5.6 Miles
Elevation: 5460 - 6000 Feet
Difficulty: Most Difficult
Open: June - October
Usage: Medium
Nearest Town: Cle Elum
Nearest Horse Camp: Ken Wilcox at Haney Meadow
Connecting Trails: 1389, 1387
Facilities at Trailhead: None

DIRECTIONS

TO THE TRAILHEAD

From Ellensburg take Reecer Road 35 north about 20 miles to the junction with Road 3521. Turn right and follow 3521 east about 2.5 miles to the trail access in Section 13, T.20N., R.18E. Reecer Road is narrow, paved, steep and has vehicle turnouts for passing.

Parking: Roadside parking.

Comments: The primary use of the trail is hiking and even though the trail has several steep sections it is still a fairly good horse trail. It crosses Drop Creek and Owl Creek but is mostly in the timber. The trail is poorly defined going up the hill near the Owl Creek trail before connecting with Trail 1389.

OLD ELLENSBURG TRAIL 1373

Trail Length: 3.6 Miles
Elevation: 5200 - 5500 Feet
Difficulty: Easy
Open: June - October
Usage: Heavy
Nearest Town: Ellensburg
Nearest Horse Camp: Ken Wilcox at Haney Meadow
Connecting Trails: 1372
Facilities at Trailhead: Horse camp, no potable water

DIRECTIONS

TO THE TRAILHEAD

Take Highway 97 north of Ellensburg for about 30 miles to Blewett Pass (formerly shown as Swauk Pass on Forest Service and Highway maps prior to 1996). Exit south onto Road 9716. Use caution as it is a turn with only fair visibility from the highway. The turn is between Highway 97 mile posts 163 and 164. Follow Road 9716 to the junction with Road 9712. This is about 4.5 miles. Take 9712 about 5 miles to the Ken Wilcox Horse Camp. Use the turnouts to let other vehicles pass on the narrow sections of this road.

Parking: Adequate for many rigs at the large horse camp.

Comments: Trail 1373 starts at Haney Meadow about a 0.5 mile ride past the entrance to the horse camp. You go past the cabin near the stock watering area. The trail goes south across the Howard Creek Trail 1372 within about 1.8 miles. It then continues to a private road outside the forest boundary. By using Trails 1373 and 1372 a loop ride to the south is possible where 1372 connects with 1381 back to the camp.

Also, Trail 1381 connects with Trail 1234 in a large meadow and 1234 can be followed to 1209 that goes back across Road 9712. Take 9712 back to Haney Meadow.

The Mount Lillian Trail 1601 if ridden with 1373 and 1372 is also a scenic trip where it goes across the top of the mountain. This connects back with 1204 and you return to the horse camp on Road 9712.

TABLE MOUNTAIN TRAIL 1209

Trail Length: 1.9 Miles
Elevation: 5440 - 5600 Feet
Difficulty: Moderate
Open: June - October
Usage: Light
Nearest Town: Ellensburg
Nearest Horse Camp: Ken Wilcox at Haney Meadow
Connecting Trails: 1234, nearby are 1205, 1373
Facilities at Trailhead: Horse camp

DIRECTIONS

TO THE TRAILHEAD

Take Highway 97 north from Ellensburg about 30 miles to Blewett (formerly called Swauk) Pass. Exit south onto Road 9716. Use caution as it is a turn with only fair visibility from the highway. Follow 9716 to the junction with 9712. This is about 4.5 miles. Take 9712 left (east) about 5 miles to the Ken Wilcox Horse Camp at Haney Meadow located in Section 13, T.21N., R.18E.

Parking: There is adequate parking for larger rigs at the horse camp entrance and at campsites.

Comments: This short trail goes southwest and connects with Trail 1234 that follows the Naneum River and provides a loop ride opportunity back to the horse camp on Trail 1381.

TRONSEN RIDGE OR MOUNT LILLIAN TRAIL 1204

Trail Length: 8.7 Miles
Elevation: 4360 - 5700 Feet
Difficulty: Moderate
Open: May - October
Usage: Medium
Nearest Town: Leavenworth or Cle Elum
Nearest Horse Camp: Ken Wilcox at Haney Meadow
Connecting Trails: 1223, 1206, 1601 (Mount Lillian)
Facilities at Trailhead: Horse camp at the south end of trail, none at
    north end

DIRECTIONS

TO THE TRAILHEAD

Take Highway 97 south from Leavenworth toward Cle Elum about 9 miles on past the junction of Highways 2 and 97 to Leavenworth and Wenatchee. Take Road 7204 (Ruby Creek) to the left or southeast. Follow 7204 for about 5 miles north to the trailhead for this trail in Section 8, T.22N., R.18E.

Parking: Roadside and a parking area are available at the north end. At the south end it is better to park at the horse camp and ride to the trailhead.

Comments: This is a ridgetop trail where water and horse feed are limited. Beyond the Magnet Creek junction the trail is rated impassable due to loose soil. The trail comes into Road 9712 at the south end and is less than 2 miles from the Ken Wilcox Horse Camp at Haney Meadow. Go to the right on Road 9712 to reach the horse camp.

Access to the south end of Trail 1204 from Road 9712 is about 1 mile past the horse camp entrance. This ride offers several miles of spectacular views of the North Cascades and Wenatchee Valley.

Aluminum Dutch Oven: pork chops and dressing,
an easy trail meal

—*Photo by authors*

Map 26

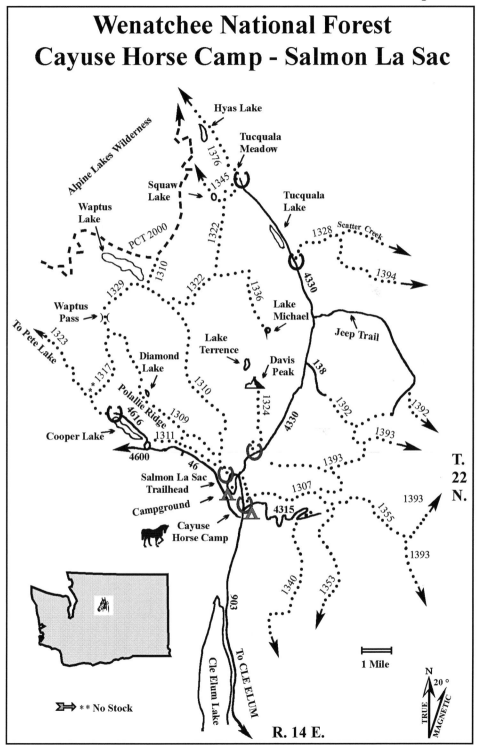

Wenatchee National Forest
Cayuse Horse Camp - Salmon La Sac

DECEPTION PASS TRAIL 1376

Trail Length: 5.0 Miles
Elevation: 3200 - 4480 Feet
Difficulty: Moderate
Open: June - October
Usage: Heavy
Nearest Town: Cle Elum
Nearest Horse Camp: Cayuse
Connecting Trails: 1345, 2000, 1066
Facilities at Trailhead: Stock water at creek, toilet, loading ramp at Tucquala Meadows

DIRECTIONS

TO THE TRAILHEAD

From Cle Elum, take Highway 903 past Cle Elum Lake and the Salmon La Sac Trailhead to Road 4330 (about 19 miles). Follow 4330 to Tucquala Meadow Trailhead located in Section 28, T.24N., R.14E. This trailhead is about 11 miles past Salmon La Sac.

Parking: Adequate for 4-5 trailer rigs.

Comments: The trailhead is at the end of Fish Lake Road 4330. Trail grade is easy to, and beyond, Hyas Lake which is about 2 miles up the trail. Past Hyas Lake to Deception Pass the trail is considered difficult for stock. Deception Pass Trail is into the Alpine Lakes Wilderness so Wilderness Regulations and permits apply. It provides access to the Pacific Crest National Scenic Trail 2000.

DAVIS PEAK TRAIL 1324

Trail Length: 5.4 Miles
Elevation: 2400 - 6500 Feet
Difficulty: Most Difficult
Open: June - October

Usage: Medium
Nearest Town: Cle Elum
Nearest Horse Camp: Cayuse
Connecting Trails: 1393.1
Facilities at Trailhead: Hitch rails, toilet

DIRECTIONS

TO THE TRAILHEAD

From Cle Elum take Highway 903 for approximately 18 miles (paved) to the Cayuse Horse Camp and continue on to the Salmon La Sac Campground about 1 mile further. Then take Road 4330 for approximately 1.5 miles and turn left onto Spur Road 134 to the trailhead located in Section 10, T.22N., R.14E. The sign to this trail is about 2 miles from the horse camp on the road toward Tucquala Lake from Salmon La Sac.

Parking: Available beyond the bridge but limited to not more than 2 trailer rigs, loop drive.

Comments: This trail crosses the Cle Elum River above Paris Creek then climbs with many switchbacks to Davis Peak. Mountain Goats may be seen in the area. The upper 1.5 miles are in the Alpine Lakes Wilderness and so Wilderness Regulations and permits apply.

JOLLY MOUNTAIN TRAIL 1307

Trail Length: 6.2 Miles
Elevation: 2400 - 6400 Feet
Difficulty: Moderate
Open: June - October
Usage: Heavy
Nearest Town: Cle Elum
Nearest Horse Camp: Cayuse
Connecting Trails: 1340, 1353, 1222, 1355
Facilities at Trailhead: Full campsites at Cayuse Horse Camp

From Cle Elum take Highway 903 approximately 18 miles (paved) to the Salmon La Sac Guard Station then take Spur Road 132. The trailhead is within the Cayuse Horse Camp located in Section 16, T.22N., R.14E.

Parking: Adequate, with turning space available at the horse camp.

Comments: This trail goes up along Salmon La Sac Creek to the junction of the Sasse Ridge Trail 1340 and then continues along the top of the ridge to Jolly Mountain. There are exceptional views on this ride.

LAKE MICHAEL TRAIL 1336

Trail Length: 6.3 Miles
Elevation: 4320 - 5600 Feet
Difficulty: Moderate
Open: June - October
Usage: Medium
Nearest Town: Cle Elum
Nearest Horse Camp: Cayuse
Connecting Trails: 1322
Facilities at Trailhead: None

DIRECTIONS

TO THE TRAILHEAD

The Cayuse Horse Camp located in Section 16, T.22N., R.14E. is reached by taking Highway 903 about 18 miles from Cle Elum past Cle Elum Lake. Access this trail from the Salmon La Sac Trailhead or Cayuse Horse Camp. Ride the Waptus River Trail 1310 north into the Alpine Lakes Wilderness for about 5 miles to the junction with Trail 1322. Follow Trail 1322 right (north) for about 2 miles to Trail 1336.

Parking: Adequate at the trailhead and horse camp.

Comments: This trail is a steep ride to an old sheep camp on the ridge between Trail Creek and Goat Creek. It then drops into Goat Creek from Lake Michael. Terrence Lake is beyond Lake Michael but the horse trail ends at Lake Michael.

PETE LAKE TRAIL 1323

Trail Length: 7.5 Miles
Elevation: 2800 - 3400 Feet
Difficulty: Easy
Open: June - October
Usage: Heavy
Nearest Town: Cle Elum
Nearest Horse Camp: Cayuse
Connecting Trails: 2000, 1329, 1317 (no horses), 1323
Facilities at Trailhead: None, but full camping facilities at the Cayuse
Horse Camp near the Salmon La Sac Trailhead

DIRECTIONS

TO THE TRAILHEAD

To reach the trailhead travel 17 miles from Cle Elum on Highway 903. About 1 mile before the Cayuse Horse Camp, turn left onto Road 46 toward Cooper Lake. Just before Cooper Lake, turn right (north) onto Road 4616 then go 1 mile on Spur Road 113 past the Owhi Campground. The trailhead is in Section 35, T.23N., R.13E.

Parking: Adequate space to park and turn around a 4-horse trailer both at the trailhead and horse camp.

Comments: There are separate trailheads for hikers and horse riders but this trail is closed to mountain bikes. Access to the Pete Lake Trail is also available from the Salmon La Sac Trailhead. Ride the Polallie Ridge Trail 1309 and the 1317 trail south or use 1309 and Trail 1329 to reach the Pete Lake area that connects to Trail 1323 further into the wilderness.

POLALLIE RIDGE TRAIL 1309

Trail Length: 8.9 Miles
Elevation: 2400 - 5500 Feet
Difficulty: Most Difficult
Open: June - October
Usage: Light
Nearest Town: Cle Elum
Nearest Horse Camp: Cayuse
Connecting Trails: 1311, 1329
Facilities at Trailhead: Cayuse Horse Camp and trailhead both have
loading ramps, hitch rails, toilet

DIRECTIONS

TO THE TRAILHEAD

Take Highway 903 for 18 miles (paved) to the Cayuse Horse Camp
and continue on for about 1 mile. The 1309 trail starts at the Salmon
La Sac Trailhead in Section 16, T.22N., R.14E. This is just beyond the
horse camp and there is a connecting trail between the Cayuse Horse
Camp and Salmon La Sac Trailhead that can be ridden if you stay at
the horse camp.

Parking: Adequate for long rigs at the horse camp. Some are pull-
through and others are pull-in, there also is a loop drive. An extra
parking area is available for 2-4 more rigs. The Salmon La Sac
Trailhead has ample parking for vehicles with trailers.

Comments: The trail climbs at a steep rate up to Polallie Ridge
and goes up and down side drainage until it drops steeply into Waptus
Pass. Repair needs are evident on this trail in areas. This will be a very
scenic ride but there is no water from Diamond Lake to Waptus Pass.
Since it is in the Alpine Lakes Wilderness, Wilderness Regulations and
permits apply.

SCATTER CREEK TRAIL 1328

Trail Length: 4.5 Miles
Elevation: 3440 - 6200 Feet
Difficulty: Moderate
Open: June - October
Usage: Light
Nearest Town: Cle Elum
Nearest Horse Camp: Cayuse
Connecting Trails: 1394
Facilities at Trailhead: None

DIRECTIONS

TO THE TRAILHEAD

From Cle Elum, take Highway 903 for 19 miles (paved) to the Salmon La Sac area. Follow Road 4330 about 6 miles toward Tucquala Lake. The trailhead is at the roadside in Section 11, T.23N., R.14E.

Parking: Roadside for 2-3 rigs maximum.

Comments: This trail climbs steeply to a junction with Trail 1394 in about 2.5 miles. It then climbs up above the head of Scatter Creek to the junction with other trails that lead into the Alpine Lakes Wilderness where there are meadows in the upper basin.

Hikers are the primary users of this trail which is outside the wilderness.

TRAIL CREEK TRAIL 1322

Trail Length: 4.7 Miles
Elevation: 2960 - 4560 Feet
Difficulty: Moderate
Open: June - October
Usage: Medium
Nearest Town: Cle Elum
Nearest Horse Camp: Cayuse
Connecting Trails: 1310, 1336
Facilities at Trailhead: Hitch rails, loading ramps, horse camp

DIRECTIONS

TO THE TRAILHEAD

From Cle Elum take Highway 903 about 18 miles (paved) to the Cayuse Horse Camp. It is 1 mile from there to the Salmon La Sac Trailhead which is 0.5 mile past a non-horse campground. Ride Trail 1310 about 6 miles into the Alpine Lakes Wilderness from the trailhead to reach the junction with Trail 1322 in Section 18, T.23N., R.14E.

Parking: Ample at the Salmon La Sac Trailhead.

Comments: Trail 1322 climbs steadily for nearly 3 miles then assumes a more gentle grade near the junction with the Cathedral Rocks Trail 1345. Horse riders, the primary users of this trail, need to carry drinking water. The trail fords the Waptus River on the south end which for hikers may be a deep crossing. Alpine Lakes Wilderness permits are needed.

WAPTUS RIVER TRAIL 1310

Trail Length: 11.2 Miles
Elevation: 2400 - 2960 Feet
Difficulty: Easy
Open: May - October
Usage: Extra Heavy
Nearest Town: Cle Elum
Nearest Horse Camp: Cayuse
Connecting Trails: 1322, 1329, 1329.1, 1310.1, 2000
Facilities at Trailhead: Complete camping at Cayuse Horse Camp

DIRECTIONS

TO THE TRAILHEAD

From Cle Elum take Highway 903 for 18 miles (paved) to the Cayuse Horse Camp. It is 1 mile further on to the Salmon La Sac Trailhead. A trail connects the trailhead with the horse camp.

Parking: Adequate for trailer rigs at both the horse camp and trailhead.

Comments: Horse riding is the primary use of this trail. Trail 1310 starts at the Trail 1309 location in Section 16, T.22N., R.14E. There are four bridges to cross on the Waptus River Trail.

WEST FORK TEANAWAY TRAIL 1353

Trail Length: 9.6 Miles
Elevation: 2800 - 5600 Feet
Difficulty: Most Difficult
Open: June - October
Usage: Medium
Nearest Town: Cle Elum
Nearest Horse Camp: Cayuse
Connecting Trails: 1307, 1355, 1340 (no space to park)
Facilities at Trailhead: None, unless Cayuse Horse Camp is used as
   the trailhead

DIRECTIONS

TO THE TRAILHEAD

From Cle Elum take Highway 903 about 18 miles (paved) to the Cayuse Horse Camp. From there use Trail 1307 going east to reach the north end of Trail 1353 in Section 13, T.22N., R.14E.

Also, from Cle Elum you can reach the south end this trail by taking Highway 10 east to Highway 97, then to Highway 970 to the Middle Fork of Teanaway Road. Follow that road to Spur Road 113 and the trailhead. It is about 21 miles from Cle Elum. You use a private road part of the distance to reach the trailhead by this route and it may be rough and some problem to travel if muddy.

There is access to the north end of this trail. It is by following Road 4315 near the horse camp to the end and then riding Trail 1340 to Trail 1353. However, there is not adequate parking on 4315. Some sections of Trail 1340 are also steep, rocky and poor footing for horses.

Parking: Ample at the horse camp on the north end. At the south end of the trail (by the private road), parking is limited but there is space to turn a 4-horse rig around.

Comments: This is a fairly good trail that has several water crossings considered difficult for hikers who are the primary users of the trail. It is a scenic ride that follows along and crosses the river several times and becomes very narrow in the high terrain with tight switchbacks. Be aware that mountain bikes have been permitted on this trail as it is not in the wilderness.

PACIFIC CREST NATIONAL SCENIC TRAIL (PCT) 2000

Trail Length: 50 Miles
Elevation: 2980 - 6020 Feet
Difficulty: Most Difficult
Open: June - October
Usage: Extra Heavy
Nearest Town: Cle Elum
Nearest Horse Camp: Cayuse
Connecting Trails: 1310, 1323, 1345, 1376 shown on Trail Maps, other connecting trails include 1013, 1033 (Mount Baker-Snoqualmie National Forest), 1331, 1339, 1329.3, 1362
Facilities at Trailhead: Vary depending on trail access location selected, Snoqualmie Pass has loading ramp and hitch rails

DIRECTIONS

TO THE TRAILHEAD

Access the south end of this 50 mile length of the Pacific Crest National Scenic Trail 2000 in the Cle Elum Ranger District by using the trailhead on I-90 at Snoqualmie Pass in Section 4, T.22N., R.11E.

Parking: Adequate for trailer rigs at Snoqualmie Pass.

Comments: This 50 miles goes from Deception Pass (Section 6, T.24N., R.14E.) in the north to Snoqualmie Pass in the south. The route is a scenic ride over ridges and into drainages that access a number of lakes. Much of the trail is showing wear and may present difficult tread for horses in some places. Hikers and horse riders often have separate trailhead entries to the Pacific Crest National Scenic Trail 2000.

Map 27

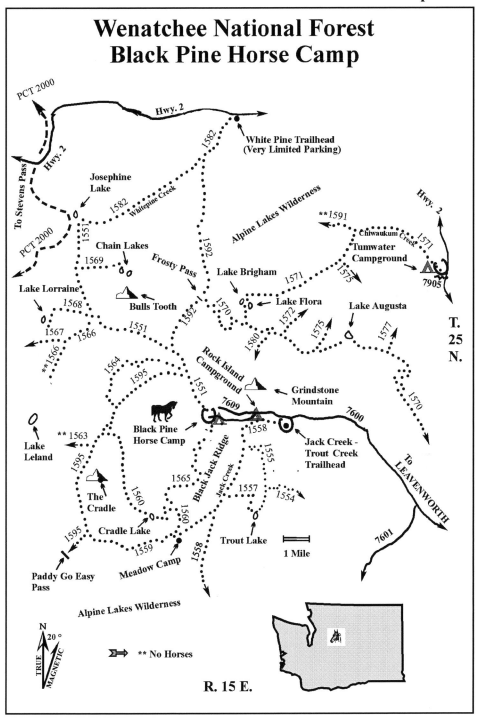

Wenatchee National Forest
Black Pine Horse Camp

PCT 2000

Hwy. 2

White Pine Trailhead
(Very Limited Parking)

1582

To Stevens Pass

Hwy. 2

Josephine Lake

1582

Whitepine Creek

Alpine Lakes Wilderness

**1591

Chiwaukum Creek

Hwy. 2

1571

PCT 2000

1551

Chain Lakes

1569

Frosty Pass

1592

Lake Brigham

1571

1575

Tunwater Campground

7905

Lake Lorraine

1568

Bulls Tooth

1551

1592

1570

Lake Flora

1572

Lake Augusta

1567

1566

**1566

1551

1580

1575

1577

T. 25 N.

1564

1595

Rock Island Campground

1551

Grindstone Mountain

7600

1570

Lake Leland

** 1563

1595

Black Pine Horse Camp

7609

1558

Jack Creek - Trout Creek Trailhead

1555

To LEAVENWORTH

The Cradle

1560

1565

Black Jack Ridge

Jack Creek

1557

1554

1595

Cradle Lake

1560

1559

Trout Lake

1 Mile

7601

Paddy Go Easy Pass

1558

Meadow Camp

Alpine Lakes Wilderness

N
20°
TRUE
MAGNETIC

⇒ ** No Horses

R. 15 E.

BLACK JACK RIDGE TRAIL 1565

Trail Length: 8.0 Miles
Elevation: 2900 - 6700 Feet
Difficulty: Most Difficult
Open: June - October
Usage: Light
Nearest Town: Leavenworth
Nearest Horse Camp: Black Pine
Connecting Trails: 1560, 1559
Facilities at Trailhead: Black Pine Horse Camp, toilets, loading ramp, hitch rails, campsites

DIRECTIONS

TO THE TRAILHEAD

Access to this camp is by taking Road 7600 south from Leavenworth past the fish hatchery to the Black Pine Horse Camp located in Section 2, T.24N., R.15E. It is about 16 miles to the trailhead which is just past the horse camp.

Parking: Ample trailer parking at either the horse camp or the stock unloading area. Do not unload at the end of road where there is a small trailhead.

Comments: Horse riding is the primary use of this steep trail that goes south into the Alpine Lakes Wilderness. The Cradle Lake Basin is closed to horse camping beyond Pablo Creek. Wilderness Regulations and permits apply but Ben Creek in Section 15 and Pablo Creek in Section 21 are good alternatives for camping.

CHIWAUKUM CREEK TRAIL 1571

Trail Length: 12.2 Miles
Elevation: 2000 - 6800 Feet
Difficulty: Moderate
Open: June - October
Usage: Medium

Nearest Town: Leavenworth
Nearest Horse Camp: None
Connecting Trails: 1570, 1591, 1575
Facilities at Trailhead: Loading ramp, hitch rail, toilet

DIRECTIONS

TO THE TRAILHEAD

Chiwaukum Creek Trail is east of the Black Pine area off Highway 2. It is reached by taking Highway 2 north from Leavenworth about 9 miles to Road 7908 on the left or west. A short 0.3 mile road leads to a gate and the trailhead parking.

The trailhead is about 1 mile past Tumwater Campground in Section 4, T.25N., R.17E. The trail follows the old road for the first 1.5 miles.

Parking: Adequate, with a loop drive suitable for 4-horse rigs.

Comments: This trail into the Alpine Lakes Wilderness has horse feed and high stock use during the high elevation hunts. Hiking is the primary use of the trail. Wilderness Regulations and permits apply.

FRENCH CREEK TRAIL 1595

Trail Length: 11.3 Miles
Elevation: 2880 - 6200 Feet
Difficulty: Moderate
Open: June - October
Usage: Heavy
Nearest Town: Leavenworth
Nearest Horse Camp: Black Pine
Connecting Trails: 1551, 1558, 1559, 1564, 1560
Facilities at Trailhead: Horse camp, hitch rails, loading ramp, toilets, campsites

DIRECTIONS

TO THE TRAILHEAD

This trail is accessed from the Black Pine Horse Camp Trailhead located in Section 2, T.24N., R.15E. To reach the horse camp, take

Road 7600 south out of Leavenworth past the fish hatchery. It is about 16 miles to the horse camp. Ride Trail 1551 to the junction with Trail 1595. It is about 2 miles out from the trailhead at the end of Road 7600.

Parking: Use the horse camp or stock unloading area near the horse camp. Parking for trailers is not available at the end of Road 7600.

Comments: This trail is into the Alpine Lake Wilderness and Wilderness Regulations on party size limits and permits apply.

Horse riders are the primary users of this trail that is brushy in spots. It does offer loop ride opportunities when used with other trails such as 1559 and 1558 from the Jack Creek-Trout Creek Trailhead off Road 7600.

ICICLE CREEK TRAIL 1551

Trail Length: 12.1 Miles
Elevation: 2900 - 4000 Feet
Difficulty: Easy
Open: June - October
Usage: Heavy
Nearest Town: Leavenworth
Nearest Horse Camp: Black Pine
Connecting Trails: 1564, 1566, 1568, 1569, 1582, 1592, 1595
Facilities at Trailhead: Horse camp with loading ramp, hitch rails, toilet, campsites, fire rings, tables

DIRECTIONS

TO THE TRAILHEAD

Icicle Creek Trail is accessed from the Black Pine Horse Camp in Section 3, T.24N., R.15E. at the end of Road 7600. Reach the trailhead by taking 7600 south out of Leavenworth. This is the road past the Leavenworth Fish Hatchery. It is about 16 miles on Road 7600 to the trailhead.

Parking: The primary trailhead area is only for cars. Use horse camp parking which has 12 pull-through sites.

Comments: Near the horse camp there is a non-camping, horse unloading area with ramp and hitch rails along the road on the right just before you reach the horse camp. A sign asks you to unload horses here and not at the road end.

This trail goes into the Alpine Lakes Wilderness and so group size regulations apply. Several trails shown on the Trail Map are not recommended for horses; Trail 1580 for example. Check with the local Forest Office before riding trails we have not described by a Trail Guide.

Grazing, tethering, hitching or hobbling any packstock within 200 feet of lakes or ponds is not permitted. This is a trip to carry pelletized feed as unprocessed grain or hay is not allowed. Note also that the Klonaqua Lakes are closed to horses.

Caution: Vandalism and theft have occurred at this trailhead so lock your rig and store valuables out of sight.

JACK CREEK TRAIL 1558

Trail Length: 11.9 Miles
Elevation: 2640 - 6450 Feet
Difficulty: Moderate
Open: June - October
Usage: Medium
Nearest Town: Leavenworth
Nearest Horse Camp: Black Pine
Connecting Trails: 1557, 1559, 1555
Facilities at Trailhead: Loading ramp

DIRECTIONS

TO THE TRAILHEAD

You reach the 1558 Trailhead by taking Road 7600 from Leavenworth past the fish hatchery. It is about 16 miles to the trailhead on Road 7600. This trail has a new trailhead located about 2 miles before the Black Pine Horse Camp. The Trout Creek Bridge from the old trail is gone. It is now called the Jack Creek-Trout Creek Trailhead and is located in Section 1, T.25N., R.15E.

Parking: Adequate for 4-6 trailer rigs and there is a small loop for turning around.

Comments: This trail can be part of about a 20 mile loop ride to the south and west that uses 1559 and 1595 to 1551 to get back to the Black Pine Horse Camp. It is about 2 miles by Road 7600 back to the Jack Creek-Trout Creek Trailhead. There is limited horse feed on the lower end of the trail so pelletized feed must be carried for overnight trips. Trail riders and hikers are the primary users of the trail.

LORRAINE RIDGE TRAIL 1568

Trail Length: 4.0 Miles
Elevation: 3240 - 5400 Feet
Difficulty: Most Difficult
Open: June - October
Usage: Light
Nearest Town: Leavenworth
Nearest Horse Camp: Black Pine
Connecting Trails: 1566, 1551
Facilities at Trailhead: Horse camp, toilets, loading ramp, hitch rails, campsites

DIRECTIONS

TO THE TRAILHEAD

Access to this trailhead is by taking Road 7600 south from Leavenworth about 16 miles. The road goes past the fish hatchery. Follow 7600 to the horse camp. Ride Trail 1551 from the horse camp to reach the junction with Trail 1566. This is about 6 miles. Take Trail 1566 to where 1568 starts with a set of switchbacks only a short distance up the 1566 trail.

Parking: Adequate at the horse camp or stock unloading area.

Comments: This is a steep trail used primarily by horse riders. Horse feed is available at the ridgetops but the only water source is at

Lake Lorraine. Pack and saddle stock are not permitted to stay within 200 feet of the lake. The trip from the horse camp to Lorraine Lake and back is about 16 miles making this a good one night trip.

MEADOW CREEK TRAIL 1559

Trail Length: 6.5 Miles
Elevation: 3600 - 5300 Feet
Difficulty: Moderate
Open: June - October
Usage: Medium
Nearest Town: Leavenworth
Nearest Horse Camp: Black Pine
Connecting Trails: 1558, 1595, 1560
Facilities at Trailhead: None

DIRECTIONS

TO THE TRAILHEAD

Meadow Creek Trail is accessed by either of two trails, 1551 or 1558. You reach the 1551 and 1558 trailheads by taking Road 7600 out of Leavenworth past the fish hatchery. It is about 16 miles to the trailhead and horse camp. Access the trail either from Trail 1595 about 1.5 miles on out Trail 1551 from the Black Pine Horse Camp or from Trail 1558. This is off Road 7600 near the Rock Island Campground where there is a horse ramp at the Jack Creek-Trout Creek Trailhead in Section 1, T.25N., R.15E.

Parking: Adequate parking at the horse camp area.

Comments: This trail is into the Alpine Lakes Wilderness and Wilderness Regulations and permits apply. It offers a loop ride when used with Trails 1551, 1595, 1560 and 1558. Horse riders are the primary users and horse feed is available. Plan to cross some boggy areas the first two miles of the trail.

SNOWALL CRADLE TRAIL 1560

Trail Length: 9.1 Miles
Elevation: 3360 - 6300 Feet
Difficulty: Most Difficult
Open: June - October
Usage: Medium
Nearest Town: Leavenworth
Nearest Horse Camp: Black Pine
Connecting Trails: 1595, 1559, 1565
Facilities at Trailhead: None, horse camp has loading ramp, hitch
rails

DIRECTIONS

TO THE TRAILHEAD

Access is by the steep 1595 French Creek Trail off the 1551 Trail
from the Black Pine Horse Camp. To reach the 1551 Trailhead, take
Road 7600 south out of Leavenworth past the fish hatchery. It is about
16 miles to the trailhead.

Ride Trail 1551 from the trailhead for about 1.5 miles to the junction with Trail 1595. Follow 1595 for about 4 miles to the junction of
Trail 1560 in Section 1, T.24N., R.14E. This ride passes the junction
with Trail 1564 on the right.

Parking: Use the horse camp or unloading area near the horse
camp. The trailhead at the end of Road 7600 is not large enough for
trailer rigs.

Comments: Horse riders are the primary users of this trail into the
Alpine Lakes Wilderness where Wilderness Regulations on party size
and stock handling apply. The Cradle Lake Basin is closed to horse
camping beyond the Pablo Creek turnoff but Meadow Camp, Ben
Creek, and Snowall Creek are good alternatives. Grazing, hitching,
tethering or hobbling are not permitted within 200 feet of Cradle Lake.

Map 28

Wenatchee National Forest
White River Falls

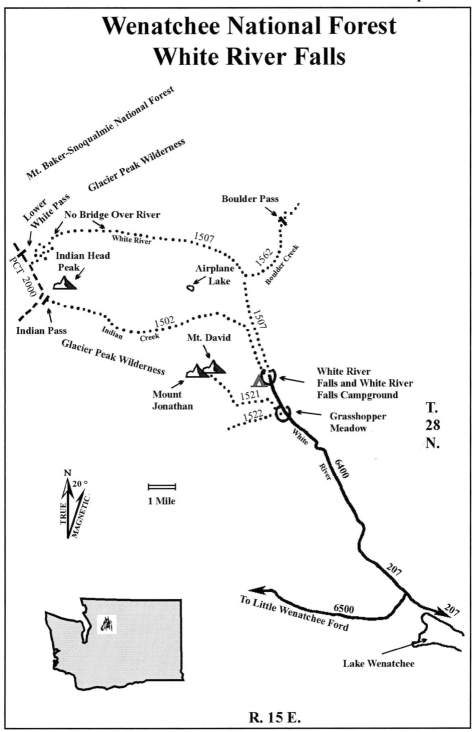

Mt. Baker-Snoqualmie National Forest

Glacier Peak Wilderness

Boulder Pass

Lower White Pass

No Bridge Over River

White River

1507

1562

Boulder Creek

PCT 2000

Indian Head Peak

Airplane Lake

Indian Pass

Indian Creek

1502

1507

Glacier Peak Wilderness

Mt. David

Mount Jonathan

1521

1522

White River Falls and White River Falls Campground

Grasshopper Meadow

T. 28 N.

White River

6400

N
20°
TRUE
MAGNETIC

1 Mile

207

To Little Wenatchee Ford

6500

207

Lake Wenatchee

BOULDER PASS TRAIL 1562

Trail Length: 9.0 Miles
Elevation: 2500 - 6200 Feet
Difficulty: Moderate
Open: July - October
Usage: Medium
Nearest Town: Leavenworth
Nearest Horse Camp: None
Connecting Trails: 1507, 1518
Facilities at Trailhead: Toilet, hitch rail, loading ramp

DIRECTIONS

TO THE TRAILHEAD

Access Trail 1562 by riding Trail 1507. You reach 1507 by following Highway 207 past Lake Wenatchee where it becomes Road 6400. Follow 6400 about 9 miles to the trailhead at the end of the road past White River Falls in Section 35, T.29N., R.15E.

Parking: There is trailer parking at the trailhead.

Comments: You ride Trail 1507 to reach the junction with Trail 1562 at Boulder Creek about 4 miles up Trail 1507. The trail usually retains snow until August in the Boulder Pass area. This trail is also the access to the Napeequa River Valley and there are difficult river crossings at the Napeequa River where it meets Trail 1518. Horse use is not recommended beyond the Napeequa River crossing and the Napeequa Valley Trail is not maintained.

INDIAN CREEK TRAIL 1502

Trail Length: 11.0 Miles
Elevation: 2300 - 5000 Feet
Difficulty: Moderate
Open: June - October
Usage: Heavy
Nearest Town: Leavenworth

Nearest Horse Camp: None
Connecting Trails: 1507, 2000
Facilities at Trailhead: Toilet, hitch rail, loading ramp

DIRECTIONS

TO THE TRAILHEAD

From Leavenworth, take Highway 2 north about 15 miles to the junction with Highway 207 to Lake Wenatchee. Follow 207 past Lake Wenatchee where it becomes Road 6400. You will pass the junction with Road 6500 about 1 mile past the lake. Keep right and follow 6400 about 9 miles to the trailhead in Section 35, T.29N., R.15.E. The last 2 miles of the road into the trailhead may be somewhat rough but it has been passable by sedan.

Parking: Ample space at the trailhead.

Comments: This trail provides access to the Pacific Crest National Scenic Trail 2000 and Indian Pass. It is usually snow free by mid-July. There is a high bridge to cross with horses as you leave the trailhead for Trail 1502. About 4 miles up the trail you ride through some brushy, boggy areas and then the last 2 miles before Trail 2000 the trail tread is eroded and narrow. Signs at the trailhead read for one route, "Indian Creek Tr. 1502, Indian Creek 2 miles, PCT 11 miles" and for the other route, "White River Tr. 1507, Boulder Pass Tr. 4 miles, PCT 15 miles."

MOUNT DAVID TRAIL 1521

Trail Length: 6.5 Miles
Elevation: 2240 - 7420 Feet
Difficulty: Moderate
Open: July - October
Usage: Light
Nearest Town: Leavenworth
Nearest Horse Camp: None
Connecting Trails: 1522 (trailhead for 1521)
Facilities at Trailhead: None

DIRECTIONS

TO THE TRAILHEAD

Take Highway 2 from Leavenworth north about 15 miles to the junction with Highway 207 to Lake Wenatchee. Follow 207 past Lake Wenatchee, it becomes Road 6400. Follow 6400 to Grasshopper Meadows about 1 mile before White River Falls Campground. Use the trailhead for Panther Creek Trail 1522. Trail 1521 starts less than 1 mile up Trail 1522 in Section 11, T.28N., R.15E.

Parking: Ample trailer parking at the trailhead.

Comments: This trail into the Glacier Peak Wilderness provides access to an old lookout site. But there is limited trail maintenance so the trail is not recommended for stock. The trail does offer excellent views of the entire district but the Mount David site is usually snow covered until the end of July. Check with the Lake Wenatchee Ranger Station for trail status.

WHITE RIVER TRAIL 1507

Trail Length: 14.9 Miles
Elevation: 2300 - 5000 Feet
Difficulty: Moderate
Open: May - October
Usage: Medium
Nearest Town: Leavenworth
Nearest Horse Camp: None
Connecting Trails: 1502, 1562, 2000
Facilities at Trailhead: Toilet, hitch rail, loading ramp

DIRECTIONS

TO THE TRAILHEAD

Take Highway 2 from Leavenworth north about 15 miles to the junction with Highway 207 to Lake Wenatchee. Turn right and follow 207 past Lake Wenatchee to Road 6400. The junction with Road 6500 is about 1 mile past the lake. Keep to the right on Highway 207, it becomes Road 6400. Follow 6400 about 9 miles to the trailhead at the end of the road which is beyond White River Falls and is in Section 35, T.29N., R.15E.

Parking: There is ample trailer space at the trailhead.

Comments: This trail provides access to the Glacier Peak Wilderness and the Pacific Crest National Scenic Trail 2000. Be aware that in the early season there may be a potentially hazardous ford crossing due to logs and high water just beyond the 11.5 mile point.

The trail tread is eroded and very narrow the last mile before Trail 2000 (PCT). The first 4 to 5 miles of the trail are usually snow free by late May. However, the upper sections near the junction with the Pacific Crest National Scenic Trail 2000 may not be free of snow until August.

Map 29

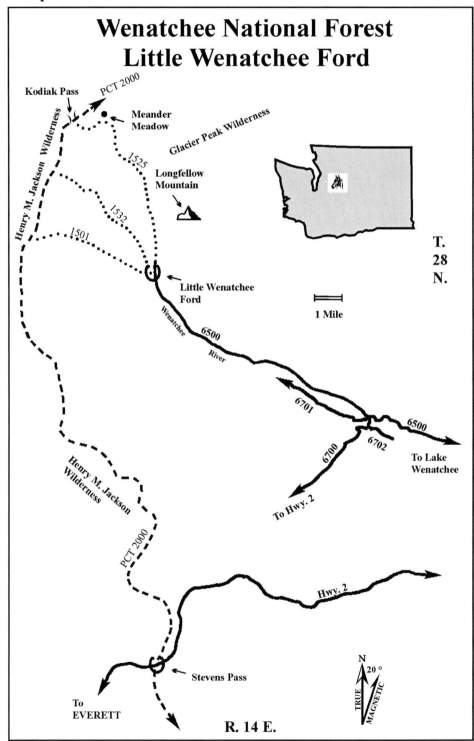

Wenatchee National Forest
Little Wenatchee Ford

Kodiak Pass

PCT 2000

Meander
Meadow

Henry M. Jackson Wilderness

Glacier Peak Wilderness

1525

Longfellow
Mountain

1532

1501

T.
28
N.

Little Wenatchee
Ford

1 Mile

Wenatchee

6500

River

6701

6500

Henry M. Jackson
Wilderness

6700

6702

To Lake
Wenatchee

PCT 2000

To Hwy. 2

Hwy. 2

N
20°

To
EVERETT

Stevens Pass

TRUE
MAGNETIC

R. 14 E.

CADY CREEK TRAIL 1501

Trail Length: 5.2 Miles
Elevation: 3000 - 4300 Feet
Difficulty: Moderate
Open: July - October
Usage: Light
Nearest Town: Leavenworth
Nearest Horse Camp: None
Connecting Trails: 1525, 1532, 2000
Facilities at Trailhead: Toilet, loading ramp, tables, fire rings

DIRECTIONS

TO THE TRAILHEAD

From Leavenworth take Highway 2 north to the junction with Highway 207 to Lake Wenatchee. Follow 207 past the lake to the junction with Road 6500. Turn left and take 6500 to the trailhead. It is about 15 miles to the Little Wenatchee Ford Trailhead located in Section 14, T.28N., R.14E.

Parking: There is a trailhead parking area but turning around with a trailer may be awkward if many cars are present.

Comments: This trail goes into the Henry M. Jackson Wilderness and provides access to the Pacific Crest National Scenic Trail 2000. Signs at the trailhead read, "Pole Mtn. Tr. 1/8 mile, PCT 7 miles and Basalt Pass Tr. 2.5 miles, Carne Mtn. Tr. 12 miles".

Cady Creek Trail 1501 can be bushy and muddy in places as it follows the valley bottom and then climbs to Cady Pass. Snow there is usually gone by mid-July.

The trailhead bridge over Cady Creek is very high and this may intimidate some inexperienced horses or packstock. Also, the bridge is nearing the end of its useful life and may not be replaced which will make this loop ride difficult for stock. You may want to call the local Forest Office for current information and comment on the potential loss of this access.

LITTLE WENATCHEE RIVER TRAIL 1525

Trail Length: 7.2 Miles
Elevation: 3000 - 5500 Feet
Difficulty: Moderate
Open: July - October
Usage: Medium
Nearest Town: Leavenworth
Nearest Horse Camp: Chiwawa
Connecting Trails: 1501, 1532, 2000
Facilities at Trailhead: Loading ramp, toilets, tables, fire rings

DIRECTIONS

TO THE TRAILHEAD

From Leavenworth take Highway 2 north to the junction with Highway 207 to Lake Wenatchee. Follow 207 past Lake Wenatchee to the junction with Road 6500. Turn left and take 6500 about 15 miles to the Little Wenatchee Ford Trailhead located in Section 13, T.28N., R.14E.

Parking: Adequate at the trailhead but turning a 4-horse trailer around may be awkward if many cars are present.

Comments: This trail goes northwest and provides access to the Pacific Crest National Scenic Trail 2000 and the Henry M. Jackson Wilderness. Upper sections of this trail are usually covered by snow until late July and horse feed is not available early in the season.

Firewood is scarce in Meander Meadows so a propane camp stove is essential when camping there. Trail 1525 (or 1501) should be ridden as the access to Trail 2000, not the steep Cady Ridge Trail 1532.

PACIFIC CREST NATIONAL SCENIC TRAIL (PCT) 2000

Trail Length: 36.1 Miles
Elevation: 4060 - 5600 Feet
Difficulty: Moderate
Open: July - October
Usage: Heavy
Nearest Town: Leavenworth
Nearest Horse Camp: None
Connecting Trails: 1502, 1507
Facilities at Trailhead: None

DIRECTIONS

TO THE TRAILHEAD

Follow Highway 2 about 35 miles west of Leavenworth to Stevens Pass. A U.S. Forest Service map of Trail 2000 (PCT) will help in the selection of a Pacific Crest National Scenic Trail trailhead to enter along the 36.1 miles in the Wenatchee Ranger District.

Parking: The parking lot at Stevens Pass is adequate but has no horse facilities.

Comments: This segment of Trail 2000 is access to both the Henry M. Jackson and Glacier Peak Wilderness. The section goes north from Stevens Pass to Lower White Pass at the head of the White River in Section 7, T.29N., R.14E.

Map 30

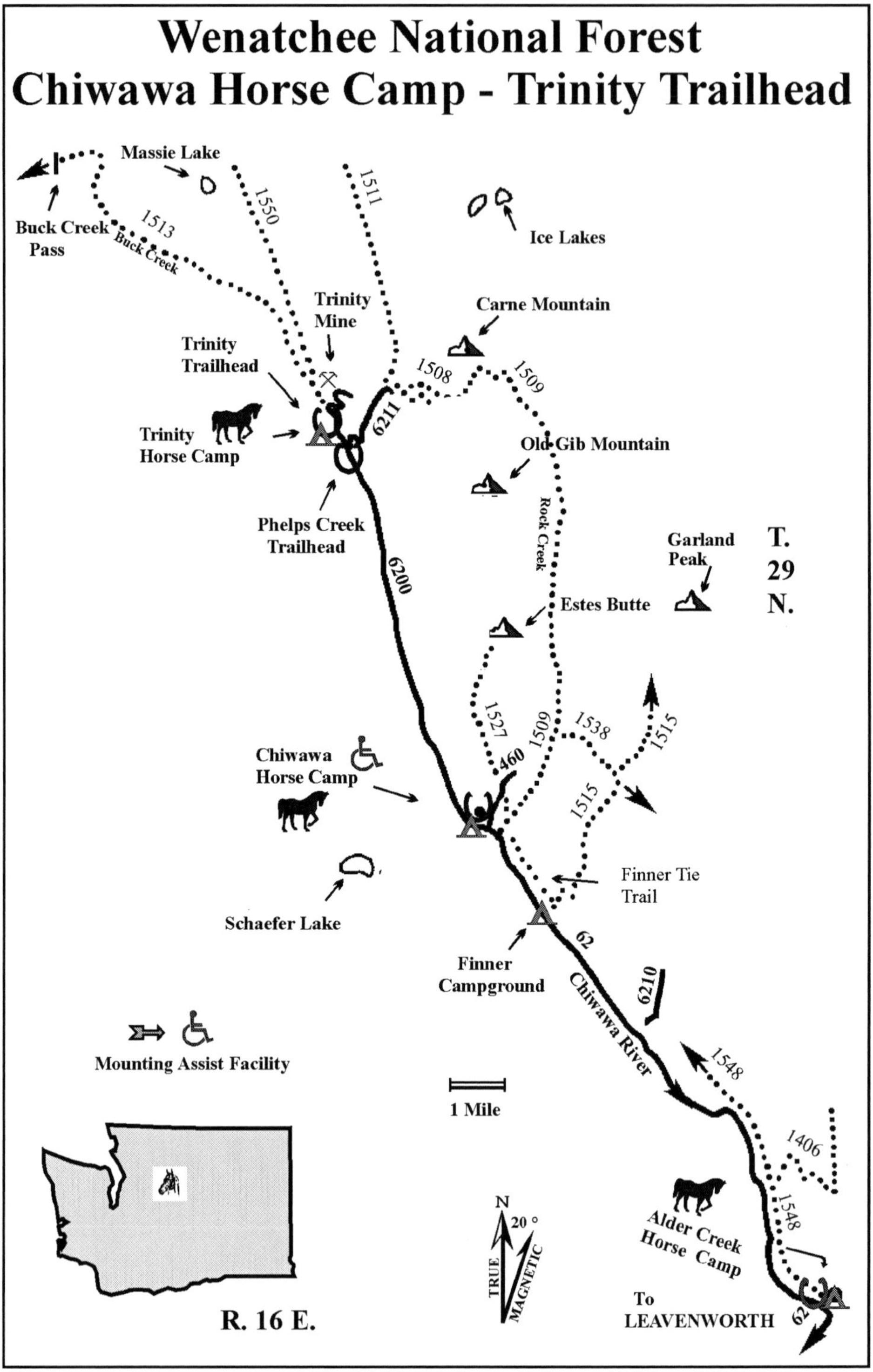

Wenatchee National Forest
Chiwawa Horse Camp - Trinity Trailhead

Massie Lake

1550

1511

Buck Creek Pass

1513

Buck Creek

Ice Lakes

Trinity Mine

Carne Mountain

Trinity Trailhead

1508

1509

6211

Trinity Horse Camp

Old Gib Mountain

Phelps Creek Trailhead

Rock Creek

Garland Peak

T. 29 N.

6200

Estes Butte

1527

1509

1538

1515

Chiwawa Horse Camp

460

Schaefer Lake

1515

Finner Tie Trail

Finner Campground

62

0129

Chiwawa River

Mounting Assist Facility

1 Mile

1548

1406

1548

Alder Creek Horse Camp

N
20°
TRUE
MAGNETIC

To
LEAVENWORTH

62

R. 16 E.

BASALT RIDGE TRAIL 1515

Trail Length: 8.5 Miles
Elevation: 2500 - 7400 Feet
Difficulty: Moderate
Open: July - October
Usage: Light
Nearest Town: Leavenworth
Nearest Horse Camp: Chiwawa
Connecting Trails: 1538
Facilities at Trailhead: Toilet

DIRECTIONS

TO THE TRAILHEAD

Take Highway 2 north from Leavenworth to the junction with Highway 207. Follow 207 for about 4 miles to the junction with Road 62 then follow 62 past Fish Lake about 12 miles to Trail 1515. This is the trailhead access at the Finner Creek Campground located in Section 6, T.28N., R.17E.

Parking: There is a small lot and roadside parking is also limited. Consider using the Chiwawa Horse Camp about 2 miles up Road 62 and then riding back to the trailhead.

Comments: This trail can be reached from the Chiwawa Horse Camp by using the Finner Tie Trail. Basalt Ridge Trail 1515 was reconstructed in 1995 to provide a day ride loop that uses the Rock Creek Trail 1509 and the Rock Creek Tie Trail 1538. This steep dry trail provides access to Garland Peak where it ties in with Trail 1408 on the Entiat Ranger District to the east. Trail 1515 usually has the snow gone by early July.

Chiwawa Horse Camp
entry sign
—Photo by authors

BUCK CREEK TRAIL 1513

Trail Length: 9.6 Miles
Elevation: 3900 - 5900 Feet
Difficulty: Moderate
Open: July - October
Usage: Heavy
Nearest Town: Leavenworth
Nearest Horse Camp: Trinity, just past Phelps Creek Campground
Connecting Trails: 1550
Facilities at Trailhead: Loading ramp, toilets

DIRECTIONS

TO THE TRAILHEAD

Take Highway 2 north from Leavenworth to the junction with Highway 207. Follow 207 for about 4 miles to the Road 62 junction. Follow 62 around Fish Lake and continue on 6200 to the Phelps Creek Trailhead in Section 27, T.30N., R.16E. The trailhead is about 23 miles from Highway 207 and Road 62 junction.

Parking: Adequate parking lot at Trinity Trailhead but limited at the new small Trinity Horse Camp.

Comments: This is a heavily used trail along Buck Creek into the Glacier Peak Wilderness with stock number and party size limited. Buck Pass at the west end of the trail near Buck Creek Pass is usually snow free by late July but is closed to horse camping.

Over Buck Pass the trail enters the Mt. Baker-Snoqualmie National Forest.

The sign at the trailhead notes the horse camping area is located on the southeast side of Buck Creek Pass. Remember to use established campsites. Also, signs at the Phelps Creek Trailhead read: "5 miles to Chiwawa Basin; Buck Creek Pass 9.5 miles; and Suiattle River Road 27 miles". The distance to Buck Creek Pass is now 10 miles due to trail changes.

CARNE MOUNTAIN TRAIL 1508

Trail Length: 3.7 Miles
Elevation: 3500 - 6500 Feet
Difficulty: Moderate
Open: June - October
Usage: Medium
Nearest Town: Leavenworth
Nearest Horse Camp: Trinity just beyond Phelps Creek Campground
Connecting Trails: 1511, 1509, 1528
Facilities at Trailhead: Loading ramp, hitch rail

DIRECTIONS

TO THE TRAILHEAD

Trail 1508 is reached by riding up the Phelps Creek Trail 1511 about 0.3 mile from the end of Road 6211.

Parking: Very limited at the Phelps Creek Trailhead located in Section 22, T.30N., R.16E. It is a narrow lot and it would be very difficult to turn a 4-horse trailer around. Use the Trinity Trailhead or the new Trinity Horse Camp just beyond the Phelps Creek Campground. This small horse camp was completed in 1996.

At the Trinity Trailhead area there is a large parking lot where the road ends at the Phelps Creek Bridge, but no camping. The Trinity Mine is beyond this location and from here the trails had to be relocated recently due to vandalism to mine property.

Comments: This trail enters the Glacier Peak Wilderness at the 3.5 mile point. By mid-July the trail is usually free of snow.

CHIWAWA RIVER TRAIL 1550

Trail Length: 5.5 Miles
Elevation: 3400 - 6900 Feet
Difficulty: Moderate
Open: June - October

Usage: Medium
Nearest Town: Leavenworth
Nearest Horse Camp: Chiwawa
Connecting Trails: 1513
Facilities at Trailhead: Loading ramp, toilet

DIRECTIONS

TO THE TRAILHEAD

Take Highway 2 north from Leavenworth to the junction with Highway 207. Follow 207 for about 4 miles to Road 62. Continue to follow Road 62 east around Fish Lake and then north to Road 6200 and on to the Trinity Trailhead located in Section 21, T.30N., R.16E.

It is about 23 miles from the Highway 207 junction to the Trinity Trailhead.

Parking: Large trailhead parking lot at Trinity Trailhead.

Comments: The access to Trail 1550 is a 1.5 miles ride up Trail 1513. The trail follows an old mining road and then is maintained to the Chiwawa Basin Trail junction. The last mile of the trail is access to Red Mountain but it is not maintained. This is not a loop ride.

Remember party size is limited for people and stock in the Glacier Peak Wilderness where Wilderness Regulations and permits apply.

ESTES BUTTE TRAIL 1527

Trail Length: 2.6 Miles
Elevation: 2470 - 5400 Feet
Difficulty: Moderate
Open: July - October
Usage: Light
Nearest Town: Leavenworth
Nearest Horse Camp: Chiwawa
Connecting Trails: 1528, 1509
Facilities at Trailhead: None, use horse camp

DIRECTIONS

TO THE TRAILHEAD

Take Highway 2 north from Leavenworth to the junction with Highway 207. Then follow 207 for about 4 miles to the junction with Road 62. Take 62 around Fish Lake about 14 miles to the Chiwawa Horse Camp near the Rock Creek Campground in Section 36, T.29N., R.16E.

Parking: Very small lot. Horse camp parking can be used.

Comments: Some segments of the trail were relocated in 1996 at the horse camp end. During the riding season, near the end of July when the snow is gone, this trail is steep and dry. It provides access to the old Estes Lookout site but now it is not maintained beyond the lookout. It does tie into the Old Gib Trail 1528 but that is also no longer maintained.

ROCK CREEK TRAIL 1509

Trail Length: 11.7 Miles
Elevation: 2500 - 6600 Feet
Difficulty: Moderate
Open: June - October
Usage: Medium
Nearest Town: Leavenworth
Nearest Horse Camp: Chiwawa
Connecting Trails: 1527, 1538, 1508
Facilities at Trailhead: None, use Chiwawa Horse Camp

DIRECTIONS

TO THE TRAILHEAD

From Leavenworth, take Highway 2 north to the junction with Highway 207. Follow 207 for about 4 miles to the junction with Road 62. The road signs read Chiwawa Valley. Road 62 follows the Chiwawa River north to the Chiwawa Horse Camp near the Rock Creek Campground. This route passes the Alder Creek Horse Camp in about 3 miles where Road 62 turns north.

Parking: Park at the Chiwawa Horse Camp for access to these trails. The actual trailhead parking for Trail 1509 is small and with cars present it will not accommodate horse trailers.

Comments: A day loop ride is possible by using Trail 1509 to connect to Trail 1538 then going south to Trail 1515 and back to Road 62. Take the Finner Tie Trail that follows the road back to the Chiwawa Horse Camp. This is a trail that is usually snow free by mid-June and the last 5 miles are usually snow free by mid-July.

Expect to meet mountain bikes on this trail along Rock Creek up to the Glacier Peak Wilderness Boundary (4.5 miles). The trailhead is in Section 36, T.29N., R.16E.

ROCK CREEK TIE TRAIL 1538

Trail Length: 1.6 Miles
Elevation: 3400 - 5200 Feet
Difficulty: Most Difficult
Open: June - October
Usage: Light
Nearest Town: Leavenworth
Nearest Horse Camp: Chiwawa
Connecting Trails: 1509, 1515
Facilities at Trailhead: Horse camp

DIRECTIONS

TO THE TRAILHEAD

From Leavenworth, take Highway 2 north to the junction with Highway 207. Follow 207 for about 4 miles to the junction with Road 62. The signs read Chiwawa Valley. This is Road 62 and leads to Road 6200 that goes to the Chiwawa Horse Camp located in Section 36, T.29N., R.17E.

Parking: Use the Chiwawa Horse Camp as parking is limited at the Rock Creek Trailhead.

Comments: The Rock Creek Tie Trail was relocated in 1995 to make it suitable for stock. It ties Trail 1509 to Trail 1515 and now makes a loop ride possible.

PHELPS CREEK TRAIL 1511

Trail Length: 7.2 Miles
Elevation: 3500 - 7000 Feet
Difficulty: Moderate
Open: July - October
Usage: Heavy
Nearest Town: Leavenworth
Nearest Horse Camp: Trinity, just past Phelps Creek Campground
Connecting Trails: 1508
Facilities at Trailhead: Loading ramp, hitch rail

DIRECTIONS

TO THE TRAILHEAD

Take Highway 2 north from Leavenworth to the junction with
Highway 207. Turn right and follow 207 for about 4 miles to the
junction of Road 62 that goes east around Fish Lake. The signs read
Chiwawa River Valley. This road follows the Chiwawa River and
becomes 6200 and goes past the Chiwawa Horse Camp. Continue on
6200 to Phelps Creek where Road 6211 takes off to the right. It is
about 1.5 miles further on to the small trailhead located in Section 22,
T.30N., R.16E.

Parking: Very limited, narrow parking area where it could be very
difficult to turn a 4-horse trailer around due to heavy use by cars.
Beyond the Phelps Creek Campground 0.1 mile, the Trinity Trailhead
area has additional parking.

Comments: This trail along Phelps Creek enters the Glacier Peak
Wilderness at 2.6 miles. It is a high use area and Wilderness Regulations apply with group size limited. The last mile of the trail and the
Upper Phelps Basin is closed to horses. This is not a loop ride, so the
return is by the same route. If planning to camp overnight, it is a good
idea to bring a propane stove as firewood is becoming scarce in this
area.

Map 31

Washington State Forests
Yacolt Burn State Forest - Rock Creek

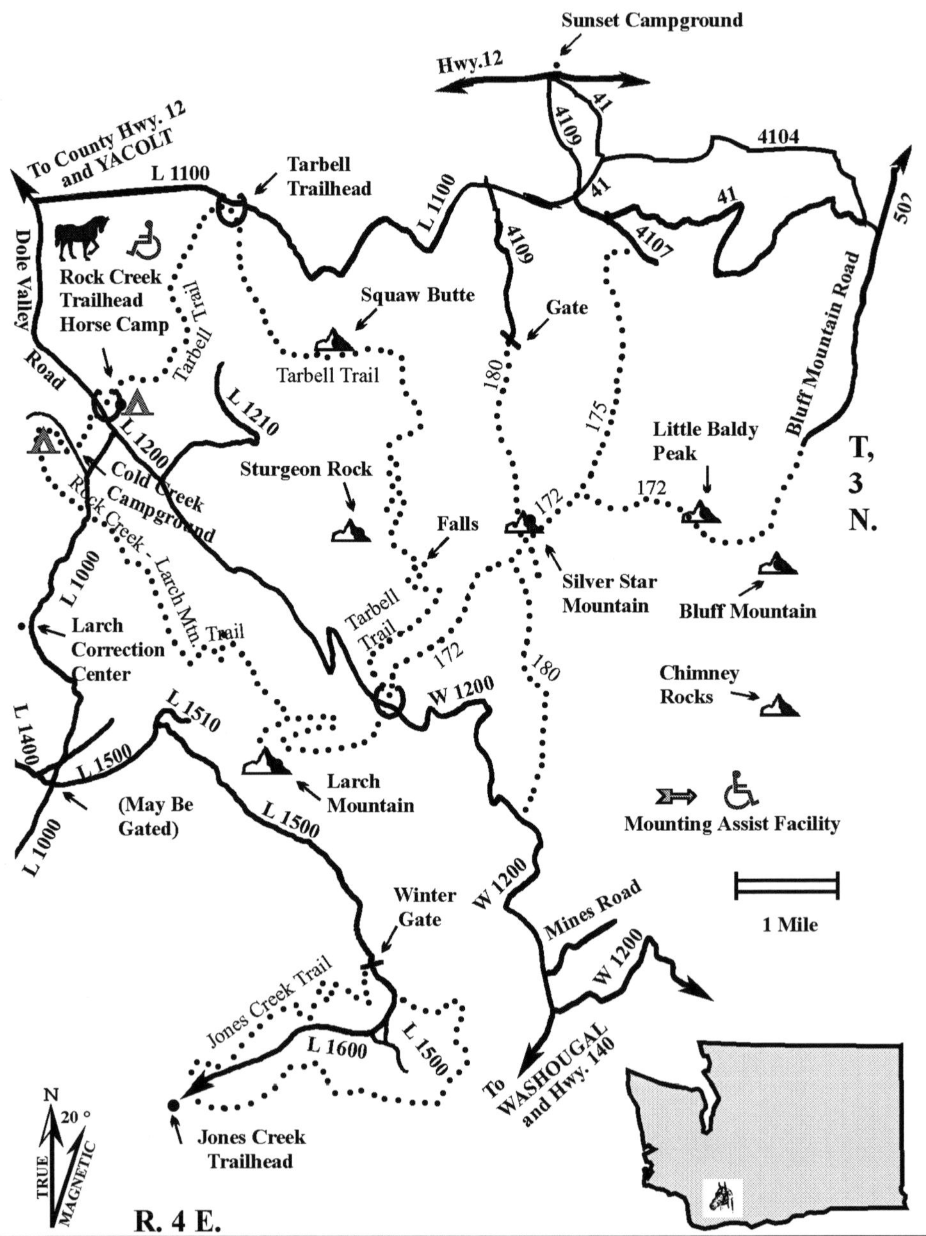

Sunset Campground

Hwy.12

4109

41

4104

To County Hwy. 12 and YACOLT

L 1100

Tarbell Trailhead

L 1100

41

4107

41

502

Dole Valley Road

Rock Creek Trailhead Horse Camp

Tarbell Trail

Squaw Butte

Tarbell Trail

4109

Gate

180

175

Bluff Mountain Road

Little Baldy Peak

T, 3 N.

L 1210

Sturgeon Rock

L 1200

Cold Creek Campground

Rock Creek - Larch Mtn.

L 1000

Falls

172

172

172

Silver Star Mountain

Bluff Mountain

Larch Correction Center

Trail

Tarbell Trail

172

180

Chimney Rocks

L 1400

L 1510

L 1500

L 1500

W 1200

Larch Mountain

(May Be Gated)

L 1000

Mounting Assist Facility

1 Mile

Winter Gate

W 1200

Mines Road

W 1200

Jones Creek Trail

L 1600

L 1500

To WASHOUGAL and Hwy. 140

N

20°

TRUE

MAGNETIC

Jones Creek Trailhead

R. 4 E.

Rock Creek Area and Horse Camp:

The Rock Creek area offers trails which require that riders and horses be in good condition. Trails lead to views of Rock Creek Canyon and the Camas City Watershed. The trail travels through forests and high brush on the way to upper sections of loop trails. There are a few waterfalls and usually some vegetation in bloom. A quiet moment at Grouse Vista may bring a serenade of grouse from the tall grass. The 23 mile loop trail connects with many logging roads so be sure and carry a map and know how to use your compass.

The bridges across the wet areas and creeks do not have side rails so your horse should be well practiced at calmly crossing a wood bridge. Some sections of the trail are steep and lead to rocky ledges that may concern an inexperienced rider or horse.

To get the most from this area know your horse's condition and its abilities.

Rock Creek Horse Camp is located in Section 9, T.3N., R.4E. in southeast Washington off I-205. Take the Battle Ground exit for Highway 503. Follow 503 north for 14 miles and turn right onto County Road 12 past the Moulton Falls. Turn right on Dole Valley Road and Rock Creek Horse Camp will be on your left after about 5 miles.

Facilities include 19 tie stalls, 6 picnic tables, toilet and drinking water.

A 23 mile loop trail is possible from the camp along with several shorter loops. This is a high use area and extra courtesy will assure a better time for everyone. Endurance riders train here in the summer so the camp fills up fast. You can call ahead to DNR for information about availability of camping space which is distributed on a first-come basis.

BLUFF MOUNTAIN TRAIL 172

Trail Length: 7.8 Miles
Elevation: 3200 - 3100 Feet
Difficulty: Most Difficult
Open: July - October
Usage: Light
Nearest Town: Camas
Nearest Horse Camp: Rock Creek
Connecting Trails: Tarbell Pump Trail, 180, 175
Facilities at Trailhead: None

DIRECTIONS

TO THE TRAILHEAD

From Vancouver take Highway 503 north through Battle Ground. About 6 miles past Battle Ground turn left (east) at the Lucia-Moulton Falls intersection onto County Road 12. Follow 12 about 11 miles to the Dole Valley Road and turn right. It will become Road L1000 after crossing Rock Creek. Continue on past Rock Creek Campground as this road now turns into L1200 0.8 mile past the Rock Creek Campground. At the intersection of Spur Road L1210 it is about 3.8 miles further to Grouse Vista. Watch mileage to avoid passing the parking area on Road W 1200! The trailhead is at the north end of the parking area in Section 24, T.3N., R.4E. The south end of the Tarbell Pump Trail is also there.

From Road 1200 North, it is just over 2 miles (mostly uphill) to the junction with Trail 180 that goes south to connect with Trail 172. Another 0.5 mile past the junction with Trail 180 the Silver Star Mountain Trail takes an easterly turn around Silver Star Mountain and follows a ridge to give a view of the Vancouver - Portland area.

Another route to the trailhead is to take Road 12 to Sunset Campground. Then follow Road 41 to the intersection with Road 502. Park here and ride south on an old road for about 2.3 miles to the trailhead at the northeast end of Trail 172.

Parking: Parking area is primitive and rough. Park along the roads at intersections and vista.

Comments: The trail winds through the 1902 Yacolt burn that covered 238,900 acres. There are deep wooded pockets of Noble fir and open areas with wild flowers.

ROCK CREEK TO COLD CREEK TRAIL

Trail Length: 6.6 Miles
Elevation: 1000 - 3500 Feet
Difficulty: Moderate
Open: May - November
Usage: Heavy
Nearest Town: Camas
Nearest Horse Camp: Rock Creek
Connecting Trails: Tarbell
Facilities at Trailhead: Horse stalls, loading ramp, hitch rails, campsites, water, toilet

DIRECTIONS

TO THE TRAILHEAD

From Vancouver take Highway 503 north toward Battle Ground. About six miles past Battle Ground turn right (east) at the Lucia-Moulton intersection onto County Road 12. Follow 12 past Moulton Falls Park to the Dole Valley Road and turn south (right) to the Rock Creek Horse Camp. Go south from the camp for 0.5 mile on Road 1000. Turn right onto Road 1300 and follow it to the camp on your left. The State Forest map may show a road to Cold Creek from the north but it is blocked.

Parking: Ample for 20 trailer rigs.

Comments: This trail begins near the entrance to the campground on the northeast side of the creek. The sign reads, "Cold Creek Campground 1.5 miles." The next mile of trail goes uphill and may be wet late into the year. The trail crosses Road 1300 and then about 0.5 mile further is Cold Creek Camp. Follow the east side of the creek and take the right fork to cross the creek on a bridge. The trail crosses the creek several times.

At Road 1000, the trail continues across the road and uphill to another fork that leads back to camp or you can follow the main trail further to Larch Mountain. Several switchbacks lead to another road. There are no signs, but the trail continues ahead to more switchbacks and a rocky bench with views of the valley floor and mountain ranges.

The trail widens onto a hillside of shale. Beyond the shale the trail is rocky to the intersection with the Tarbell Trail at Larch Mountain. Views to the north are of Rock Creek Canyon and to the south of the City of Camas Watershed.

This trail connects with 172 to Silver Star Mountain and a series of switchbacks make this a steep and rugged ride. Views are of Mount St. Helens, Mt. Hood, Mt. Rainier, Three Corner Rock, Vancouver and Camas.

ROCK CREEK TO TARBELL PUMP TRAIL

Trail Length: 2.6 Miles
Elevation: 1000 - 1600 Feet
Difficulty: Moderate
Open: May - November
Usage: Heavy
Nearest Town: Camas
Nearest Horse Camp: Rock Creek
Connecting Trails: Tarbell, Rock Creek, Larch Mountain, 172
Facilities at Trailhead: At Tarbell Pump, picnic and camp area, water, toilet

DIRECTIONS

TO THE TRAILHEAD

From Vancouver take Highway 503 north toward Battle Ground. Follow 503 past Battle Ground about 6 miles and turn right (east) at the Lucia-Moulton intersection onto County Road 12. Follow 12 past Moulton Falls Park to the Dole Valley Road on the right. Turn south (right) to the Rock Creek Horse Camp. Go south from the camp for 0.3 mile and turn left on Road 1200. Next go about 0.5 mile and take the left fork of the "Y" in the road and continue for 4 miles on Road L1210. Tarbell is at the junction of Road 1100 in Section 34, T.4N., R.4E.

Parking: Small area for 3 to 4 rigs and some roadside parking.

Comments: Access to the trail at Rock Creek is at the north end of the Day Use area. Just across the grassy area the trail leads to the north bank and climbs in a northerly direction for its entire length. The creek is wide and shallow with a rocky bottom that makes for easy crossings but the bank is steep on the north side. This is a spot to leave room for the horse in front to get up the bank before you start. The trail is well marked, crossing several small bogs with bridges so stay on the trail which continues to Tarbell Pump across Road L1216 and later across Road L1215.

TARBELL PUMP TRAIL

Trail Length: 13.9 Miles
Elevation: 1000 - 1600 Feet
Difficulty: Most Difficult
Open: May - November
Usage: Heavy
Nearest Town: Camas
Nearest Horse Camp: Rock Creek
Connecting Trails: Tarbell to Rock Creek, 172, Rock Creek to Cold Creek
Facilities at Trailhead: At Rock Creek Horse Camp, tie stalls, drinking water, campsites, toilet

DIRECTIONS

TO THE TRAILHEAD

From Vancouver take Highway 503 north toward Battle Ground. About six miles past Battle Ground at the Lucia-Moulton intersection turn east onto Road 12. Follow 12 past Moulton Falls Park to the Dole

Valley Road and turn south (right) for about 2 miles to the junction with Road L1100. Follow Road L1100 for about 2 miles to Tarbell Pump in Section 34, T.4N., R.4E.

Parking: Ample, with camp area and roadside parking.

Comments: This well marked trail from the Tarbell Trailhead to Larch Mountain goes through timber, brush, huckleberries, beargrass and Indian Paintbrush depending on the season. It climbs to an overlook on the Rock Creek drainage. After the first waterfall on this trail, a long section of switchbacks ends with a crossing of Coyote Creek followed by more steep switchbacks. Sturgeon Rock can be seen to the west.

At 3100 feet elevation the trail descends to another waterfall at Grouse Creek and to Trail 172 to Silver Star Mountain. This section has steep, rocky sections that are narrow in places. At the junction with Road L1200, the trail is difficult to locate for a short distance. After that it turns west and skirts Rock Creek Canyon with views of Larch Mountain, Sturgeon Rock and Pyramid Rock. The trail is wide but rocky with shale outcrops for the next 2.8 miles until it intersects with Rock Creek at Larch Mountain. The going will be slow, so know your ability and that of your horse if riding this section.

Other Trail Users
—Photos courtesy of Washington State Department of Natural Resources

Map 32

Washington State Forests
Yacolt Burn State Forest - 3 Corner Rock

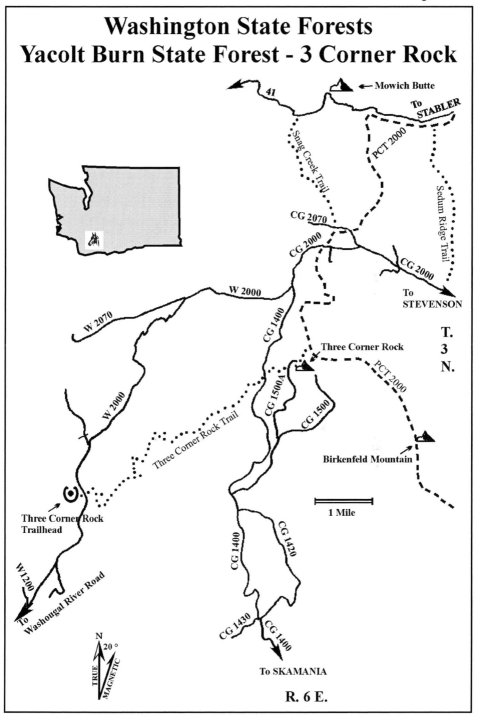

THREE CORNER ROCK TRAIL

Trail Length: 12.0 Miles
Elevation: 900 - 3500 Feet
Difficulty: Most Difficult
Open: July - October
Usage: Heavy
Nearest Town: Washougal
Nearest Horse Camp: Rock Creek
Connecting Trails: 2000
Facilities at Trailhead: Loading ramp, stalls, hitch rails, toilets

DIRECTIONS

TO THE TRAILHEAD

From Vancouver take Highway 14 east to Washougal. Go north from Washougal on Highway 140 along the Washougal River Canyon to the Washougal River Road. At the steel bridge take the West River Road north to the junction with the 2000 Road which goes to the trailhead. The trailhead is about 23 miles from Washougal in Section 31, T.3N., R.6E.

Parking: Ample at the Trailhead.

Comments: Trails in this area are designed for horse and hikers. The Three Corner Rock Trail goes from the Washougal River through the old Yacolt Burn (Yacolt Burn State Forest) to the site of the former Three Corner Rock fire lookout tower. The Pacific Crest National Recreation Trail 2000 is 0.8 mile beyond the site. A horse water trough is available at the junction of Trail 2000 and the Three Corner Rock Trail. Surrounding views are spectacular from Three Corner Rock. Hikers, mountain bikes and horses are all permitted on this trail.

Several crossings of Stebbins Creek, the bridges and a number of switchbacks test a horse's condition. There is a road crossing at about 7.5 miles just before the climb up to Three Corner Rock.

Map 33

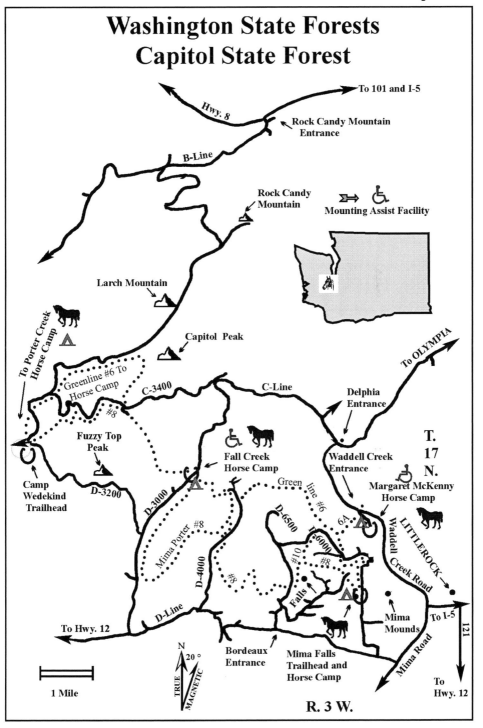

Washington State Forests
Capitol State Forest

To 101 and I-5

Hwy. 8

Rock Candy Mountain
Entrance

B-Line

Rock Candy
Mountain

Mounting Assist Facility

Larch Mountain

Capitol Peak

To Porter Creek Horse Camp

Greenline #6 To Horse Camp

C-3400

C-Line

Delphia
Entrance

To OLYMPIA

#8

Fuzzy Top
Peak

Fall Creek
Horse Camp

Waddell Creek
Entrance

Margaret McKenny
Horse Camp

T.
17
N.

Camp
Wedekind
Trailhead

D-3200

D-3000

Green line #6

Mima Porter #8

D-6500

6A

Waddell Creek Road

LITTLEROCK

#10

#600

#8

D-4000

#8

Falls

Mima
Mounds

To I-5

121

To Hwy. 12

D-Line

N
20°

TRUE

MAGNETIC

Bordeaux
Entrance

Mima Falls
Trailhead and
Horse Camp

To
Hwy. 12

Mima Road

1 Mile

R. 3 W.

CAPITOL STATE FOREST

This area has five horse use areas, Margaret McKenny, Porter Creek, Fall Creek, Mima Mounds and Camp Wedekind and Fall Creek Day-Use area. See the Book section on Horse Camps.

Capitol State Forest located 15 miles east of Olympia is a 84,000 acre multiple use area managed by the Washington State Department of Natural Resources (DNR). Multiple use means that horseback riding, hiking, trail bike riding, camping and hunting and a rifle range co-exist with timber harvest. Clearcuts and harvested stands are in various phases of regeneration and growth. An excellent topographic map of the forest has a color code system to designate horse use trails. To reach the area take I-5 to the Littlerock Exit 95 and follow Highway 121 west to Littlerock.

From high ridges on the forest the Puget Sound is visible as well as the Olympics, Cascades, Mount St. Helens, Mt. Rainier, and Mount Adams. An added feature in the area is the Mima Mounds geological site near the Mima Horse Camp. There is speculation on the origin of this geological phenomenon.

The five camps designed for horse use may have some construction evident, especially Fall Creek Horse Camp where parking is being expanded. All have parking, fire rings, toilets and horse holding facilities. The trails are well signed and in good shape most of the time although there can be muddy stretches during the wetter times of the year. Most of the competing use from trail bikes has been separated from the horse use through thoughtful management by DNR. Please limit your stay to no more than 7 days.

Primary ride opportunities from each horse camp and loop rides are identified on the Trail Map. Many horseback activities are scheduled for this area during the riding season so check with the DNR as to planned events.

CAPITOL FOREST TRAILS AND CAMPS OPEN TO HORSES

Trail length: Extensive miles are available from each camp
Elevation: 100 - 2660 Feet (Capitol Peak)
Difficulty: Moderate
Open: Year Around
Usage: Light mid-week, very heavy on event weekends
Nearest Town: Littlerock
Nearest Horse Camp: 5 horse camps and 1 day use area
Connecting Trails: Well signed loop trail rides from each horse camp. For example, use the Green Line 6 trail as a starting base at Margaret McKenny Camp
Facilities at Horse Camp: See Book section on horse camps

MARGARET McKENNY HORSE CAMP: (Mounting Assist Ramp)
FALL CREEK HORSE CAMP
PORTER CREEK HORSE CAMP
CAMP WEDEKIND CAMP (Group Gatherings)
MIMA FALLS CAMP
FALL CREEK DAY-USE CAMP (Mounting Assist Ramp)

Map 34

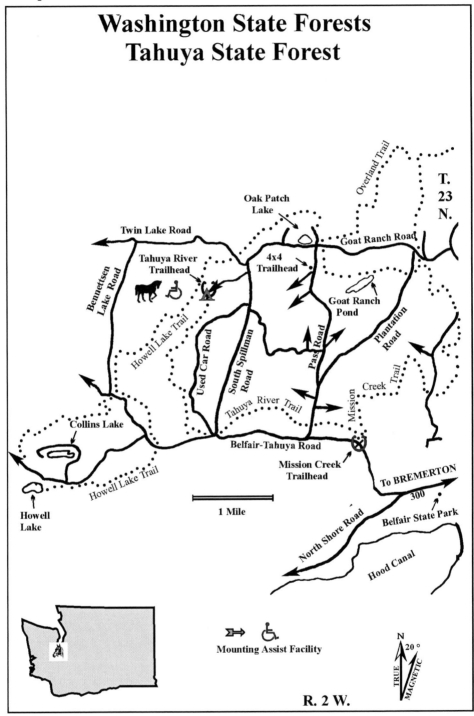

Washington State Forests
Tahuya State Forest

Overland Trail

T.
23
N.

Oak Patch
Lake

Twin Lake Road

Goat Ranch Road

Tahuya River
Trailhead

4x4
Trailhead

Bennettsen Lake Road

Goat Ranch
Pond

Howell Lake Trail

Used Car Road

South Spillman Road

Pass Road

Plantation Road

Creek Trail

Tahuya River Trail

Mission

Collins Lake

Belfair-Tahuya Road

Mission Creek
Trailhead

To BREMERTON

300

Howell Lake Trail

1 Mile

Belfair State Park

Howell
Lake

North Shore Road

Hood Canal

Mounting Assist Facility

N
20°

TRUE
MAGNETIC

R. 2 W.

TAHUYA RIVER CAMP and MISSION CREEK TRAILHEAD

Trail Length: Over 37 Miles of multiple use trails
Elevation: 100 - 500 Feet
Difficulty: Moderate
Open: Year around, temporary closures for logging
Usage: Heavy
Nearest Town: Belfair (north of Shelton)
Nearest Horse Camp: Tahuya River Camp
Connecting Trails: Howell Lake, Tahuya River, Mission Creek, Overland
Facilities at Trailhead: Drinking water, toilet at Tahuya River Trailhead

DIRECTIONS

TO THE TRAILHEAD

From Bremerton take Highway 3 south to the junction of 3 and Road 300. Follow 300 (North Shore Road) approximately 6 miles to the junction with Tahuya Road. Mission Creek Trailhead is within 2 miles in Section 35, T.23N., R.2W. It provides a day use only staging area to the multiple use trails. There are no toilets at the Mission Creek Trailhead.

Parking: Adequate at Mission Creek Trailhead for horse rigs.

Comments: The Tahuya River Camp in Section 21, T.23N., R.2W. is the only designated horse camp in the Tahuya State Forest. It has 11 campsites that fill quickly during the summer and for horse events. There are 20 horse corrals so the camp is primarily used by horse riders although other users are permitted. When the horse camp is full trail riders can park at any of the trailheads and tie horses to trailers, not trees, and stay to ride. There are no campsites at these alternate trailheads.

The trails are in several user classes that are intended to provide some separation between 4-wheel users (called two track trails) and horses, motor bikes and bicycles (called single track trails). Watch for these different trail signs. The Tahuya State Forest Recreation Map does not show the primitive level single track trails.

The forest has 37 miles of multiple use year-round trails so expect to meet hikers, mountain bikes and motorized equipment. Avoid any user-built trails that may lead you off the official Grey Diamond and Blue Diamond marked trails.

Howell Lake, Tahuya State Forest
—Photo courtesy of Washington State Department of Natural Resources

Map 35

Washington State Forests
Tiger Mountain State Forest

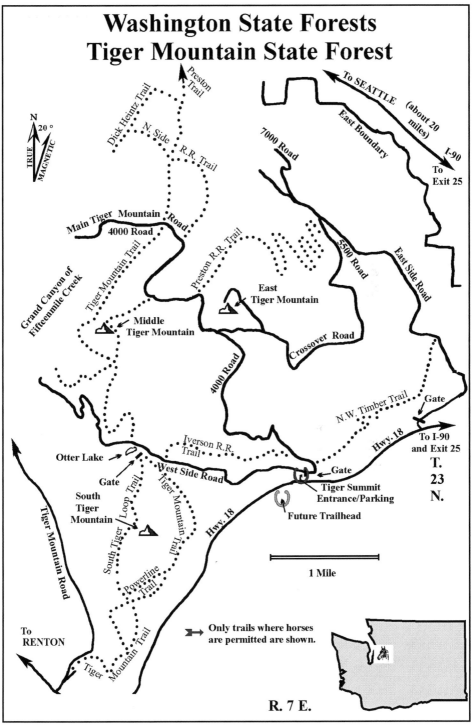

N 20°
TRUE MAGNETIC

To SEATTLE (about 20 miles)
I-90
To Exit 25

East Boundary

7000 Road

Preston Trail

Dick Heinz Trail

N. Side R.R. Trail

Main Tiger Mountain Road

4000 Road

Tiger Mountain Trail

Preston R.R. Trail

5500 Road

East Side Road

East Tiger Mountain

Grand Canyon of Fifteenmile Creek

Middle Tiger Mountain

Crossover Road

4000 Road

N.W. Timber Trail

Gate

Hwy. 18

To I-90 and Exit 25

T. 23 N.

Iverson R.R. Trail

Otter Lake

West Side Road

Gate

Tiger Summit Entrance/Parking

Gate

Future Trailhead

South Tiger Mountain

South Tiger Loop Trail

Tiger Mountain Trail

Tiger Mountain Road

Powerline Trail

Hwy. 18

To RENTON

Tiger Mountain Trail

1 Mile

Only trails where horses are permitted are shown.

R. 7 E.

TIGER MOUNTAIN STATE FOREST

Trail Length: 35 Miles
Elevation: 400 - 2600 Feet
Difficulty: Difficult
Open: Year around
Usage: Heavy
Nearest Town: Renton, also 15 miles from Seattle
Nearest Horse Camp: None
Connecting Trails: Many short loop trails
Facilities at Trailhead: None

DIRECTIONS

TO THE TRAILHEAD

From Renton access the Tiger Summit Entrance and the Tiger Mountain Trail on the south side of the forest by taking the Maple Valley Highway 169 east for 10 miles to Maple Valley. Next follow Highway 18 northeast 3.5 miles to the Tiger Mountain Trail. From here it is 3.1 miles further to the Tiger Summit Entrance located in Section 20, T.23N., R.7E.

From Seattle, going east on I-90, take Exit 25 onto Highway 18. Follow 18 south for 4.3 miles along the east side of Tiger Mountain State Forest to the Tiger Summit Entrance. State Forest literature states a new trailhead is planned for near here.

There is also access to Tiger Mountain Trail just 0.3 miles up SE Tiger Mountain Road at the south end of the forest. This is only 3.1 miles from the trailhead where Highway 18 meets SE Tiger Mountain Road.

Parking: Very limited for trailer rigs.

Comments: There are no horse camping facilities in this State Forest and many of the trails for horses, hikers and mountain bikes have seasonal closures.

The 13,000 acre forest covers Tiger Mountain and is another part of the Washington State DNR Trust Lands. It is comprised of several land segments that have other names and access regulations. A DNR map of the forest area will help ensure your enjoyment and protection.

Map 36

Washington State Forests
Green Mountain State Forest

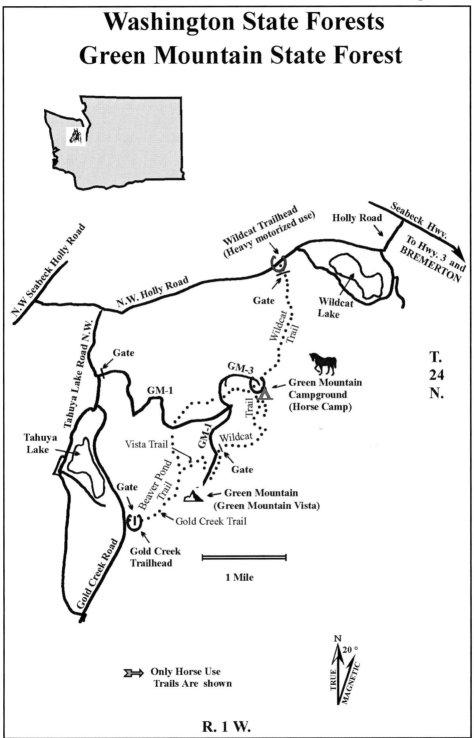

T.
24
N.

Only Horse Use
Trails Are shown

1 Mile

R. 1 W.

GREEN MOUNTAIN STATE FOREST TRAILS

Trail Length: 8.5 Miles
Elevation: 500 - 1690 Feet
Difficulty: Moderate
Open: Year Around
Usage: Moderate to Heavy
Nearest Town: Bremerton
Nearest Horse Camp: Green Mountain Vista Campground
Connecting Trails: See Trail Map for loop trails
Facilities at Trailhead: Toilets

DIRECTIONS

TO THE TRAILHEAD

Access from Bremerton (on Highway 3) is by taking Kitsap Road north 1.1 miles to North Lake Way. Turn right and proceed for 1.1 miles to the Seabeck Highway. Turn left and follow Seabeck Highway 3 miles to N.W. Holly Road. The Wildcat Trailhead (north end of forest) will be on your left in 1.8 miles in Section 3, T.24N., R.1W. This trailhead has heavy use from bikers so trail riders usually continue on to the Gold Creek Trailhead in Section 20.

Gold Creek Trailhead is reached by continuing on Holly Road about 2.5 miles to Tahuya Lake Road N.W. Turn left and follow Tahuya Lake Road N.W. for about 1.3 mile to the junction with the Gold Creek Road that goes along the east side of Tahuya Lake. Gold Creek Trail is about 1.5 mile past that road junction on Gold Creek Road.

Campgrounds in the State Forest are by trail access only and there is no overnight camping at the trailheads where you park.

Parking: Adequate at trailheads for horse trailers, Gold Creek has the most parking space.

Comments: This is another working State Forest with a system of trails for hikers, horse riders, mountain bikes and motor bikes in various mixes. Although there are two trailheads in this forest, neither trailheads or campgrounds provide for overnight stay with horses and it is necessary to carry your own drinking water. This area was re-opened in 1993 after a closure due to extensive vandalism. Stewardship is the camping emphasis now.

A loop ride is possible but there is always the potential for meeting logging trucks and heavy equipment as you cross roads. While the trails are open seven days a week year-round, the campgrounds are open at various times based on the seasons and are by trail access only.

Bridge needs repairing: report the problem
—Photo courtesy of Washington State Department of Natural Resources

Chapter 6

MAP AND COMPASS

Trail Riders Can Keep From Getting Lost: There must be a reason why almost every list of what riders should carry in the back-country includes a compass. Is it because people get lost?

People can and do get lost. But knowing how to use a compass can keep you from staying lost. If you have never owned a compass, this chapter will give you an idea of the type to buy. If you already carry a compass on the trail but have never tried it, this chapter will show you how it works and how to use it. Don't give up. Work your way through the various steps. It does take practice to learn to use a compass. This chapter is intended to give you the skills to practice and use a compass, and read a map. The two go together.

We begin this chapter with some reminders about backcountry travel that relate to not getting lost and to using a map and compass. Before there is a need to use the compass, we can learn from others why they have gotten lost and maybe avoid the same mistakes. Here are reasons that people get lost.

1. They lacked knowledge about the area selected for the trail ride. They did not study the area or gather information about it so they did not recognize road junctions, trail crossings or land features.
2. They never looked back over the route just traveled so they did not recognize a location on the return trip. (Even on known trails this is a good practice.)
3. They were forced to take an unplanned route because of bad weather or a person's physical condition, the route was blocked by snow or downed timber, or a horse became injured.

4. They got excited or panicked over some situation like an injury, unexpected severe weather, or not being able to get back to camp before darkness.

5. They lacked map and, especially, compass skills and the confidence to use either.

Be Aware: A good way to keep track of where you are as you trail ride is to talk with companions about the area. Be aware of things you see like unusual tree snags, trail hazards, rock formations, and small creeks crossed. We were once riding between two lakes in a northwest National Forest wilderness. At one of the lakes, a small party of riders crossed the creek and reined up to let us pass with our two pack horses. As greetings were exchanged, they asked which lake they had just passed. They were on a day ride and expected to make a loop ride back to their camp. The trouble was the loop could not be easily ridden that day in the daylight left. Even with their topographic wilderness map they had lost recognition of the lakes they had passed and were unable to determine their location.

Start being aware before leaving your vehicle or camp since that is when everyone knows their location. Take the time to look around and see what the area nearby looks like. What is the trail like? Is a creek flowing in the same direction you were traveling when you left camp? What is the road direction at the campsite? *Be aware!*

It is a good idea to start being aware even before you leave home. Do that by letting someone know your destination and probable route. One search was for a party of three after a family emergency at home. Their trail ride route had changed in the wilderness and several days were lost in the Forest Service's effort to locate them.

You may never have had such a problem on a trail ride. But if there are times when you would like to understand a bit more about how to read a map and use a compass, this chapter should help. It provides several approaches to map and compass techniques. Included are both basic and general information on how to read a map, use a compass, apply an azimuth reading to your map (that just means a direction or bearing in degrees) and more. An introductory level of map and compass knowledge can help you identify a mountain, or select the next campsite; it may be important to you and your group for safety, or maybe you just want to know how to use the thing!

This may be the first horse trail riding book that includes a chapter about map and compass use. The techniques described in the printed information received when you purchase a compass may vary from these techniques. Decide which is the most practical and easiest for you to use. These methods are presented in the same manner used in classes for mounted search and rescue volunteers and for saddle club members. There are also some well-written books on map and compass use and you are urged to look to them for additional study. There are general comments about maps before the compass is discussed. We suggest you skim the map information even if you are fully comfortable with maps.

Information Covered

Map types to use
How to find where you are on your map—Land Survey
What a map tells you—Legend
Contour lines—Intervals
Compass types and how to read them
Declination—what it is and how and why to take it into account
True North and Magnetic North
Orienting your compass to Magnetic North—Practice
Orienting your map to True North—Practice
Which peak is that?
How to follow compass direction (azimuth) or put it on your map
What is the direction to a peak or between landmarks?
Back sighting
Where am I?—Triangulation
List of some essential items to carry

Trail rides can be greater fun, and probably safer, if we know how to read a map and use a compass. Experienced riders know that even though they never expect to have to leave a trail, there is the possibility of a sudden snowstorm, a foggy, rainy day, or a trail route change that will cause them to pull out the map and reach for the compass. If you are already experienced with map and compass maybe these pages can help you share knowledge with others. The Boy Scouts have it right: Be Prepared!

So how do we start? What type of map do we use?

It is hard to imagine any trail ride without several maps along. There are three map types trail riders can use. **(1)** state highway maps show how to drive to the area but are no help on the trail; **(2)** U.S. Forest Service recreation maps show ranger stations and other constructed features, plus streams, peaks, trailheads, campgrounds, roads and trails. **(3)** essential topographic maps contain the information on the forest recreation map plus contour lines to show differences in elevation. (More on contour lines later in the chapter.) Many National Forest wilderness maps and all U.S. Geological Survey (U.S.G.S.) maps (Quads) are topographic maps. Several companies now produce the maps of public lands and these are also usually topographic. Each trail rider (as well as hiker, camper or hunter) should carry—and know how to read and follow—a topographic map for the area they plan to enjoy.

Map Legend: A map legend is more helpful than some trail riders may realize. It gives the map scale, the date of information on which the map is based, and the elevation change between contour lines. A sketch will usually show magnetic and true north arrows with the degrees of declination for the map area. In addition, the legend may include, with many others, symbols for road quality, horse camps, trailheads, campgrounds, facility sites, streams, swamps, peaks, waterfalls, and Forest Service or other land management offices.

Since most trail riders take the time to learn the quality of road they will travel into the area, the map date is important because it is a clue to what may be road and trail changes. National Forest trails and roads are often being relocated, are closed, or are even dropped from the trail and road system for a variety of reasons. Carry the latest edition of the map for the area you plan to visit. Older maps remain of use for recognizing abandoned routes not shown on later maps.

Map Scales: Maps are drawn to scale. That means a certain distance on the map represents a certain distance on earth. Because a map represents, at a reduced size, a part of the earth's surface, the amount of reduction is the map's scale. A common recreation map scale is one inch to the mile where one inch on the map represents one mile on the ground. This is written 1:62,500 (62,500 being the approximate number of inches in a mile). The map legend will usually present the scale as a bar or ruler where the length represents some distance on the ground, for example, a 1-inch bar may represent 1 mile. A few maps are now drawn to metric scale, as 1:100,000, where one centimeter on the map represents one kilometer on the ground. Here is the time to remember that there are approximately 2.5 centimeters to the inch and 1.6 kilometers to the mile.

A popular and useful topographic map type is the U.S. Geological Survey (U.S.G.S). Quad series with a scale is 1:24,000. One inch on the map represents 2,000 feet on the ground (so 12 inches x 2,000' =24,000). This is a larger scale than 1:62,500 (1 inch to the mile). With a scale of about 2.5 inches to the mile, the map of 1:24,000 contains more detail and is easier to read. Trail riders should know the scale of their map and be able to estimate distance and riding time when trail miles are not shown on the map.

Land Survey - How to read where you are on a map: Trail riders tend to use land survey language to find places on a map and describe a place to meet or camp so a bit of background may help you understand the survey words of section, township and range.

The lines that form the grids across a map represent land surveys that started in the Northwest in the 1800s. Western lands were surveyed into six-mile squares called townships. There are 36 starting points in the western United States that were established for surveys. That point for Washington and Oregon was a marker placed at what is now called Willamette Stone State Park located on Skyline Boulevard in the hills above Portland, Oregon. This survey monument was set in place in the mid-1800s at the intersection of two lines. The east-west one is called the Willamette Baseline and the north-south one is called the Willamette Meridian.

Other survey lines were run at six-mile intervals parallel to the east-west baseline and to the north-south meridian. The first row of townships (north) above the baseline is called Township 1 North (T.1 N.). The first row (south) below the baseline is Township 1 South (T.1 S.). You find these noted on the side margins of maps. Survey lines that run north and south are called range lines and are numbered consecutively east and west of the Willamette Meridian. They are noted at the top and bottom of a map. The first range column or tier east of the meridian is called

Range 1 East (R.1 E.) and the first tier west is named Range 1 West (R.1 W.) These are shown in *Figure 1*. All trail maps in the book show a township (T) and range (R) number to help you locate the trail map area on a larger recreation map.

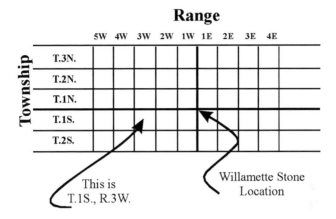

Figure 1. Township and range lines

A six-mile square township is further divided into 36 sections, which are one mile on each side. *(Figure 2)* (There are occasional exceptions related to errors in surveys and as they approached other survey starting points.)

**Figure 2.
How sections are
numbered**

6	5	4	3	2	1
7	8	9	10	11	12
18	17	16	15	14	13
19	20	21	22	23	24
30	29	28	27	26	25
31	32	33	34	35	36

Sections are numbered starting with *1* in the upper right or northeast corner and continue to *36* in the lower right or southeast corner. Most maps show either just those two section numbers or all 36 numbers.

Sections are a mile square and can be divided into smaller units to describe land ownership or some location like a trail junction. For example, in *Figure 3*, a trail location past the lake would be described as being in the Southeast 1/4 of the Southeast 1/4 of Section 11. It would be written as; SE 1/4, SE 1/4, Sec. 11, T.3N., R.7E. Other parts of the section are also named as examples.

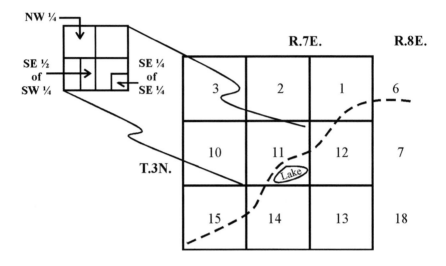

Figure 3. Locating areas in a section

Contour Lines on a Topographic Map: Contour lines on a map are brown and represent equal elevation on the ground. They convert a recreation map into a topographic map. Each line is the height or elevation above sea level; every fifth line is darker and labeled with the elevation, such as 5,600 feet. The difference in elevation from one line to another is the *contour interval*, noted in the map legend as C.I., along with a statement of the interval, such as *80 feet*. The lines are drawn closer together on steep ground, a clear signal that a trail across them will mean hard work for the trail horse. While a trail along them will mean a steep-sided hill below and above the trail. You can also tell the shape of features like a hill, pass or ridge from contour lines. Contour lines point down a ridge but point up a stream. Carry and use a topographic map in order to help know what is ahead in the ride.

The one-page copy of part of a topographic wilderness map at the end of this chapter has a scale of 2.0 inches to the mile (1:31,680). The following features are identifiable by contour lines on the page: A is a peak top; B is a steep ridge; C is a stream; D is a steep hill; E is a saddle area between two peaks; F is a steep trail area; and G is a gentle slope. Can you visualize the shape of the feature?

Compass; Often Number 1 on the Essential Lists

This simple but reliable instrument comes in many sizes and shapes. All have one thing in common: a magnetized needle that points to a place on earth where there is a strong magnetic attraction (magnetic north). *Figure 4* shows the parts of a compass.

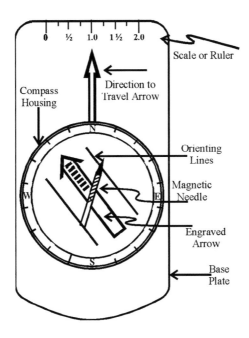

Figure 4. Compass parts

The magnetic needle is balanced so that it rotates in a housing with a rim usually marked in two-degree increments. The letter N, or the numerals 0 or 360 represents north. Since north, east, south and west are each 90 degrees apart, east is at 90 degrees, south is at 180 degrees and west is at 270 degrees.

The methods in this chapter are based on the hand-held compasses available to trail riders for about $10 to $50. Some popular brands are Silva, Brunton and Suunto. Each has a ring with clear degree markings that rotates over a housing containing the magnetic needle. The housing is on a strong plastic base with an arrow or line to indicate the direction of travel. Some models feature scales or rulers to measure map distance, and a magnifying lens to read small print. While all compasses point to magnetic north, some—like the pocket watch or wrist watch styles, military-lensatic types, ones on ornamental key chains, and those that are part of other items, like match holders or thermometers—are more difficult to use in map reading.

Now things get a bit more complex because the magnetic compass needle will align with any nearby metal. To get an accurate reading, you need to hold a compass away from items like binoculars, knives, cameras, or even saddle horns with metal under the leather. Obviously, accurate compass reading is impossible with your map and compass laid out on the hood of the pickup. But stay out of the trap of some who have refused to believe their compass! If you are concerned that the compass isn't working, or that your reading isn't accurate, just move a metal object like a pocket knife past the needle and see if it follows the metal. If it does, the compass is working. To be sure, carry an inexpensive spare compass as a backup.

Declination - The Arrow Diagram in the Map Legend: If we plan to use a map and compass together we need to know something about *declination*. The first basic point to know is that the compass needle points to the earth's magnetic north, located in the Hudson Bay area. The second basic point to know is that the top of the map is North. The third basic point to know is that maps are drawn (and land surveyed) based on true north, located at the North Pole.

Since magnetic north and true north are not the same, it is necessary to correct for the difference which is usually called declination. There are several techniques for accounting for declination. Two similar ones are discussed in this chapter. Sometimes material included with a purchased compass describes the method that uses the map grid lines and the lines in the compass base plate to account for declination. If you find that method easier to follow, do so.

Figure 5 shows the magnetic north and true north locations in relation to Vancouver, Washington, which has 20 degrees declination.

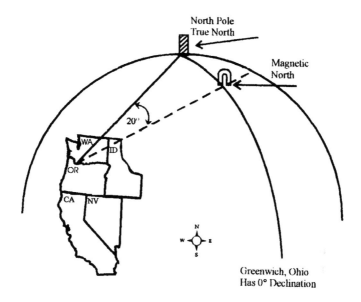

Figure 5. Magnetic and true north locations

The solid line is true north and the dashed line is magnetic north. The difference is 20 degrees as drawn for Vancouver, Washington.

Declination changes across the United States. The lines of declination are called isogonic lines. A declination of close to 21 degrees would be used in the most northeastern part of Washington, and close to 18 degrees in the southeastern corner of the state. There are places in the United States where the North Pole and magnetic north are in-line, where there is 0 degree declination and no correction is needed. This Agonic line runs approximately from the North Pole down the through the length of Florida. We are not concerned with it in the Northwest.

The map legend usually contains a drawing similar to the one in *Figure 6.* It gives the reader the declination for the map area. All trail maps presented in this book contain a similar diagram for either 19 or 20 degrees. For trail riding in Washington, using any declination closer than 19 or 20 degrees is probably impractical.

Figure 6. True north, magnetic north and degrees of declination

Correcting for Declination: Now we need to account for declination. If the compass you purchased allows you to make or preset the needed declination correction within the compass housing, future compass readings are already corrected to true north. To make the correction, turn a small screw usually found on the compass housing ring to set the required declination.

Less expensive plate-type compasses do not have the internal set screw adjustment, but they can be adapted to correct for declination by adding a piece of masking tape or by making a small scratch mark onto the plastic base plate. (Try the masking tape first. It can be replaced by a scratch mark later.)

•Hold the compass level and point the direction or travel arrow away from you.

•Turn the housing ring to set 0 or 360 at the direction-to-travel arrow on the plate compass (do not worry about the magnetic needle in this step).

•Place a piece of masking tape on the base plate next to the dial so the tape covers the area from about 18 to 22 degrees. (The degrees of 18, 20, and 22 are selected for this example because they cover the declination across Washington.)

•Carefully put an ink mark at 18, 20 and 22 degrees on the tape. If you decide to make a scratch mark on the plate do not use the tape, just put a small scratch mark at 20 degrees.

•These marks now become part of how you read and set the compass. They become the point on the housing ring at which you read ALL DIRECTIONS to a landmark or where you set ALL DIRECTIONS that are to be followed with the compass. Now you do not have to wonder, "Do I add or subtract the degrees of declination from the reading on the compass?" Do neither. Just read the degrees at the scratch mark. *Figure 7* shows a plate compass with 18, 20 and 22 degree scratch marks added.

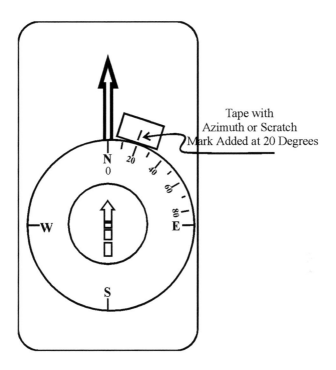

Figure 7. A plate compass without internal declination adjustment marked to correct for declination

The method pretaining to declination and map orientation contained in literature often included with the purchase of a compass need not be repeated here. That method will show you how to account for declination using the lines inside the compass housing with the lines on the map. We find the scratch technique and boxing the needle to be more direct and easy to understand. But both approaches work and give accurate readings when used with care.

To this point, you have been getting the compass ready to use more easily. Before making some compass readings, consider how to use the direction-to-travel arrow. It is important to know that the line in the center of the base plate is the direction of travel to take as you ride off. The words "keep the needle boxed" are used through the next few paragraphs; boxing the needle is described after *Figure 8*. The example in *Figure 8* is intended to convince even the most experienced trail rider or hiker that declination has to be part of compass use.

Example: You unload your horse where the trail crosses the road and plan to go across rocky country to reach a lake said to have great fishing, stock feed, and campsites. You were told the lake is over a mile wide and just three miles north of where the trail and road cross. Without map and compass knowledge you might say "Why not follow the compass needle to the lake, after all it points north doesn't it? Besides, it's late and over five miles by the trail around to the lake."

You park, and ride due north according to your magnetic compass needle but do not correct for the 20 degree declination for the area.

Surprise! If you just follow the compass needle as it points to magnetic north, without considering declination, you will miss the lake! Here is why. **FOR EVERY DEGREE OF DECLINATION NOT USED YOU WILL BE OFF ABOUT 92 FEET PER MILE OF TRAVEL**. That means for a 20 degree declination x 92 feet error per declination degree x 3 miles traveled, the line of travel will be off the destination by 5,520 feet, well over a mile. You may have ridden right by the lake! Even on a route toward the middle of the lake it could have been missed by over half a mile to the east if you just followed magnetic north and did not correct for 20 degrees declination.

Orient Your Compass to Magnetic North: Although you do not follow the compass to magnetic north, it can help you understand your location. This next quick operation is intended to make you aware of your location in relation to north before you even leave camp or trailhead. Here are the steps to orient to magnetic north.

Turn the dial so the N or 360 is at the center line (travel direction line) on the plate. Next, hold the compass in front of you with the travel direction arrow pointed away. Turn yourself until the magnetic needle comes over the engraved arrow on the compass plate (this is the "box the needle" step). Remember it is the red needle end that points North.

When both arrows point the same direction and are boxed, you are facing magnetic north. (We will not use magnetic north after we have set declination. We are more interested in true north.)

Now, stay in the same spot and make a mental note of some feature out the end of the compass that is in line with the direction of travel arrow. We will refer to it again in the next paragraph.

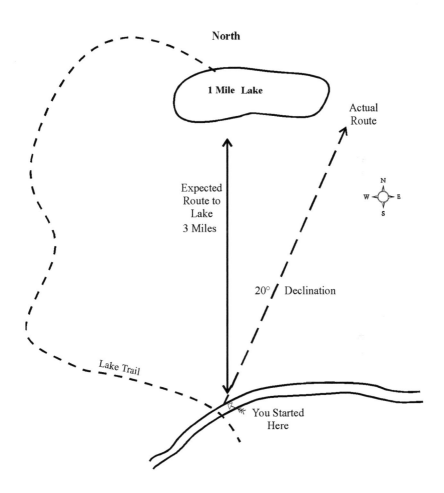

Figure 8. Follow north to the lake

Orient to True North, the North to Use: To orient a compass to true north means to have it in the same position relevant to the ground as maps are drawn. This is the direction you use when working with map and compass. To orient a compass to true north when that compass does not have the means to pre-set declination:

    (1) Rotate the dial until the 360 degree or N is at the scratch mark made for the declination for your area. (Assume the scratch mark is 20 degrees.)

    (2) Next, hold the compass level with the travel arrow pointing away and turn yourself until the magnetic needle and engraved arrow are again together. The magnetic needle should be directly over the arrow and pointing the same direction (boxed).

You have now boxed the needle and face true north. *Now see how far you face to the left (west) from the feature picked out and noted above on the magnetic north line.* To ride this true north, ride in the direction the travel arrow points and keep the needle boxed at the 20 degree scratch mark that has corrected for declination.

Remember, for all plate compasses, keep the needle boxed when following a bearing.

If you have a compass of each type, compare a direction that is taken using the scratch mark technique to the same direction taken with internal declination capability. The direction-to-travel arrow will point the same direction. The results will be the same. The direction to travel for both is always where the travel arrow points, NOT the direction the needle points. To stay on a direction or bearing means keeping whatever setting was made at the appropriate compass mark. At the same time, the needle and arrow must stay boxed.

To Follow a Compass Direction, When You Are Not Going True North: The techniques are the same even if you want to travel at some direction other than 0 degrees (true north). If the desired direction was 140 degrees (southeast), set the 140 at the declination 20 degree scratch mark, keep the needle boxed, and ride the direction indicated by the travel arrow. Remember the travel arrow must be pointed away from you. Again, if the compass is the type that can be pre-set for declination, place the 140 degree at the travel arrow and then ride the travel arrow direction but still keep the needle boxed. This same set of steps apply to any compass direction you select to travel.

Sighting Along the Way and Looking Back: If it is important to ride a certain direction, no one wants to—or probably needs to—keep an eye on the compass all the time. In order to stay on the azimuth or direction line being ridden, take a sighting on some feature ahead like a special rock formation, big tree or clump of trees that is directly in-line with the direction of travel, then ride to it without consulting the compass. At that feature, use the compass again to locate another one in the line of travel. Each time make sure the needle stays boxed over the engraved arrow and that the dial did not move off the azimuth setting you selected to travel. In this way, in the one-mile lake example, we would have gone from landmark to landmark all in a rough line at 0 (or 360) degrees which was now true north.

When you arrive at one of these in-line landmarks, check the accuracy of your riding by taking a look back (back sight) to the last feature. Do this without turning the dial on the compass. Just turn and face in the opposite direction and box the needle in reverse. This means that the magnetic needle will still be pointing in the same direction, BUT the engraved arrow in the housing is now pointing in the opposite direction. By sighting back along the travel arrow you should be looking close to the last feature used as a landmark.

This serves as a check on the accuracy of travel. If the features are not in line, you have the option of returning to an earlier feature and re-riding to your present location. However, more than likely, all you need to do to get in line is to shift left or right a few feet until the needles are boxed, but pointing in opposite directions. Remember it is not essential to ride in a straight line from one landmark to another. It is important that you safely work your way across the land, protect the resource and get to the next landmark.

What Is the Direction to a Peak or Other Landmark? When you see a distant feature. like a peak or some trail going over a ridge, and want to determine the direction (or azimuth) to it:

(1) Point the compass direction-to-travel arrow at the peak or landmark.

(2) Hold the compass steady and turn the compass dial until the engraved arrow is under the magnetic needle and points the same direction. This "boxes the needle" and sets the direction (or azimuth) to the feature.

(3) Now lower the compass and, for internal set declination compasses, read the degrees (direction) at the travel arrow, or read the degrees at the scratch mark on other compasses. Both readings should be the same.

Map Direction Between Two Locations: One commonly asked question is, "What direction do I travel to get from one location to another?" To determine that on a map, you can either use a compass or try a standard half-circle (180 degree) protractor of the type used in school.

Use a compass to check the direction to a landmark
—Photo by authors

Protractor: Remember that north is at the top of a map and the map has already been corrected for declination so a degree reading by protractor is based on true north. This can be done on any type of surface, even a pickup hood, since there is no magnetic influence on the protractor accuracy only your reading and care in alignment. What is necessary is to be sure that the 0 degree end of the protractor is lined up to the top along a north-south line on the map and the 90 degree point is to the east. Always check your reading against the fact that a 90 degree reading is east, a 180 degree reading is south, a 270 degree reading is west, and there are only 360 degrees in a circle.

Compass: When you use a compass to get the direction between two locations, remember to do it away from metal.

(1) Place the map on the ground and orient it to true north as described earlier.

(2) Lay the compass straight-edge along the line from one location to the one to which you want to determine the direction. The travel arrow should point to the second location. If the compass edge does not span the distance between the two locations, use a straight-edge.

(3) With the compass held steady along this direction, rotate the housing to box the magnetic needle over the travel arrow. Again, be sure the two arrows are pointing the same direction.

(4) Now pick up the compass and read the direction from one landmark to the other at the scratch mark. (Remember to read the direction or azimuth at the travel arrow line for an internal adjustment compass.)

Orient Your Map before You Leave a New Trailhead or Camp: Help other riders. When you are ready to ride away from a camp or vehicle, take a few minutes for one small map and compass exercise. Orient your map. When you orient a map and compass to true north you take the time to consider not only how the country looks but the trail direction. This simple process will help build confidence in your map and compass skills. Besides it makes you think about where you are before you ever start up the trail. It becomes more than just knowing that you are at some camp, trailhead or other jumping off place for a day ride. It is another part of *being aware* of what is around before starting a trip.

To orient a map to true north set the 0 or 360 degree on the scratch mark (or at the travel arrow for internal declination set compass). Place the compass on a north-south line of the map. (In this exercise the travel arrow should point toward the top of the map.) Next, rotate the map and compass together until the two compass arrows, magnetic and engraved, are boxed. That is all there is to it. The map now is oriented with the way the land was surveyed. Test that by looking out from your location on the map to some feature you see. It should be on the map in the same line of vision, unless it is so far away to be off the map.

Which Peak is That? Use your compass skill to identify an unknown mountain. If it is on your map, you can find out which one it is with the following:

(1) Orient the map to true north.
(2) Hold the compass and point the travel arrow at the landmark in question while you rotate the compass dial to box the needles.
(3) Now read the direction to the landmark at the scratch mark (or read at the travel arrow for internal-set declination).
(4) Place the straight edge of the compass plate at your location on the map and pivot the compass around the location to box the needle. A pencil makes a good pivot point. The compass edge, or a line drawn along the edge, will pass through the landmark of interest if your readings are accurate.
(5) Find the name of the peak on a line drawn out along the edge of your compass.

I See Two Known Landmarks, but What Is My Location? When you have to ask this question, it sort of means you are "turned around a bit"! But the question can be answered if the map you are carrying has the known landmarks on it.

Suppose you left the trail and are not sure where camp is located. This next technique, *triangulation,* will allow you to determine your approximate location when there are two known landmarks and they are also shown on your map and you know where you want to end up.

(1) Orient your map to True North.
(2) Take an azimuth reading to one of the landmarks using the methods explained earlier. (See "Which Peak is That?" above.)
(3) Without changing the dial, place the compass edge at the landmark on your map and pivot the compass around the landmark point until you box the magnetic needle over the engraved arrow.
(4) Draw a straight and fairly long line along the edge of compass that passes through the landmark.

(5) Pick up the compass and take the azimuth reading to the other landmark and do the same thing with that reading.

(6) Place the compass edge at the second landmark on your map and pivot the compass until you again box the needle.

(7) Draw another line along the compass edge.

(8) Where the two lines cross on the map will be your approximate location if readings have been carefully made and placed on the map.

To get back to camp, place the edge of the compass on the map (still oriented to true north) at the point where the two drawn lines cross and at the camp location. Hold the compass steady and turn the dial to box the needle. Read the direction to camp at the scratch mark (or travel line for internal-set declination.) Travel that reading to camp without moving the dial. Keep the needle boxed. This is illustrated in *Figure 9.*

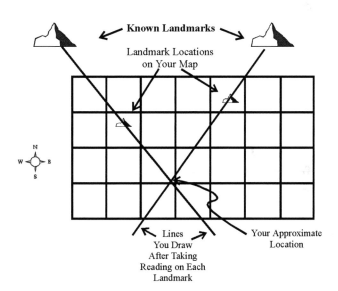

Figure 9. Known landmarks on map used to find your location

Practice Course: Convince yourself that you can follow a compass bearing on foot or horseback. Start from a mark on the ground. Set 120 degrees on your compass. Box the compass needle and walk 100 steps. Place a marker. Add 120 degrees to your original setting and box the needle. Walk 100 steps at 240 degrees and place another marker. Add 120 degrees to your last setting, box the needle and walk another 100 steps. You should arrive back at the original mark. Try riding this or a longer version and keep your compass needle boxed .

Direction Without a Compass: There are a number of ways to roughly tell direction without a compass. The shadow-tip method is fun, quick, and accurate. Put a two to three-foot stick vertically into the ground at a fairly level spot so a distinct shadow is cast. Mark the shadow tip with a stone or twig. Wait about 10 to 15 minutes until the shadow moves a few inches. Mark the new position of the shadow tip like the first. You can do one or two more intervals or just draw a straight line through the first two marks made at the shadow tip. This line drawn is an east-west line. Since the sun rises in the east and sets in the west, the shadow tip moves in the opposite direction. So the first shadow tip mark is always west and the second or last is east. Next, draw a line from the east-west line perpendicular (90 degrees) to the stick base. This is a north-south line. On a cloudy day spread a white handkerchief on the ground to catch the shadow. Tapping the stick helps find the shadow .

You can also use a watch with hands. Point the hour hand at the sun. Halfway on around between the hour hand and 12 o'clock is a rough approximation of north. At night the north star (Polaris) indicates true north since it is directly over the North Pole and keeps that position. The last two stars in the cup of the Big Dipper point to Polaris, about three to four hand widths away.

Ten Essentials: We wrap up this chapter with our version of the *10 essentials* things to have on a trail ride. They easily fit into a small cantle bag or saddle bags. Some duplicates end up in a vest or pocket.

1. Compass (two)
2. Maps (topographic)
3. Water and iodine purification tablets
4. Sharp knife
5. Whistle
6. Space blanket with cord
7. Matches and striker paper in container
8. Matches in another container

9. Fire starter material
10. First aid kit

A compass is not difficult to use and like many things (including throwing a Double Diamond hitch) requires practice and an occasional refresher on techniques. Buy a topographic map of your favorite backcountry area and practice with it around home. You can orient it to true north, use a compass or protractor to get directions to a feature, scale the trail distance, check out trail steepness and learn the features before ever setting foot in the wilderness. What better way to plan and dream of the summer trips while waiting for the snow to melt.

Always remember riders can get seriously lost just by not paying attention to where they are going and where they have been! In the end, we should really be responsible for ourselves.

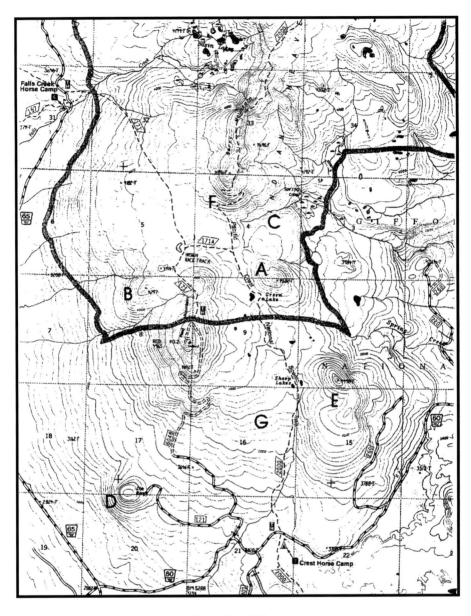

Practice Map

DIRECTORY OF HORSE CAMPS
AND TRAIL MAP NUMBERS

Trinity Horse Camp, Map 30
Alder Creek Horse Camp. Map 30
White Pass Horse Camp, Maps 22 & 7
Lion Rocks Springs, Map 25
Cayuse Horse Camp, Map 26
Deep Creek Horse Camp & Trailhead, Maps 23 & 22
Buck Meadows, Map 24
Black Pine Horse Camp, Map 27

DIRECTORY OF TRAIL GUIDES BY MAP NUMBERS

COLVILLE NATIONAL FOREST

GIFFORD PINCHOT NATIONAL FOREST

OKANOGAN NATIONAL FOREST

OLYMPIC NATIONAL FOREST

WENATCHEE NATIONAL FOREST

Fifes Ridge Trail 954
Kettle Creek Trail 957
Mesatchee Creek Trail 969
Pleasant Valley Loop Trail 999
Union Creek Trail 956

Hereford Meadow Trail 1207
Keenan Meadow Trail 1386
Manastash Lake Trail 1350
Shoestring Lake Trail 1385
Taneum Ridge Trail 1363

Devils Gulch Trail 1220
Mission Ridge Trail 1201
Naneum Wilson Trail 1371
Old Ellensburg Trail 1373
Table Mountain Trail 1209
Tronsen Ridge Trail or Mount Lillian Trail 1204

Deception Pass Trail 1376
Davis Peak Trail 1324
Jolly Mountain Trail 1307
Lake Michael Trail 1336
Pete Lake Trail 1323
Polallie Ridge Trail 1309
Scatter Creek Trail 1328
Trail Creek Trail 1322
Waptus River Trail 1310
West Fork Teanaway Trail 1353
Pacific Crest Trail 2000

Black Jack Ridge Trail 1565
Chiwaukum Creek Trail 1571
French Creek Trail 1595
Icicle Creek Trail 1551

Jack Creek Trail 1558
Lorraine Ridge Trail 1568
Meadow Creek Trail 1559
Snowall Cradle Trail 1560

Boulder Pass Trail 1562
Indian Creek Trail 1502
Mount David Trail 1521
White River Trail 1507

Cady Creek Trail 1501
Little Wenatchee River Trail 1525
Pacific Crest Trail 2000

Basalt Ridge Trail 1515
Buck Creek Trail 1513
Carne Mountain Trail 1508
Chiwawa River Trail 1550
Estes Butte Trail 1527
Rock Creek Trail 1509
Rock Creek Tie Trail 1538
Phelps Creek Trail 1511

WASHINGTON STATE FORESTS

Yacolt Burn State Forest
Bluff Mountain Trail 172
Rock Creek to Cold Creek Trail
Rock Creek to Tarbell Pump Trail
Tarbell Pump Trail

Three Corner Rock Trail

Capitol State Forest
Capitol Forest Trails & Camps Open to Horses

Appendix 1

TRAIL AND PACK STOCK REGULATIONS

Recreation stock use regulations on National Forest Lands tend to change and become more restrictive every year to protect the land and resources from overuse. Trail riders need to make it a practice to check with the local Forest Service office or other public land management agency for current regulations. The trails and horse camps in this book are covered by one or more of the following public lands use-regulations in Washington. We each have the responsibility of making sure a trip meets any new or changing regulations.

•Stock can be watered at lakes and streams, but in most areas are not allowed to graze or be tied in any manner within 200 feet of a lake shoreline whether hitched, hobbled or tethered.

•Stock feed carried into a designated wilderness must be certified as processed. Hay certified weed free is not adequate and is not considered processed.

•The William O. Douglas, Goat Rocks, Norse Peak and the Alpine Lakes Wilderness party size limit is 12 heartbeats. There also may be specific site restrictions as stock is not permitted in the Alpine Lakes Enchantment Permit area of the Alpine Lakes Wilderness.

•Starting in 1995 camping in the Alpine Lakes Wilderness with pack and saddle animals became, in some cases, prohibited or limited to marked sites within 0.5 mile of many lakes and areas. Further, stock are not to be tied to trees under six inches in diameter (eight inches is better) or to larger trees for more than four hours. Use a high-line and keep stock eight feet from each tree.

Within the Lake Chelan-Sawtooth Wilderness, Okanogan and Wenatchee National Forests, hitching or tying any pack or saddle stock to any tree for an overnight period is prohibited. Further, hitching or tying stock to any object, including a high-line where the point of tie is within eight feet of any tree, for an overnight period, is prohibited within the Lake-Chelan Wilderness, Okanogan and Wenatchee National Forests and in unroaded portions of the Twisp Ranger District in the Foggy Dew and Crater Creek drainages of the Okanogan National Forest.

Permits for overnight trips may be necessary for an area to be visited. Check with the local Forest Service office for requirements.

Some horse camps have a limit as to the number of head of stock that can be kept in each campsite. The limit is three to four horses at the Wenatchee National Forest Naches Ranger District horse camps and trailheads. The Black Pine Horse Camp on the Leavenworth District has a limit of five head per camp. Check horse camp regulations when you park.

As of April 1993, these specific entry and use restrictions were being applied to designated wildernesses in Washington State:

All Washington State, Cascade Mt. Range Wildernesses within Gifford Pinchot National Forest, Wenatchee National Forest, Mt. Baker-Snoqualmie National Forest, and Okanogan National Forest.

•Entering or being in all wilderness, except the Lake Chelan-Sawtooth and Pasayten wildernesses, with a group consisting of a combination of persons and pack and saddle animals exceeding 12 in total number.

•Entering or being in the Lake Chelan-Sawtooth or Pasayten Wilderness with a group consisting of more than 12 persons or more than 18 pack and saddle animals. Group limit for any wilderness in the Olympic National Forest is "12 persons and/or 8 head of livestock."

•Possessing or transporting livestock feed other than processed feed.

•Grazing any pack or saddle animals within 200 feet slope distance of the shoreline of any lake.

•Hitching, tethering, or hobbling any pack or saddle animals within 200 feet slope distance of the shoreline of any lake.

Appendix 2

U.S.F.S. AND D.N.R. DIRECTORY

U.S. Forest Service and Washington DNR addresses and phone numbers are as follows:

Colville National Forest, 765 S. Main, Colville, WA 99114, 509-684-7000
Colville District, 765 S. Main St., Colville, WA 99114, 509-684-7010
Kettle Falls District, 255 West 11th., Kettle Falls, WA 99141, 509-738-6111
Newport District, 315 N. Warren, Newport, WA 99156, 509-447-3129
Republic District, 180 N. Jefferson, Republic, WA 99166, 509-775-3305
Sullivan Lake District, 12641 Sullivan Lake Rd., Metaline Falls, WA 99153, 509-446-7500

Gifford Pinchot National Forest, 10600 NE 51st Circle, Vancouver, WA 98682, 360-891-5000
Mt. Adams District, 2455 Highway 141, Trout Lake, WA 98650, 509-395-3400
Mount St. Helens National Volcanic Monument, 42218 NE Yale Bridge Rd., Amboy, WA 98601, 360-274-2100
Packwood District, 13068 U.S. Hwy 12, Packwood, WA 98361, 360-494-0600
Randle District, 10024 U.S. Hwy 12, Randle, WA 98377, 360-497-1100
Wind River District, M.P. 1. 23R Hemlock Rd., Carson, WA 98610, 509-427-3200

Mt. Baker-Snoqualmie National Forest, 21905 64th Avenue W., Mountlake Terrace, WA 98403, 206-775-9702
Darrington District, 1405 Emmens St., Darrington, WA 98241, 360-436-1155
Mt. Baker District, 2105 Highway 20, Sedro Woolley, WA 98284, 360-856-5700
North Bend District, 42404 SE North Bend Way, North Bend, WA 98045, 206-888-1421
Skykomish District, 74920 NE Stevens Pass Hwy., Skykomish, WA 98288, 360-677-2414
White River District, 857 Roosevelt Ave. E., Enumclaw, WA 98022, 360-825-6585

Okanogan National Forest, 1240 S. 2nd Ave., Okanogan, WA 98840, 509-826-3275
Tonasket District, 1 West Winsap, Tonasket, WA 98855, 509-486-2186

Methow Valley District, 502 Glover, Twisp, WA 98856, 509-997-2131

Olympic National Forest, 1835 Black Lake Blvd. S.W., Olympia, WA 98512, 360-956-2300

Hood Canal District, N.150 Lake Cushman Rd., Hoodsport, WA 98548, 360-877-5254

Quilcene District, 20482 Highway 101, Quilcene, WA 98376, 360-765-2200

Quinault District, 353 South Shore Road, Quinault, WA 98575, 360-288-2525

Soleduck District, Rt.1, Box 5750, Hwy 101, Forks, WA 98331, 360-374-6522

Wentachee National Forest, 215 Melody Lane, Wenatchee, WA 98801, 509-662-4335

Chelan District, Rt. 2, Box 360, Chelan, WA 98816, 509-682-2576

Cle Elum District, 803 W. 2nd St., Cle Elum, WA 98922, 509-674-4411

Entiat District, 2108 Entiat Way, Entiat, WA 98822, 509-784-1511

Lake Wenatchee District, 22976 State Hwy 207, Leavenworth, WA 98826, 509-763-3103

Leavenworth District, 600 Sherbourne St., Leavenworth, WA 98826, 509-548-6977

Naches District, 10061 Highway 12, Naches, WA 98937, 509-653-2205

Washington State Regions:

Olympic Region, 411 Tillicum Lane, Forks, WA 98331, 360-374-6131

Central Region, 1405 Rush Rd., Chehalis WA 98532, 360-748-2383

South Puget Sound Region, P.O. Box 68, 28329 SE 448th St., Enumclaw, WA 98022, 360-825-1631

Northwest Region, 919 N. Township St., Sedro Woolley, WA 98284, 360-856-3500

Southwest Region, P.O. Box 280, 601 Bond Rd., Castle Rock, WA 98611, 360-577-2025

Northeast Region, P.O.Box 190, 225 S. Silke Rd., Colville, WA 98114, 509-684-7474

Southeast Region, 713 E. Bowers Rd., Ellensburg, WA 98926, 509-925-8510

Appendix 3

REFERENCES

Horse Sense on National Forest Pack Trips. USDA Forest Service, Northern Region, P.O. Box 7669, Missoula, MT 59807. 1986. Pamphlet.

Horse Sense: Packing Lightly on Your National Forests. USDA Forest Service, Pacific Northwest Region, P.O. Box 3623, Portland OR 97208. Pamphlet.

Salmo-Priest Wilderness Guidebook: USDA Forest Service, Colville National Forest, Colville, WA 99114. 37pp.

Techniques and Equipment for Wilderness Horse Travel With Stock: USDA Forest Service, Missoula Equipment Development Center, Missoula, MT 59807. October 1993. 60pp.

Washington Outfitters and Guides Association (WOGA), 22845 N.E. 8th, Suite 331, Redmond, WA 98053.

Leave No Trace, Minimum Impact Guide: BackCountry Horsemen of Washington. Pamphlet.

Packin' In on Mules and Horses. Smoke Elser and Bill Brown. Mountain Press Publishing Co., Missoula, MT. 1980. 158pp. Illust.

Load 'Em Up, Tie 'Em Down. Gordon Jesse Walker. Craft Printers Inc., Klamath Falls, OR 97601. 1980. 41pp. Illust.

Hypothermia, Frostbite and Other Cold Injuries, Prevention, Recognition, Pre-Hospital Treatment: James A. Wilkerson M.D., Cameron C. Bangs M.D., and John S. Hayward, PhD. The Mountaineers, Seattle, WA 98134. 1986. 105pp.

Map and Compass Recreation Aid 2: USDA Forest Service Portland, OR 97208, April 1965, 11pp. Illust.

Staying Found: The Complete Map and Compass Handbook. June Fleming. The Mountaineers, Seattle, WA 98134. 1994. 158pp. Illust.

Be Expert With Map and Compass: The Orienteering Handbook: Bjorn Kjellstrom. Charles Scribner's Sons, New York. 1976. 214pp. Illust.

Appendix 4

TRAIL RIDING CATEGORIES

Trail difficulty is the degree of challenge a trail presents to an average rider's skill and physical ability. Difficulty is a function of the steepness, cross slope, tread and clearing widths, elevation change and natural hazards. The four levels, with symbols, being put into place by the Forest Service are:

Easy: Limited skill and challenge required to travel trail. (Persons with disabilities should not need assistance).
Previously described as "Easiest."

Moderate: Some skill and challenge required to travel trail. (Persons with disabilities may require some assistance).
Previously described as "Moderate."

Difficult: High degree of skill and challenge to travel trail. (Persons with disabilities will require some assistance).
Previously also described as "Difficult."

Most Difficult: Very high degree of skill and challenge to travel trail. (Persons with disabilities will require assistance and trail may be inaccessible to some users).
These trails may be open to stock, but unsafe due to current conditions, trails are commonly described as "Not Recommended for Stock."
Previously also described as "Most Difficult."

Level Of Use Categories: Level of usage is measured by experience in terms of number of people met (encounters per day). There are separate levels for wilderness and for non-wilderness areas.

Usage Level	Encounters Per Day	
	Wilderness	Non-Wilderness
Light	0-3	0-5
Medium	4-9	6-15
Heavy	10-18	16-50
Extra Heavy	18+	50+

Appendix 5

MAP SOURCES

The sources for other maps that cover the trails shown in *Trail Riding and Pack Trips in Washington* are listed by the name and number of each of the 36 Trail Maps.

Trail Map 1: **Colville N.F.; Boulder-Deer Creek Summit**
Colville N.F. map; USGS Quads Boundary Mtn., Mt. Leona and Copper Butte.

Trail Map 2: **Colville N.F.; Sherman Pass South**
Colville N.F. map; USGS Quads Sherman Peak, Edds Mtn. and Bear Mtn.

Trail Map 3: **Colville N.F.; Salmo - Priest Wilderness**
Colville N.F. map; Colville and Idaho Panhandle N.F. Salmo - Priest Wilderness map; USGS Quads Gypsy Peak, Salmo-Mtn., Pass Creek and Helmer Mtn.

Trail Map 4: **Gifford Pinchot N.F.; Walupt Lake**
Gifford Pinchot N.F. map; Goat Rock Wilderness map; PCT Washington Southern Portion map; USGS Quads Packwood Lake, Old Snowy Mtn., and Walupt Lake; Green Trail Map; Packwood.

Trail Map 5: **Gifford Pinchot N.F.; S. W. Slopes of Mount Adams**
Gifford Pinchot N.F. map; Mount Adams Wilderness map; PCT Washington Southern Portion map; USGS Quads Trout Lake, Mount Adams West, Mount Adams East and Green Mtn.; Green Trail Map; Mt. Adams West.

Trail Map 6: **Gifford Pinchot N.F.; Keenes Horse Camp**
Gifford Pinchot N.F. map; Mount Adams Wilderness map; PCT Washington Southern Portion map; USGS Quads Mount Adams West, Mount Adams East, Green Mountain and Glaciate Butte; Green Trail Maps; Mt. Adams West and Walupt Lake.

Trail Map 7: **Gifford Pinchot N.F.; Packwood Lake**
Gifford Pinchot N.F. map; Goat Rocks Wilderness map; PCT Washington Southern Portion map; USGS Quads Packwood Lake, Old Snowy Mtn., White Pass and Packwood; Green Trail Maps; Packwood and White Pass.

Trail Map 8: **Gifford Pinchot N.F.; Indian Heaven Wilderness**
Gifford Pinchot N.F. map; Indian Heaven Wilderness map; PCT Washington Southern Portion map; USGS Quads Lone Butte, Sleeping Beauty and

Gifford Peak; Green Trail Maps; Wind River, Lone Butte and Mt. Adams West.

Trail Map 9: **Gifford Pinchot N.F.; Trapper Creek Wilderness**
Gifford Pinchot N.F. map; Trapper Creek Wilderness map; PCT Washington Southern Portion map; USGS Quads Blue Mountain and Termination Point; Green Trail Maps; Lookout Mtn. and Wind River.

Trail Map 10: **Gifford Pinchot N.F.; Siouxon Area**
Gifford Pinchot N.F. map; USGS Quads Siouxon Peak and BareMtn.; Green Trail Map; Lookout Mtn.

Trail Map 11: **Gifford Pinchot N.F.; Lewis River Area**
Gifford Pinchot N.F. map; USGS Quads Spencer Butte, Quartz Creek Butte and McCoy Peak; Green Trail Maps; Lone Butte and Mount St. Helens.

Trail Map 12: **Gifford Pinchot N.F.; Kalama Horse Camp - Mount St.Helens**
Gifford Pinchot N.F. map, Mount St. Helens National Volcanic Monument map.

Trail Map 13: **Okanogan N.F.; Upper Twisp River - Methow Valley**
Okanogan N.F. map; PCT Washington Northern Portion map; USGS Quads Doe Mtn., Mazama and Robinson Mtn.; Green Trail Maps; Washington Pass and Mt. Logan.

Trail Map 14: **Okanogan N.F.; Twisp River - Black Pine Lake**
Okanogan N.F. map; Lake Chelan-Sawtooth Wilderness map; USGS Quads Twisp West, Hoo Doo Peak, Oval Creek, Thompson Ridge, Midnight Mtn. and Gilbert; Green Trail Maps; Buttermilk Butte and Stehekin.

Trail Map 15: **Okanogan N.F.; Pasayten Wilderness - Andrews Creek East**
Okanogan N.F. map; Pasayten Wilderness map; USGS Quads Horseshoe Basin, Bauerman Ridge, Coleman Peak and Corral Butte; Green Trail maps; Horseshoe Basin and Coleman Peak.

Trail Map 16: **Okanogan N.F.; Pasayten Wilderness - Andrews Creek**
Okanogan N.F. map; Pasayten Wilderness map; USGS Quads Remmel Mtn., Ashnola Pass, Mt. Barney and Billy Goat Mtn.; Green Trail maps; Coleman Peak and Billy Goat Mtn.

Trail Map 17: **Okanogan N.F.; Pasayten Wilderness - Billy Goat Pass**
Okanogan N.F. map; Pasayten Wilderness map; USGS Quads Ashnola Mtn., Ashnola Pass, Tatoosh Buttes, Mt. Lago, Lost Peak and Billy Goat Mtn.

Trail Map 18: **Okanogan N.F.; Pasayten Wilderness - Hidden Lakes**
Okanogan N.F. map; Pasayten Wilderness map; USGS Quads Frosty Creek, Tatoosh Buttes, Pasayten Peak, Slate Peak, Robinson Mtn. and Mt. Lago; Green Trail maps; Jack Mountains and Pasayten Peak.

Trail Map 19: **Olympic N.F.; LeBar Horse Camp - Skokomish River**
Olympic N.F. map; USGS Quads Mt. Tebo NE, Mt. Tebo NW and Grisdale NE; Green Trail maps; Mt. Tebo and Grisdale.

Trail Map 20: **Olympic N.F.; Tubal Cain - Mount Townsend**
Olympic N.F. map; USGS Quads The Brothers, Tyler Peak, Mt. Walker, Mt. Jupiter and Mt. Washington; Green Trail maps; Tyler Peak and The Brothers.

Trail Map 21: **Olympic N.F.; Mt. Muller - Littleton Loop**
Olympic N.F. map (not on current Forest map, trail is new, use temporary
Recreation Guide map from Soleduck Ranger District, Forks, WA); USGS
Quads Snide Peak, Mount Muller; Green Trail maps; Lake Crescent and
Pysht.

Trail Map 22: **Wenatchee N.F.; White Pass Horse Camp**
Wenatchee N.F. map; Gifford Pinchot N.F. map; William O. Douglas Wilderness
and Goat Rocks Wilderness maps; PCT Washington Southern Portion map;
USGS Quads White Pass, Spiral Butte, Cougar Lake, Bumping Lake, Rimrock Lake and Timber Wolf Mtn.; Green Trail map; White Pass.

Trail Map 23: **Wenatchee N.F.; Norse Peak Wilderness - Bumping Lake**
Wenatchee N.F. map; William O. Douglas and Norse Peak Wilderness maps;
PCT Washington Southern Portion map; USGS Quads Bumping Lake, Norse
Peak, Goose Prairie and Old Scab Mtn.; Green Trail maps; Bumping Lake
and Lester.

Trail Map 24: **Wenatchee N. F.; Buck Meadows - Manastash Lake**
Wenatchee N.F. map; USGS Quads Frost Mtn., Quartz Mtn. and Manastash
Lake; Green Trail maps; Manastash Lake, Easton and Cle Elum.

Trail Map 25: **Wenatchee N.F.; Ken Wilcox Horse Camp at Haney Meadow**
Wenatchee N.F. map; USGS Quads Swauk Pass, Mission Peak, Tipoff and Reecer
Canyon; Green Trail map; Liberty.

Trail Map 26: **Wenatchee N. F.; Cayuse Horse Camp - Salmon La Sac**
Wenatchee N.F. map; Alpine Lakes Wilderness map; PCT Washington Northern
Portion map; USGS Quads Cle Elum Lake, Davis Peak, Polalie Ridge and
The Cradle; Green Trail map; Kachess Lake.

Trail Map 27: **Wenatchee N. F.; Black Pine Horse Camp**
Wenatchee N.F. map; Alpine Lake Wilderness map; PCT Washington Northern
Portion map; USGS Quads Sterns Pass, The Cradle, Chiwaukum Mtns.
and Jack Ridge; Green Trail maps; Stevens Pass and Chiwaukum Mtns.

Trail Map 28: **Wenatchee N. F.; White River Falls**
Wenatchee N.F. map; Glacier Peak Wilderness map; PCT Washington Northern
Portion map; USGS Quads Lake Wenatchee, Mount Daniel, Doe Mtn., Clark
Mtn. and Trinity; Green Trail Maps; Benchmark Mtn., Glacier Peak and
Holden.

Trail Map 29: **Wenatchee N.F.; Little Wenatchee Ford**
Wenatchee N.F. map; Glacier Peak Wilderness map; PCT Washington Northern
Portion map; USGS Quads Mount Howard and Mount Daniel; Green Trail
Maps; Labyrinth Mtn., Benchmark Mtn., Wenatchee Lake and Glacier Peak.

Trail Map 30: **Wenatchee N. F.; Chiwawa River Horse Camp - Trinity
Trailhead**
Wenatchee N.F. map; Glacier Peak Wilderness map; PCT Washington Northern
Portion map; USGS Quads Clark Mtn., Trinity, Holden and Suiattle Pass;
Green Trail maps, Glacier Peak and Holden.

Trail Map 31: **Washington State Forests; Yacolt Burn State Forest -
Rock Creek**

Washington State DNR, Yacolt Burn State Forest Map; Gifford Pinchot N.F. map; USGS Quads Yacolt and Dole.

Trail Map 32: **Washington State Forests; Yacolt Burn State Forest - 3 Corner Rock**

Washington State DNR, Yacolt Burn State Forest Map; Gifford Pinchot N.F. map; USGS Quads Yacolt and Dole.

Trail Map 33: **Washington State Forests; Capitol State Forest**

Washington State DNR, Capitol State Forest and Lower Chehalis State Forest map.

Trail Map 34: **Washington State Forests; Tahuya State Forest**

Washington State DNR, Tahuya State Forest map.

Trail Map 35: **Washington State Forests; Tiger Mountain State Forest** Washington State DNR, Tiger Mountain map.

Trail Map 36: **Washington State Forests; Green Mountain State Forest** Washington State DNR, Green Mountain State Forest map.

ABOUT THE AUTHORS

The authors, like many of you, are life-long horse owners and avid trail riders who have ridden over 300 miles on back-country trails each year for the past 20 years. Day rides, week-end trips and extended pack trips with their horses have included trips to National Forests and Wildernesses in Washington, Oregon, Idaho, Montana, Arizona, Utah and Wyoming. Both are members of the Backcountry Horsemen of Washington (BCHW) and Oregon Equestrian Trails (OET).

R.O. (Dick) Woodfin is a retired U.S. Forest Service researcher, has done field work in all the western states, and is a member of a mounted sheriff's posse and past president of the Oregon Association of Mounted Posses. He is active in search and rescue (SAR), and teaches map and compass to mounted SAR groups and to saddle clubs. He was one of the founding members of Oregon Equestrian Trails (OET), an organization with goals similar to BCHW.

LaDonna Woodfin is an office manager for a nurses' union. She was raised in Washington on the Egner family cattle ranch in the Danville area just south of the Canadian border. She rode

alone 2 miles on horseback from the ranch to the school bus stop and back, in all weather as a first grader. She hitched and drove teams of horses used for ranch work and was a self-taught trick rider performing at Washington fairs and rodeos during her high school years.

Authors Dick and LaDonna Woodfin

A FINAL THANKS

In closing we warmly remember Miley, Barb, Lexina, Reb, Beanie, Hobo, Tequila, Poco, Catcher and Rooster, four-legged friends who contributed to this Book by their unfailing performances of doing what a good trail horse or pack horse should do. Go where they are pointed and get you there safely. They met all the challenges of steep, grinding trails, bogs and a couple of wrecks, as well as black bear in camp in Wyoming's Fitzpatrick and Teton Wildernesses; bands of domestic sheep drifting across camp in Utah's High Uintas Wilderness; elk and deer through camps; Big Horn Sheep on the trail at 10,500 feet in Wyoming; grizzly bear on the trail in the Montana's Bob Marshall Wilderness; high, flooding rivers in Idaho's River of No Return Wilderness; moose in Utah; snowstorms in the Eagle Cap Wilderness in Oregon; snow drifts in the William O. Douglas Wilderness; massive thunder storms in the Pasayten Wilderness; rattlesnakes and bear in Hells Canyon; hobbled horses scooting back to camp at sight of a black bear in Idaho's Sawtooth Wilderness; and many, many more — but got us back all in one piece.